Caring as Healing:
Renewal Through Hope

Caring as Healing: Renewal Through Hope

Edited by
Delores A. Gaut
and
Anne Boykin

National League for Nursing Press · New York
Pub. No. 14-2607

ISBN: 0-88737-607-X

The views expressed in this publication represent the views of the authors and do not necessarily reflect the official views of the National League for Nursing.

Library of Congress Cataloging-in-Publication Data

Caring as healing : renewal through hope / edited by Delores A. Gaut and Anne Boykin.
    p. cm.
    Papers presented at the 15th International Human Caring Research Conference in Portland, Oregon, May 1993.
    Includes bibliographical references.
    Pub. no. 14-2607.
    ISBN 0-88737-607-X
    1. Nurse and patient—Congresses. 2. Caring—Congresses.
3. Healing—Congresses. 4. Ritual—Therapeutic use—Congresses.
I. Gaut, Delores A. II. Boykin, Anne. III. International Human Caring Research Conference (15th : 1993 : Portland, Or.)
RT86.3.C37 1994
610.73—dc20   94-5923
                                                        CIP

This book was set in Palatino by Eastern Composition, Inc. The editor and designer was Nancy Jeffries. Northeastern Press was the printer and binder. The cover was designed by Lauren Stevens.

Conference logo design by Connie Harrison, St. Vincent Hospital, Portland, Oregon.

Printed in the United States of America

We dedicate this book to the nurse scholars from around the world who have engaged in the study of human care and caring as the unique and essential characteristic of nursing practice. A special word of appreciation to the pioneer group who met some 15 years ago, and through mutual support, research presentations, and critique, developed the foundational knowledge of caring that now serves as the basis for further studies; to the first officers and board members who organized and directed what is now known as The International Association of Human Caring, Inc.; and to the members of the Association for their continued support and involvement. Lastly, a special thank you to the behind the scenes peer reviewers who have assisted the editors over the years with the research papers presented at the Annual Caring Research Conferences. Their time, energy and expertise have been essential to the final production of ten quality, peer-reviewed publications.

Delores Gaut
Anne Boykin

Contents

Introduction

Caring as Healing: Renewal Through Hope was selected as the theme for the 15th International Human Caring Research Conference to bring nursing scholars together to explore the healing power of care and hope for clients, for communities, and for nurses as care providers. The theme provided a forum for nursing scholars from around the world to have creative dialogue, to share stories, and to collectively explore the concept of caring as healing, the benefits of healing rituals and modalities, and the value of hope from a patient's perspective. The conference setting and activities provided the opportunity for participant nurses to experience a variety of personal healing rituals and modalities.

The logo for the 1993 Human Caring Research Conference, pictured on the cover of this book, was designed by Connie Harrison, MS, RN, a member of the Steering Committee from St. Vincent Hospital in Portland, Oregon. It denotes the theme of the conference. The design is an American Indian symbolgram representing a healing person with caring hands.

The University of Portland School of Nursing, St. Vincent Hospital and Medical Center, and the International Association for Human Caring (IAHC) hosted the Caring Research Conference on the University of Portland campus in Portland, Oregon in May, 1993. Faculty, alumni, staff, and administrative nurses from these three organizations worked together for over two years to plan, coordinate, and present the conference.

An historical link and commitment to caring fostered the cooperation of these sponsoring organizations. The University of Portland School of Nursing, established in 1934 as the first baccalaureate nursing program in the State of Oregon, was developed from the diploma school of nursing at St. Vincent Hospital and uses caring as a foundation of its curriculum. The Department of Nursing at St. Vincent Hospital developed a "Mobile Model" conceptual framework for nursing practice with care/caring concepts as an integrating force. Dr. Delores Gaut, as President of the IAHC and a visiting Professor of Nursing at the University of Portland, provided the guidance, framework, and vision essential for the conference.

The beautiful 92-acre residential campus of the University of Portland located on a bluff overlooking the Willamette River and the city of Portland provided the setting for the conference planners to create a caring environment that reflected the theme. Participants experienced the healing rituals of the American Indians of the Northwest through the words of a storyteller and the traditional Native American dances. Workshops provided the opportunity to experience the healing art of clay and of journaling, the healing expression of dance, the healing ritual of Tai Chi, and concepts of therapeutic touch. Comfortable dormitory housing encouraged networking, dialogue, and the celebration of a caring community.

It was an honor for the University of Portland to host the Human Caring Research Conference. A Catholic institution, the mission of the University is to support a community of scholars by providing excellence in teaching, a commitment to justice, and service to the community. This mission promoted the theme of the conference and the philosophy of the International Association for Human Caring, that care and caring are the essence of nursing and form the central core of the profession. The Chapel of Christ the Teacher on campus provided the location for a community mass celebration involving many of the conference participants.

There are many persons to thank for the success of the conference, but a very special thank you to Dean Patricia Chadwick for extending the invitation to hold the conference at the University of Portland, and to Mr. Larry Scruggs, for providing direction for campus services; to Kathy Johnson, Sylvia McSkimming and Connie Harrison of St. Vincent Hospital for their invaluable time and energy as members of the Steering Committee; and lastly to all of the volunteers from St. Vincent Hospital and the students from the University of Portland School of Nursing for their energy and assistance in making things run smoothly and on time. Because of everyone's effort, participants evaluated the conference as "one of the best" they had ever attended. The participants explored the concept of care as healing and the value of hope from a patient's perspective. Just as importantly, they personally experienced the healing powers of a caring community.

Susan R. Moscato, EdD, RN
Adjunct Assistant Professor
University of Portland
School of Nursing
Portland, Oregon

Preface

This publication represents the excellent papers presented at the 15th Caring Research Conference held in Portland, Oregon in May, 1993. Nursing scholars from Australia, Canada, Finland, New Zealand, Scotland, United Kingdom, and the United States, came together for creative dialogue and exploration of caring as healing and personal renewal through hope. The book is organized within the three major themes of the conference—healing rituals, healing modalities, and the value of hope from the patient's perspective. The conference offered the participants opportunities to personally experience a variety of health and healing rituals, and a section of this book includes the formalized stories of three workshop leaders as they explored healing through clay, dance, and storytelling. The book concludes with invited papers that were relevant to the themes of the conference.

The book begins with the inspiring work of Dr. Katie Eriksson, "Theories of Caring as Health," (Chapter 1). A creative reflection on the essence of human caring, Dr. Eriksson approaches the topic from a holistic perception of what it means to be a fully human person. The philosophical, theoretical and epistemic focus will challenge researchers, theorists, and nurse practitioners interested in caring and health.

The section on healing begins with the work of Francelyn Reeder, (Chapter 2), "Rituals of Healing." She invites the reader into reflecting on ritual through historical eyes, and discusses the making, breaking, and remaking of ritual throughout life. In Chapter 3, Joan Engebretson invites the reader to listen to the, "Voices of Healing" to learn messages from nurses who are concerned with caring and expanding nursing models to focus on healing as well as curing.

In Chapter 4, "Living Nursing's Values in Nursing Practice," Marilyn Parker presents an ongoing study that explores and describes nursing's values expressed by practicing nurses when asked the question, "What values do you hold most dear about nursing practice?" This existential investigation presents the enduring beliefs of nurses as lived rituals of caring. Charlotte Barry's paper, "Nursing Values Expressed in Caring Rituals" (Chapter 5) further explores living nursing values. Examining common rituals of bathing, combing hair, changing linen, Barry also uses storytelling to uncover meaning and significance of caring rituals that provide comfort and a shared knowing of interconnectedness.

Monica Nebauer (Chapter 6), presents one client's perspective in "Healing Through Therapeutic Touch." Using a case study approach to understand the lived experience of a person receiving therapeutic touch over time, the author provides not only the details of the process, but the client's inward journey of self-discovery, maturing, and healing.

Lynette Sheppard (Chapter 7) presents the perspective of nurse-healers in her paper, "Art and Beauty as Healing Modalities." Drawing from a qualitative research study of nurse healers, and her own experience as nurse and artist, the author discusses the power of symbols in healing and caring, and through the voices of nurse-healers, describes how art and beauty play profound roles in the healing process. Returning to the client's perspective, Cynthia Russell's "Care Recipient's Voices: Elders' Dependency Work" (Chapter 8) attempts to clarify the client's meanings of care, describe how clients seek and negotiate for care, and identify how clients act to influence their care relationships.

The evening workshops were an invitation to experience healing and caring rituals. The next three chapters were written by leaders of three of those sessions, Marilyn Parker (Chapter 9), "The Healing Art of Clay," Carol Picard (Chapter 10), "The Healing Expression of Dance," and Karen Vaught-Alexander (Chapter 11), "The Healing Art of Journaling." I trust the readers will find these chapters a rich source of reflection and an invitation to engage in creative healing rituals.

The next three papers address the theme of Hope. Linda Brown's (Chapter 12) "Healing as Hope," presents a patient's perspective of the many dimensions of hope as it is experienced in the reality of illness. In this paper, the author examines the meanings and structure of hope and identifies critical components of the experience of hope from the stories of individuals in search of healing as they face the realities of illness and suffering.

Chapter 13 is a very special personal story of "A Journey With

Breast Cancer" by A. Lynne Wagner. This is a beautiful, open, honest, and inspirational story of a painful experience. The author's storytelling as a re-living of the experience has a healing effect not only for herself, but also for those with whom it is shared. Lynne's story is an account of a human journey, lived in suffering, but molded into a colorful picture of hope.

The last chapter of this section (14) "Hoping for the Best" by Philip Darbyshire describes a study of "live-in" parent's experience in a large Scottish pediatric hospital. Using a combination of fieldwork, individual and focus group interviews with both resident parents and nurses, the study revealed the crucial importance of nurses' caring practices in helping parents adjust to being resident with their sick child.

The last set of papers includes authors who were accepted for the conference poster session, and have since completed their studies for publication. Rosze Barrington (Chapter 15), "A Naturalistic Inquiry of Post-Operative Pain After Therapeutic Touch," presents a thoughtful study of the therapeutic use of self through therapeutic touch with patients experiencing post-operative pain phenomena. The method used by the author draws upon some current models of application that are qualitatively sound derivatives of descriptive phenomenology.

In Chapter 16, "Harmony: The Path to Health," Carol Simonson invites the reader to a crosscultural dialogue on harmony or *hozho*, as the Navajo explain health. The author proposes to look at harmony as descriptive of the path toward and the destination of anyone seeking health.

Mary-Therese Dombeck in Chapter 17, "Dream Sharing: A Narrative Approach to Self-Care" asks the reader to consider dream telling as a social experience and a ritual of self-care. Based on the theoretical foundations of interactive groups and dream telling as healing symbolic storytelling, the author describes how a dream group can be a supportive and growth producing experience.

Janet Lakomy (Chapter 18) also examines healing in her paper, "Healing Rituals Experienced by Persons Living With AIDS." Utilizing phenomenology, the author addressed the question, "What are the healing rituals experienced by persons living with HIV-related infections?" Further questions about healing, and healing rituals and activities provided the researcher with emergent themes and upon further reflection, a description of the group's universal experience with healing rituals.

In Chapter 19, Maureen Propst and her colleagues, Laura Schenk and Sherry Clairain present a research study with the focus of caring in a specified setting—that of the birthing experience. The study, "Caring as Perceived During the Birth Experience," is a phenomenological approach to understanding the woman's lived experience during the intrapartum period.

The final paper (Chapter 20) "Caring and Learning: A Mosaic" by Kathryn Stewart Hegedus suggests that nurse faculty have a special responsibility to participate in the overall picture or mosaic of learning through caring and empowering actions. Shared student/teacher activities such as the evaluation of clinical learning is highlighted.

A special word of appreciation to all of the authors and peer reviewers for the excellent scholarship, continuing support, and advancement of the goals of the International Association for Human Caring. A special thank you also to all of the readers who have purchased this book. A percentage of the proceeds from the sale of this book is returned to the Association and provides some financial support for the annual Caring Research Conferences.

This publication would not have been possible without the assistance of Anne Boykin, my co-editor and now President of the IAHC, and the continuing support and expertise of Allan Graubard, Editorial Director of the National League for Nursing Press, and Nancy Jeffries, editor. Through combined efforts, this publication once again, furthers the goals of developing and expanding caring knowledge and research for the profession and discipline of nursing.

Delores A. Gaut, PhD, RN
Immediate Past President
IAHC, Inc.

Peer Reviewers

Agnes Aamodt, PhD, RN, FAAN
Professor Emerita
University of Arizona
College of Nursing
Tucson, AZ

Nancy Case, PhD, RN
Undergraduate Program Director
Regis College
School of Nursing
Englewood, CO

Linda Dietrich, MS, RN
Director of Professional Practice
Kaiser Sunnyside Medical Center
Portland, OR

Kathryn G. Gardner, MSN, RN
Director of Nursing Research
Rochester General Hospital
Rochester, NY

Cheryl Demerath Learn, PhD, RN
Lecturer
University of New Mexico
College of Nursing
Albuquerque, NM

Madeleine Leininger, PhD,
   RN, FAAN
Professor
Wayne State University
College of Nursing
Detroit, MI

Ruth M. Neil, PhD, RN
Assistant Professor
University of Colorado
School of Nursing
Denver, CO

Marilyn E. Parker, PhD, RN
Florida Atlantic University
College of Nursing
Boca Raton, FL

Francelyn Reeder, PhD, RN
Associate Professor
University of Colorado
Health Sciences Center
School of Nursing
Denver, CO

Doris Riemen, PhD, RN
Treasurer, IAHC, Inc.
Big Sandy, TX

Sister M. Simone Roach, PhD, RN
Researcher/Lecturer
Scarborough, Ontario
Canada

Gwen Sherwood, PhD, RN
Assistant Dean for Educational
   Outreach
University of Texas-Houston
School of Nursing
Houston, TX

Peer Reviewers

Sue A. Thomas, EdD, RN
Professor, Department of Nursing
Sonoma State University
Rohnert Park, CA

Kathleen L. Valentine, PhD, RN
Director of Evaluation
University of Wisconsin
Eau Claire, WI

Robin J. Watts, PhD, RN
Head, School of Nursing
Curtin University of Technology
Perth, WA
Australia

Zane Wolf, PhD, RN
Associate Professor
LaSalle University
School of Nursing
Ardmore, PA

Contributors

Karen Vaught-Alexander, PhD
Associate Professor of English and
Integrated Writing Program
Director
University of Portland
Portland, OR

Rosze Barrington, MS, ANP, CS, RN
Adult Nurse Practitioner
Native American Rehabilitation
Association
Indian Health Clinic
Portland, Oregon

Charlotte Barry, MSN RN
Adjunct Faculty
College of Nursing
Florida Atlantic University
Boca Raton, FL

Linda Brown, PhD, RN
Research Assistant Professor
Department of Psychosocial Nursing
University of Washington
Seattle, WA

Sherry Clairain, MSN, RN, C
Instructor
University of Mississippi
School of Nursing
Jackson, MS

Philip Darbyshire, PhD, RSCN
Lecturer in Health and Nursing
Studies
Department of Health and Nursing
Studies
Glasgow Caledonian University
Glasgow, Scotland

Mary-Therese Dombeck, PhD, RN
Assistant Professor of Nursing
University of Rochester
School of Nursing
Rochester, NY

Joan Engebretson, DrPH, RN
University of Texas
Health Sciences Center-Houston
School of Nursing
Houston, TX

Katie Eriksson, PhD, RN, Docent
Professor of Caring Science
Department of Caring Science
Abo Akademi University
Vasa, Finland

Delores A. Gaut, PhD, RN
Visiting Professor
University of Portland
School of Nursing
Portland, OR

Kathryn Stewart Hegedus, RN,
DNSc
Assistant Professor
University of Connecticut
Storrs, CT

Janet M. Lakomy, PhD, RN
Associate Professor
University of Texas at Tyler
Division of Nursing
Tyler, TX

Susan R. Moscato, EdD, RN
Adjunct Assistant Professor
University of Portland
School of Nursing
Portland, OR

Monica Nebauer, PhM, RN
Australian Catholic University
(QLD Div.)
Mitchelton, Brisbane
Queensland, Australia

Marilyn E. Parker, PhD, RN
Associate Professor
College of Nursing
Florida Atlantic University
Boca Raton, FL

Carol A. Picard, MS, RN, CS
Assistant Professor
Fitchburg State College
Fitchburg, MA

Maureen G. Probst, PhD, RN
Associate Professor
University of Mississippi
School of Nursing
Jackson, MI

Francelyn Reeder, PhD, RN, CNM
Associate Professor
University of Colorado
Health Sciences Center
University of Colorado
School of Nursing
Denver, CO

Cynthia K. Russell, PhD, RN, CS
Assistant Professor
College of Nursing
The University of Tennessee
Memphis, TN

Laura K. Schenk, MSN, RN
Instructor
University of Mississippi
School of Nursing
Jackson, MS

Lynette C. Sheppard, RN, CHT
Owner-Consultant
Haynes-Sheppard
Petaluma, CA

Carol L. S. Simonson, PhD, RN
Associate Professor
Georgia Southern University
Statesboro, GA

Jane A. Smith, MN, RN
Assistant Administrator
Patient Care Services
St. Vincent Hospital and Medical
Center
Portland, Oregon

A. Lynne Wagner, MSN, RN, C,
FNP
Assistant Professor
Fitchburg State College
Fitchburg, MA

Foreword

In the fast paced environment of today's world, it is indeed appropriate to research the concept of human caring. Most of our values are established when we are very young. Having respect and caring for one another begins with those significant life experiences in our early years. Kitty Davis, an author, of San Diego, California aptly describes such an event in her life:

> *Every child should have a mulberry tree to play around. My brothers and I did in the '20s and '30s on our farm. Seeing the tree get leaves was thrilling, and then the berries were yummy in pie, jam, and for throwing at each other and squashing under our feet. So we had purple feet to show each other.*
>
> *My younger brother and I were two years apart. The mulberry trees were life saving for us. When we got in trouble, which was most of the day, Mom would chase us up the mulberry trees, we would daydream and feed each other mulberries, never knowing mom didn't have to worry about us when we sat in the tree dreaming. One time my dad was sitting in the yard, and we threw mulberries down the ventilator and he came, all purple and he raised his fist and said 'I'll get you' and we stayed up in the tree a long time and laughed ourselves sick. Having a purple dad was so funny, even now at 69 years of age I can laugh at his purple sight—all mulberry-looking, and yelling his head off. We used to join hands and dance around the mulberry trees.*

So remember the children in your research on caring, as it is in our relationships in our younger years that the seed for future behaviors is planted.

Jane A. Smith, MN, RN
Assistant Administrator
Patient Care Services
St. Vincent Hospital and Medical Center
Portland, Oregon

REFERENCE

Davis, K. (1993). Good Times, in J. Maynard (Ed.), *Domestic Affairs,* Spring, 1993, *1*,(8), 5. Keene, New Hampshire.

Part I

Theories of Caring as Health

1

Theories of Caring as Health

Katie Eriksson

We are in a period of a paradigm shift in nursing toward a more historical and a more caring paradigm. A paradigm shift presupposes a change in the core of the theory. Do we have the courage for this change? Throughout the 1980s and continuing into the 1990s caring research has been directed to search for answers to the most basic questions about human caring. The internal problems of the science are today of most importance. Caring science needs scientific precision, i.e., distinct approaches to basic ontological, theoretical, and methodological questions. It is surprising how little attention these questions have been afforded in the international caring science debate. Caring science has not succeeded in separating itself from the medical-technical paradigm and forming a really distinct paradigm of its own. Only in the last few years have we seen discussion on a more concrete level, allowing for the development of an autonomous and humanistic orientation of caring science. Basic research within caring science clearly, therefore, needs more attention today (cf. Eriksson, 1988; Leininger, 1980; Lanara, 1981; Roach, 1984; Watson, 1985).

A CARING PARADIGM

My basic assumption is that the utmost aim of caring is to alleviate the patient's suffering, and therefore the nature of caring is to promote healing and health. I am building the presentation of my caring paradigm on Ford's (1975) components of a paradigm (Figure 1.1).

FIGURATION OF FACTS AND BASIC BELIEFS

The focus of this presentation is on the figuration of facts and basic beliefs for an ontological, humanistic model of caring and nursing, a "caritative caring model."

The basic concepts are:

1. The human being
      Patient
      Carer/Nurse

2. Suffering and health

3. The caritas motive—the ethics of caring

4. Caring
      Compassion
      Invitation and commitment to the caring relation
      Faith, hope and love

5. The caring communion

The Human Being

The human being is a whole of body, soul, and spirit. By spiritual is meant the phenomena which can be existential (not necessarily theistic) and religious (according to different religions). This view of the human being can provide for more caring possibilities. It also can provide for a more open view of knowledge than, for example, a view of the human being which does not recognize a spiritual dimension.

Human dignity means an inner freedom and a responsibility for one's own life and for other persons' lives. In its deepest sense—coherent with the meaning of life—a person's primary task is to be able to minister, to exist for another person. This idea is supported by, for

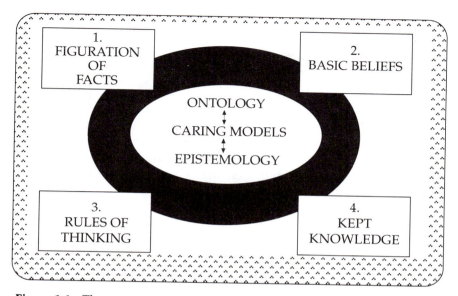

Figure 1.1 The components of a caring paradigm.

1. ***Figuration of facts***   or the researcher's conception of the world and of science. In the figuration of facts the researcher's conception of the "caring world" and of "caring science" is manifested in an inner structure or picture of caring. The basic concepts are defined and delineated out of this manifestation.

2. ***The basic beliefs***   are presented in basic assumptions; theses concerning the ontological foundation. The figuration of facts and the basic beliefs describe the ontology of caring and caring science.

3. ***Rules of thinking***   or the researcher's orientation in research methology and rules for conclusions.

4. ***Kept knowledge or body of knowledge***   The figuration of facts, basic beliefs and the rules of thinking direct the manifestation of the epistemology—the view of knowledge in caring science, models, and theories of caring.

instance, E. H. Erikson (1985), Lévinas (1988), and Tillich (1952). In this sense, health is a way to this ministering, but health cannot be the aim of caring (cf. Eriksson, 1981, 1987, 1989).

The Patient   The concept of a patient means a suffering person. The idea of health is consistent with the idea of the human person, i.e., one's conception of self and existence. Being healthy means being whole, experiencing oneself as a whole person. The experience of wholeness implies in its deepest sense an experience of "holiness"; reverence for one's own life, for oneself as a human being, and as someone unique.

As far as is known, caring, in many instances, is an objective, impersonal concept in the sense that health personnel do not sufficiently have regard for the unique, individual human being. One does not respect the human person and the individual's right to form one's own life. My responsibility for *the other*, i.e., the nurse's responsibility for the patient, is the ability to guarantee the patient the responsibility for his or her own life. This is my responsibility for another person's life. Love presupposes that I would not leave *the other* alone (cf. Lévinas, 1988).

The Carer/Nurse   The caring, caritative love, is based on the fact that nurses try to serve by seeing and confirming *the other*, i.e., taking responsibility for the patient. In that sense, this presupposes deliberate spiritual reflection. One is aware of the real value of human beings and their holiness. This idea is historically rooted in nursing, which I hope will be firmly established in the 1990s and become a lodestar for nurses in the future. In its deepest meaning, it is every nurse's wish to work on the basis of an inner motive of love (Eriksson, 1990).

Suffering and Health

The Esssence of Suffering   Nursing as a humanistic discipline means that a caring science has its roots in all aspects of human life. Suffering is part of human existence. Suffering can be explained in many ways, depending on which view is chosen. All suffering, however, has one common denominator, which is that suffering in some sense is *a dying*. Suffering is not a feeling or a pain, suffering is more fundamental, it is a state of being (Eriksson, 1992d; Lindholm & Eriksson, 1993).

Suffering   The human being is constantly in a fight between good and evil, suffering and pleasure. Evil reveals itself in many ways, sometimes getting the better of a person, who may find the suffering unendurable since it is unmotivated, i.e., it is in conflict with the sense of goodness, of ethics. This bad suffering can make deep wounds in a human being. The suffering person, the patient (the word patient derives from a word for suffering), needs care that makes the suffering endurable. The human being tries to get away from the unendurable suffering by escaping suffering, by entering illness or perhaps denying it, closing it in or becoming immovable to be able to stand it.

A human being must be able to perceive love in order to suffer. Suffering in the present is related to the human ability to suffer. An ability to suffer is a condition for human growth and sound development. A person's ability to suffer may to some extent have disappeared. Frankl (1987) considers it important to help a suffering person to have ability to suffer. Through suffering a human being comes in contact with the basic conditions of life, and through suffering a human being can grow to understand the meaning of suffering. The ability to suffer is not based on an understanding of why, but on the courage to perceive the actual feeling. By all the premature explaining and excusing, we deprive the human being of the possibility to perceive suffering and thereby face suffering and possibly grow through it.

Suffering in itself has no meaning, but people could, having lived through it, realize that it was in fact meaningful to do so. There is a great danger that we all too soon give suffering a purpose in order to explain it away, or that we think that suffering can be alleviated by giving it meaning.

The alleviation of suffering presupposes a recognition and confirmation of suffering in its different shapes and expressions, and an understanding in its deepest sense. Many questions arise as we stand before a suffering human being. Our interest is directed toward the suffering human being in the caring process, the patient. Do we see the suffering and how it is expressed? How is the nurse prepared to alleviate the patient's suffering? These and many other questions formed the basis of suffering-research (Eriksson, 1992d; Lindholm & Eriksson, 1993).

The Model: Drama of Suffering Findings from suffering-research has revealed that there is suffering in caring. There is a suffering not specifically connected with illness, but with human existence. The faces of suffering are so many that suffering becomes intangible and impossible to reach. Still, one of the most important things is to have the courage to admit that suffering exists and to try to reach it. Experiences described by the nurses often show that there are ways to understand suffering human beings. A model of suffering in caring has been created through the research. We call the model "the drama of suffering." Every single suffering is a drama of various degrees of substance and intensity. The drama is formed by "the acts"; confirming; being in suffering and becoming in suffering (reconciliation or un-reconciliation) (cf. Eriksson, 1992d; Lindholm & Eriksson, 1993).

The first act is shaped by the extent to which the nurse is able to confirm the patient's suffering. She can either see and accept the suffering, or she can overlook and try to explain it away because she is not able, or lacks the courage to see it. The second act consists of the nurse's ability to permit suffering, to let the patient remain suffering, to be able to suffer with and share in the patient's suffering. The third act could lead to a reconciliation where suffering is part of a new wholeness, but it could also lead to non-reconciliation. Non-reconciliation is a new disappointment to the suffering person. It means not having been received and been confirmed in suffering, which leads to the suffering becoming rigid and sinking deeper and deeper into the human being, not as a natural part of the person, but as something strange and frightening.

The Essence of Health   Little by little a guiding principle has emerged about the essence of health. Some central premises have been developed. A "final" concept of health, an ontological model, has developed when studying health by interviewing several hundred people and through abductive logic. Abductive logic was developed by the American philosopher Charles Peirce. Peirce (1958) developed a theory of "inquiry," a process of thinking. A conviction, belief, is confused by new experiences and doubt arises about the unwillingness which tries to find its way out, to find a new conviction which is similar to the new experiences. Having found a new conviction, the process of thinking settles down until new impulses arise. This process is characteristic of the scientific method and its goal is to provide convincing evidence that all reasonable human beings cannot doubt. Peirce (1958) calls this logical reconstruction speculative rhetoric.

Toward an Ontological Model of Health   By an ontological model of health we mean a way toward health that is an integral part of life and being of the human person, a true experience of wholeness. To experience oneself as whole implies an inner sense to experience holiness, to feel veneration for one's own life, for oneself as a human being, and thus someone unique. To make a person feel holy, it is assumed that the person is in contact with an innermost core, one's spirituality and religiousness (cf. Eriksson, 1989; Frankl, 1987).

The concept analysis of health suggests that there are different dimensions and levels of health. We presuppose that there is a third perspective in addition to the clinical/medical and the holistic ones (cf. Nordefeldt, 1991). This concept of health we call ontological. By this we mean a concept of health that derives from health as growing toward a deeper oneness (cf. Eriksson, 1992c).

The purpose of an ontological health model is to provide a deeper perspective for understanding true health. We assume three different dimensions of health: health as behavior, health as being, and health as becoming.

Health as Behavior, to Have Health   In the first dimension a person thinks in terms of "having health," or health as behavior or doing. One judges one's health on the basis of external, often objective criteria. One often connects health with a certain behavior, living in a healthy way and avoiding anything that could endanger one's health. One is concerned with problems connected to illness.

The persons we assume to be functioning in this dimension are totally absorbed by this in their way of thinking and acting. For others, who are functioning in the dimension of becoming or being, this dimension does not play an important role, though it still is there. Going through different models of health promotion, one notices that most of the models deal with this dimension of health.

Health as Being   Health as being implies a state of health and is characterized by a search for some kind of balance or harmony in the inner state. One understands the connection between physiological, psychological and social factors, between body and soul, and between internal and external factors. Needs are a manifestation of existence and biological life. Desire goes deeper than need and beyond the spoken word.

Persons we assume to be functioning in this dimension have their mind set on reaching a state of equilibrium and harmony. It becomes essential to them to fulfill their needs. They also want balance in their own relations and different life situations. Most of the caring models could be assigned to this category, which emanates from the human wish to adapt and seek for the fulfillment of needs.

Health as Becoming   Health as becoming starts with the assumption that the human being is always becoming something, he or she is shaped or reshaped but is never complete (cf. Bergson, 1928). Growing toward health means that a person becomes whole on a higher level of integration, achieving in the sense of holiness. Frankl (1987) associates oneness with the spiritual. According to him, it is only the spiritual person who creates oneness and wholeness in the being we call human. The wholeness one creates is a physical, mental and spiritual wholeness. It is the spiritual that forms the true essence of the human being (Frankl, 1987, p. 27). These are human beings that are determined by their goals, and not driven by coincidence and external circumstances. They become more and more their own true essence. Becoming implies a higher state of awareness (cf. Newman, 1986). The experience of holiness is an important source of energy in an individual, and in order to be a whole person, one must be able to return to the original state of (experienced) wholeness. E. H. Erikson (1985) calls this process rebirth. Eliade (1968) called it re-creation, and Tillich (1952) sees it as the basis of existence and source of courage for everything. In this essential experience one will find the source of belief and hope which together with love provides central sources of energy. This person feels freedom and vitality and can live as a complete and whole human being. He or she lives in peace and wants to live and to grow. In order to be able to talk about health as wholeness, there has to be a dimension of "being" as well as a dimension of "becoming." This means an active consciousness of one's own health, i.e., health is part of a person, something within a person. A person has to have the courage to cross the borderline of doing and being, and enter the definite freedom of becoming, the courage to surrender to one's own inner self (cf. Eriksson, 1992c).

Buber (1963) discusses the difficulties connected with the struggle of the person in surrendering to an inner being. Anything a human being should do should be done with all of one's being so that nothing of one's self will be omitted. Those who cannot collect themselves in this way cannot be harmonious creatures and find peace.

The persons we assume to be living on this level concentrate on questions of life. They know suffering but try to reconcile it with the circumstances of life. It could be crises as well as moments of happiness that lead a human being to a better understanding of the terms of existence.

Existing on the level of becoming, the human being is an integral oneness; one part cannot be separated from another. Movement in becoming changes between integration and disintegration. The integration can emerge by internal or external forces. The innermost center that expresses itself through desire must grow in relation to the external fields, the needs, and the social instinct.

Suffering and health belong together. If suffering and health are regarded as natural parts of life, then suffering must be a part of health. We know that suffering can be unendurable. But through facing suffering we learn to endure it, and the experience becomes a positive resource in life. Unendurable suffering in turn cripples us and prevents us from growing. Health is endurable suffering.

Health presupposes a suffering that is endurable (cf. Eriksson, 1992d). The unendurable suffering or the unnatural suffering that causes wounds that will not heal may momentarily be forgotten but will always be carried around and will always exist as potential for suffering in time and space.

The Caritas Motive—The Ethics of Caring

The idea and origins of caring have come under consideration during the last few years. The caritas motive can be traced through semantics, anthropology, and the history of ideas.

The concept of "caring" is connected with the concept of "love." The English word "cherish" (which means to hold dear, feel or show love for) originates from the Latin word "carus" (in English: "care," "caring") which means love. "Caritas" means human love and charity (Nygren, 1972). Anthropologically, every human being has a desire to give and to recieve love (cf. Lévinas, 1988). The history of ideas states that the foundation of the caring profession through the ages has been an inclination to help and minister to those suffering (Eriksson, 1992a).

Caring is also the essence of humanity and the basic constitutive phenomena of human existence (cf. Leininger, 1980; Roach, 1992; Watson, 1988). True caring is not a form of behavior, not a feeling or a state, it is a being. The caritas motive, the idea of caring as an expression of human love and charity, is one of the ideas that has been shaping caring for hundreds of years (Vonhoff, 1962). There is hardly any other guiding idea, however, that has been so invisible in nursing practice. True caring is not just an abstract thought, a philosophy, or an ideology; the performance of caring is a most tangible work, encountering suffering in real situations, being there.

The caritas motive, as the basic motive of caring, implies the core, i.e., responsibility for another person in caritative caring. In other words, true caring is based on human love. This does not mean, however, that caring science disregards the fact that technology also is necessary in nursing. The core of nursing is caring; the author holds that the components of caring are purging, playing, and learning in a spirit of love, truth, and hope (Eriksson, 1987).

Ethical Motive   Caring is in itself ethics (cf. Nodding, 1984). The true, ethical element does not appear until one enters into a real relation with another person. The ethical foundations, frames and models we may carry with us, in some form, but only as premises or a potential; and it is not enough for us to have knowledge of the ethical premises, they also have to be integrated with our basic disposition (cf. Eriksson, 1992b).

Our ethics are determined by our ethical motive. Can a person's ethics vary from one situation to another? When it comes to the application of ethical rules and principles ethics may vary, but the fundamental ethical standpoint is an integral part of a person's entity. We could distinguish between three dimensions in a person's ethical dimension, which are connected to the ethical motive: social motive, humanistic motive, and caritas motive (Figure 1.2).

The different motives represent different dimensions within what we might call the ethical human being and, at the same time, they reflect different levels or depths in both our human relations and above all, our caring. What matters is our standpoint in life, the responsibility and liberty of human beings, and how far we are prepared to go in sacrificing ourselves for another.

A great deal of today's human interaction has a social motive. Human interaction tends to become reduced to a superficial social responsibility. We want to intervene and correct the behavior we do not accept, but in a deeper sense we are not prepared to take care of the person; our motives are not very profound.

The humanistic motive is based upon humanity and goodness. Nurses have a professional responsibility for human needs and human existence. They are prepared to help within certain limits. We defend human freedom in the sense that we gladly pass the responsibility on to someone else.

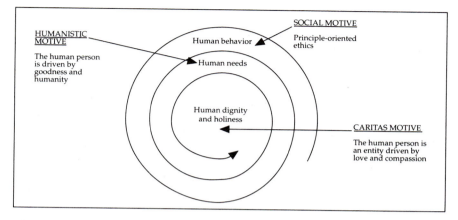

Figure 1.2   Nurse's ethical motive.

The most profound motive is the "caritas" motive, which makes one act out of love and compassion, while also demanding responsibility for one's own inner development. Caritative caring means putting "caritas" into use, and using it for the human being, health, and life. In the professional sense, it means using it for a certain purpose, i.e., for the person who is more or less suffering, or in some kind of distress and need. Caritative caring is a manifestation of the love which "just exists," and which has a caring effect through its very existence in a caring culture. Love is in essence genuinely good by nature. The human suffering is sometimes unendurable, and therefore it might be difficult for love to penetrate suffering and pain. Suffering, pain, sorrow, and evil do not per se change the very essence of love, but they can exclude positive experiences. The caring, caritative love, is based on the fact that we always try to save the "distinction," by seeing "the other," and taking responsibility for an other. In that sense, the love is total ethic. This presupposes deliberate spiritual reflection and awareness of the real value of the person and of that person's holiness. This is the historically rooted nurse I hope will be rediscovered in the 1990s and become a lodestar for nurses in the future.

Caring

The caritas motive is the core of caring. Compassion is the force, which motivates a person to care. "So much compassion—so much care." The substance of caring is faith, hope, and love. The invitation opens the act of caring. The core of nursing is caring—a deep human and professional communion. The idea of caring is to alleviate suffering in a spirit of "caritas," i.e., in faith, hope, and love.

Compassion True caring is based on compassion. Compassion will emerge in the meeting between suffering and love. The nurse's ability to feel compassion emerges from personal experiences of suffering and love. One does not acquire compassion by advanced skills and techniques. Roach (1992) defines compassion as a way of living born out of an awareness of one's relationship to all living creatures; engendering a response of participation in the experience of another; a sensitivity to the pain and brokenness of the other; a quality of presence which allows one to share with and make room for the other. Compassion involves a simple, unpretentious presence to each other.

The Invitation The basic structure for all kinds of caring is the relationship between the patient and the nurse. In a caring relationship the ethical element is contained even in our invitation (cf. Kierkegaard, 1928), i.e., in the way we "invite" the patient to the relation. The "ethical" appears, among other things, in the correlation between the invitation offered to the patient and subsequently the way in which the patient is accepted into this relationship. What is significant in caring, as opposed to, for example, therapy, is that there ought to be a constant invitation to the patient. This means that the nurse, by her basic attitude, signals "Welcome," "I am here" and "I am here for You." The ethical in caring is to invite the patient as a guest of honor.

Faith, Hope, and Love During life humans need some "basic food." This basic food is faith, hope, and love. The premise that health is faith, hope, and love, derives its origins from the assumption that individuals throughout their lives need faith, hope, and love in order to be able to mature and grow as natural human beings. According to E. H. Erikson (1985), faith, hope, and love are different forms of the basic human virtue which, in different life phases, emerge as predominant resources when the natural development is improved (compare also May, 1972, 1983). The premise about health as belief, hope, and love could be formed as faith, hope, and love in the benefit of health (Eriksson, 1987).

Faith for the benefit of health cannot prevent non-health, but it helps to adopt a trustful position toward existence. Faith is dependent on the will of the subject. Faith and health belong together. Hope as wish, prospect, and expectation aims at future. Hope as faith confidence, waiting, and consolation gives a person strength in the present. The connection with *friend* is interesting. One can assume that a friend (either concrete or abstract) means hope. Anyone with a real friend has someone to trust.

Hope is a motion between hope and hopelessness. According to Fromm (1968), the human being experiences hope consciously and hopelessness unconsciously. Hopelessness puts hope in motion. One should not be aware of hopelessness where it is not mingled with conscious hope. Spinoza (1983) defines hope as a varying mind governed by our concepts of something in the future or past, the outcome of which is not entirely certain. The ability to hope means that a person has not given up, that he or she believes in the future.

Who would not principally admit the need for love, growth, development, and health? Everybody has a vision about the essence of love and an imagination about its meaning just for one's self and one's health. But paradoxically, we know that one has an ability to admit love, to really dare to believe in love and let it benefit one's own health. The devoted, claimless care and caring are the basis for will and wish, or actually for our hope (cf. May, 1972). Even if health is faith, love and hope from a caring science perspective, health can only be understood in relation to suffering.

The Caring Communion

If the basic assumption is that caring communion is the context of caring, it may be supposed that communion is the source of power and meaning in caring. It is this inner context which is the basis for the inner desire to care.

According to a lexical definition, communion means "the act of sharing, an intimate relationship with deep understanding" (Webster's New World Dictionary, 3rd Edition). We are born to live in communion with others. Communion is the basis for human society (Buber, 1963; May, 1983; Tillich, 1952). One logical consequence of this premise is that all forms of caring are variations on human communion (Eriksson, 1992a).

Joining in communion means creating possibilities for the other. Lévinas (1988) suggests that considering someone as one's own son implies crossing the border of "the possible." This is a relationship which perceives the other person's possibilities as if they were one's own. It means the ability to shake off the liability of one's own identity and something which is just one's own, and move toward something which is no longer one's own but which belongs to oneself. It is one of the deepest forms of communion, according to Lévinas (1988). It is fatherhood.

Descriptions of caring situations in an empirical research study (Eriksson, 1990) include caritative elements. At the heart of caring communion there are different prerequisites which appear to be most important for its experience. Heading the list is a genuine, mature, and professional attitude. This is something more than basic neighborliness and friendship. The professional attitude implies responsibility, genuineness, courage, and wisdom.

Caring communion requires meeting in time and space, an absolute, lasting presence. Time as a quantity is of no great significance, but the quality of shared time with the other is important. This kind of time experience is not objectively connected with time experiences in general; it has more to do with the ability to achieve an absolute experience of presence.

The substance of caring communion can be summarized as the art of making something very special out of something less special. Caring communion is a creative act which can imply different forms and contents, but it is characterized by intensity, vitality, openness, and possibilities.

The meaning of caring communion can be summarized as the ability to do good for another person. It is the source of power and meaning in caring which is the basis for the inner desire to care. In its deepest meaning it is every nurse's wish to be guided by an inner motive (Eriksson, 1992a).

SUMMARY

The premises for the caring model presented here include:

1. The human being is a whole of body, soul, and spirit. By spiritual we mean spiritual phenomena which can be existential (not necessarily theistic) and religious (according to different religions). This view of the human being can provide for more caring possibilities. It also can provide for a

more open view of knowledge than, for example, a view which does not recognize a spiritual dimension.

2. In my view, human beings are religious although everyone has not personally accepted this dimension. By religious we mean here a person's longing for and dependence on something outside oneself, something transcendent, a God or an abstract other.

3. Human dignity means an inner freedom and a responsibility for one's own life and for other persons' lives. In its deepest sense—coherent with the meaning of life—a person's primary task is to be able to minister, to exist for another person.

4. Health is more than the absence of illness. To be healthy is to be whole, to experience and feel whole as regards body, soul, and spirit. Health is part of life. Health has no meaning unless life has meaning. Health is consistent with endurable suffering.

5. The basic category—that which motivates every kind of caring—is suffering.

6. Caring is based on the motive of caritas, which through compassion awakens a desire to alleviate another's suffering.

7. The basic structure for all kinds of caring is the relationship between the patient and the nurse. This relationship is an invitation and it is the way of acceptance of the other into the relationship.

8. A caring communion is the essential context of caring and it will occur in an unselfish relationship with the other (between the patient and the nurse), when the patient and the nurse have an interest in common, to help the patient.

9. Caring is naturally a manifestation of human love. The core of caring is purging, playing, and learning in a caritative disposition, i.e., in a spirit of faith, hope, and love.

10. The basis for every kind of caring is unconditional caritative ethics, i.e., a responsibility and a desire to do what is good, that which springs from the nurse's basic attitude toward caring.

The relation between the basic concepts describes the conceptual model. Basic concepts direct the figuration of facts in the caring reality, i.e., *what* we see or what we want to see. The reality of what we see or want to see is based on our thinking and values. Basic concepts determine the substance—the core of the theory. In different theories of caring and nursing, we can find different basic concepts. The conceptual model and the main theses describe our ontology.

In developing the discipline of nursing and caring science, the goal of a discipline is to get close to the core, the very essence of the actual reality, i.e., to provide good care. Today we must develop the true core of the theory in order to be able to change the paradigm in caring practice and caring science. Concretely, this means returning to the original idea of caring, caring characterized by human love as the heart of technological care.

Caring is defined by its ontology. As nursing evolves, it is increasingly important to clarify its ontological foundation as both prerequisite to, and interactive with, its caring epistemology, methology, and praxis.

REFERENCES

Bergson, H. (1928). *Den skapande utvecklingen*. Stockholm: Wahlström & Widstrand.

Buber, M. (1963). *Jag och Du*. (Original title 1924: Ich und Du.) Stockholm: Bonniers.

Eliade, M. (1968). *Heligt och profant*. Stockholm: Verbum.

Erikson, E. H. (1985). *Den fullbordade livscykeln*. Stockholm: Natur och Kultur.

Eriksson, K. (1981). *The Patient Care Process—an Approach to Curriculum Construction within Nursing Education. The Development of a Model for the Patient Care Process and an Approach for Curriculum Development Based on the Process of Patient Care*. Helsinki: Department of Education, University of Helsinki, No. 94.

Eriksson, K. (1987). *Vårdndets idé*. (The Idea of Caring.) Stockholm: Almqvist & Wiksell.

Eriksson, K. (1988). *Caring Science as a Discipline.* Reports from Department of Caring Science, No 1. Åbo: Åbo Akademi.

Eriksson, K. (1989). *Hälsans idé.* (The Idea of Health.) Stockholm: Almqvist & Wiksell.

Eriksson, K. (1990). *Pro Caritate. Caritative Caring—A Situational Analysis and Empirical Study Concerning the Existence of Caritative Caring.* Reports from Department of Caring Science. Åbo: Åbo Akademi.

Eriksson, K. (1992a). *Caring Communion.* In Gaut, D. A. (Ed.) *The presence of caring in nursing,* pp. 201–210. New York: National League for Nursing Press.

Eriksson, K. (1992b). *Caring Ethics.* 6th Biennial Conference of the Workgroup of European Nurse Researchers, 23–26, 9, 1992, Madrid. Abstract.

Eriksson, K. (1992c). *Multidimensional Health.* International Research Conference of Nursing: Promoting Health, 9–11,9, 1992, London. Abstract.

Eriksson, K. (1992d). The alleviation of suffering—The idea of caring. *Scandinavian Journal of Caring Sciences,* 6, 2, 119–123.

Ford, J. (1975). *Paradigms and fairy tales: An introduction to the science of meaning.* Volume 1. London: Routledge & Kegan Paul.

Frankl, V. (1987). *Gud och det omedvetna.* Psykologi och religion. (Original title: Der unbewusste Gott. Psychoterapie und Religion.) Stockholm: Natur och Kultur.

Fromm, E. (1968). *Kärlekens konst.* Stockholm: Natur och Kultur.

Kierkegaard, S. (1928). *Dagbok.* Stockholm: Svenska Diakoniföreningens förlag.

Lanara, V. (1981). *Heroism as a nursing value: A philosophical perspective.* Athens: Sisterhood Evniki.

Leininger, M. (1980). Caring: A central focus for nursing and health care services. *Nursing & Health Care,* 1(3), 135–143, 176.

Lévinas, E. (1988). *Etik och oändlighet.* Stockholm-Lund: Symposion Bokförlag och tryckeri AB.

Lindholm, L., & Eriksson, K. (1993). To understand and to alleviate suffering in a caring culture. *Journal of Advanced Nursing,* Summer 1993.

May, R. (1972). *A Search for the Sources of Violence.* (Sw. transl. 1974. Makt och oskuld. Stockholm: Bonniers.)

May, R. (1983). *Den omätbara människan: om människosynen i existentialistisk psykologi och terapi.* Stockholm: Bonniers. (Original title: The Discovery of Being: Writings in existential psychology.)

Newman, M. (1986). *Health as expanding consciousness.* St. Louis: C. V. Mosby Company.

Nodding, N. (1984). *Caring: A feminine approach to ethics/moral education.* Berkeley: University of California Press.

Nordefeldt, L. (1991). *Hälsa och värde.* Stockholm: Thales.

Nygren, A. (1972). *Meaning and method.* London: Epworth Press.

Peirce, C. S. (1958). *Collected Papers,* vols. 1–8. 1931–1958. Cambridge, MA: Harvard University Press.

Roach, M. S. (1984). *Caring: The human mode of being, implications for nursing.* Toronto, Canada: The University of Toronto. Monograph series.

Roach, M. S. (1992). *The human act of caring: A Blueprint for the health professions.* (Rev. ed.) Ottawa: Canadian Hospital Association.

Spinoza, B. 1983. *Etik.* Göteborg: Daidalos.

Tillich, P. (1952). *The courage to be.* Yale University Press. (Sw. transl. Modet att vara till. Stockholm: AB Tryckmans.)

Vonhoff, H. 1962. *I kamp mot nöd. Barmhärtighetens historia.* Stockholm: EFS-förlag.

Watson, J. (1985). *Nursing: Human science and human care, A theory of nursing.* Norwalk: Appleton-Century-Crofts.

Webster's New World Dictionary of American English. (3rd ed.) New York: Webster's New World.

Part II

Rituals of Healing

2

Rituals of Healing: Ever Ancient, Ever New

Francelyn Reeder

In David Cohen's inspiring book, *The Circle of Life* (1991), the introduction tells us the images collected represent an essential moment in the subject's experience. Gabriel García Marquez (Cohen, 1991) suggests that the viewer must see ritual with historical eyes, in order to move from partial understanding to deeper richness.

> For it is not merely that the instants portrayed here—births, comings of age, marriages and deaths—are important ones. It is that they are predictably important, repeatedly important, important in the same way throughout history, as billions of human beings attempt to navigate the same life crises as regularly as clockwork, and it is that this predictability and repetition present society with a tremendous opportunity. The occasion to meticulously, painstakingly, thicken the air—to assign meaning, and to do so again and again, adding here, adjusting there, until the end result is the group of ceremonies we call the Rites of Passage—rituals of such surpassing power, complexity and joy, that they sometimes seem to transcend normal experience and leave us a sense of humankind partaking of the divine (VanBiema, 1991).

This chapter will express the point of view of an educator, researcher, and practitioner on the topic of healing ritual. Using a hermeneutic view, I will emphasize *mindfulness* and *integrity* of the *cosmic self in ac-*

tion. I propose these elements are common to the making, breaking, and remaking of ritual throughout life. In talking about rituals of healing, a return to the nature of ritual as it is manifest across time and culture is necessary. A grand view is enlightening and provides a glimpse of implications for nursing as a practice discipline, specifically as ritual is relevant to the manner in which practice ideals are lived in the service of others.

I invite readers to become reflective through a centering process, and suggest that features of our own lives serve as referents linking meaning to those I discuss as I review ritual in Western society. Notice where Western society has been, where we are now, and where we may be in the future. It is not my intention to present an in-depth anthropological study of ritual, but rather to awaken insights, recognizable to you, through thoughtful interpretation of prevalent voices on the topic.

WHAT IS RITUAL?

The planning committee chose the term *ritual* for this discussion instead of any of the familiar terms to nursing such as *method, approach,* or *praxis of healing*. Their choice delights me! Although I have used the title "Natural Healing Modalities" for a course being taught at the University of Colorado, ritual says it better and captures the essential features of caring practice expressed by nursing scholars in the caring literature. Let me say what I mean by ritual through a few ancient and new voices on the topic. I will then explain why I believe ritual has become important, again, for western society!

On the larger scale of life, Margaret Mead suggested that, "The essence of ritual is the ability of the known form to reinvoke past emotion, to bind the individual to his own past experience, and to bring the members of the group together in a shared experience" (1972, p. 127). Such an anthropological perspective affirms the view that ritual (the known form) reflects and creates the values of a culture just as Hildegard of Bingen envisioned through the mandala, "All Beings Celebrate Creation" (Fox, 1985, p. 74).

Recently, Jeanne Achterberg, writer and author in transpersonal medicine, eloquently emphasized, "Rituals for healing have the purpose of giving credence and significance to life's transitions; they provide maps of form and guidance for behavior during perilous times when bodies, minds, and spirits are broken" (1992, p. 22). Further, Achterberg observes, "The acts of ritual allow people to share their common experiences and to give visible support to one another. The symbols and events of healing ritual cement the healer/healee bonds and engender faith and hope that the passage into the place of whole- ness, harmony, or relief of suffering will be achieved" (p. 158). An example is provided again through the mandala of Hildegard, "The Man in Sapphire Blue: A Study in Compassion" (Fox, 1985, p. 22). These assumptions are inherent in ritual and provide meaning and im- portance to a culture. When the meaning of a ritual breaks down, the ritual itself breaks down, and people cast it aside, seeking elsewhere for sources of transformation in their lives.

Achterberg (1992) warns "A wide range of cultural and temporal diversity in symbols is . . . to be expected because all symbols must address the current metaphor or myth (or paradigm) if they are to have any power to communicate or represent the unseen worlds" (p. 158). Without clues to an unseen world, is it any wonder that ritualistic be- havior in nursing was met with resistance and replaced by deliberative nursing in the 1960s? Or that today a one-sided fascination and ease with high technology in the health care arena is being challenged and balanced by efforts in nursing? Re-emphasis on the art and humanistic nature of compassionate caring is visible in the development of theo- ries of practice. Perhaps, in summary, one could say the nature of rit- ual healing requires a mutual relationship, a partnership. The words of an Aboriginal Australian woman express this mutuality of attitude well:

> *If you have come to help me*
> *You are wasting your time.*
> *But if you have come because*
> *Your liberation is bound up with mine,*
> *Then let us work together.*
>
> Brencato, 1990

At face value, very few of us would disagree that the ritual features mentioned are good, desirable, and constructive. However, in every- day speech, the word "ritual" often is used to connote repetition of empty, meaningless forms or actions. Attention to the underlying responses to ritual reveal patterns of breaking, keeping, and remaking of rituals.

The Breaking of Ritual   Evidence of growing discomfort and outright rejection of rituals in the United States arose in the 1960s, for example, against countless societal conventions and perfunctory religious practices. These responses were evident during the Vietnam war and following the monumental changes in the Catholic Church conferred by the Second Vatican Council. Counterculture movements increased in number. Signs and symbols of a different identity emerged and challenged the status quo with diversity and extremes in behavior, values, and dress! A cry for recognition of a different identity was expressed! The need for more flow and flexibility of structures in the church and society was voiced. Pope John XXIII at this time in history ushered in a new world view, one that opened the doors and windows in the church that effected a vitality and renewal of spirit that would change the lives of the people of God for the next century. Provisional structures which had been created over many previous centuries were reevaluated in light of the needs of the times and changes were made to simplify the rules and obligations affecting the daily life of the people. Celebration of the Mass was no longer celebrated in Latin, but instead a spirit of community was created through the vernacular language of the people. A change in ritual language was said by many to have an enormous impact on their sense of belonging and understanding of the meaning behind the sacred rituals, one that empowered their daily lives.

Major changes in governance within the communities of the faithful were decentralized, with authority to be participatory and collaborative; decisions were made through processes of discernment. Roles and relationships were based on respect for every person, recognized with human dignity. This shift meant rituals of behavior associated with hierarchical structures depended less on conformity of exterior sign, gesture, and symbol but more on interior unity of spirit through love. A renewed emphasis on the importance of the individual required greater attention to processes in which unique voices would be heard, and opened the development of opportunities for personal growth and fullness of life to everyone. Intentional communities were characterized by persons who experienced renewal of spirit and energy to live for purposes larger than themselves, and to participate in social change, protection of human rights, and overcoming of social injustices and violence. Changes in governance brought balance to the lives of people, expressed in a new motif to: Think globally and act locally. In other words, the story was being retold by participation of the people, by the people, and for the people.

Today, sexist language presents a challenge for change because noninclusive language symbolizes a long history of oppression and injustice in women's lives not only in the church but also in society. If change at the level of ritual language is effected, there is hope that emancipation and human development at the level of life itself will occur.

Serious study and reflection on evolutionary or revolutionary changes in the history of humankind have been described as "breaking out of the procrustean bed of obsolescence" (Rogers, 1970, p. 28). When the purpose or meaning of ritual ceases to exist for people, like an albatross around the neck, ritual can take on a destructive influence for a major group in society. What happens? Does ritual lose meaning? Or do people with changed consciousness change ritual meaning? Several reasons from various perspectives could be given to explain why or how rituals loose their meaning. Can you think of rituals in your life that became sources of embarrassment, or even pain, yet for others these same rituals continued to have meaning?

I would propose that a shift in interpretation relates to making public what has been private. That is, growth in self awareness and global consciousness is a plausible outcome after an experience of having what you thought was private, suddenly presented in the public media. This happened in the Church when the revered leader, Pope John XXIII, took the public stand that human dignity has social implications. For example, Vatican II reaffirmed the dignity of the person, and restored practices that would encourage individuals to take responsibility for their own actions, rather than to be oppressed or rendered silent by rules that lack the Spirit. In this light, ritualistic behavior is distinguished from *authentic rituals of healing* in the church and elsewhere. For example, in nursing, full participation of persons involved in a ritual of healing requires mindful consideration of all individual needs and preferences. Ethical codes of conduct are reminders, but simple conformity to behavior or imitation of gestures characteristic of a protocol is not enough! People will suffer rather than be healed or helped from mindless, heartless robotic actions.

Taking personal responsibility for actions with others transforms the private interest into the public, cultural interest. When long-respected rituals of a culture are broken by a large number from that culture, the meanings embedded in the ritual can be antiquated. If rituals are not made fresh and relevant over time with renewal of connections with current life, such rituals cannot be expected to address the hunger people have for meaning in their lives. After a period of time with suppressive structural rituals, where there is a failure to rejuvenate and transform ritual, there often follows a desire by the people for simplicity, to create or rediscover the root connection of life. Complex, ornate, detailed rituals tend to overwhelm the uninitiated.

Perhaps the reason for such rejection of ritual can be traced back to the simple failure of leaders/educators to *tell the story* behind the ritual; an action easily included at the time symbol and action are being performed. Has the story became too complex and difficult to retell because the contemporary use of language, competing social practices and values are too diverse from one another? Where is the truth? Your own story reveals the answer to the breakdown of ritual in your own life. The rituals which remain meaningful to me are the ones shared in family, community, and professional celebrations that relate to the major transitions in life shared by the people I knew. They are rituals that expressed affirmations and renewed commitment to shared values at significant moments in my life.

Keeping and Remaking Ritual   In contrast to breaking with rituals that have an apparent poverty of meaning, there definitely are other responses. Rarely are rituals in society simply dropped from life. Several studies on ritual in the home indicate families are replacing meaningless rituals with new ones, however simple or complex (McGuire, 1988; Imber-Black & Roberts, 1992; VanBiema, 1991). It seems, the integrity of the self in community action is created through ritual making and in turn enacts the rituals. Think of yourself in caring situations and observe. As long as rituals are meaningful, the cycle of making, keeping, breaking, and remaking ritual repeats itself. Such dynamic renewal has the potential to be efficacious for reconciling the private and public realms of meaning within a group as a whole (Wolin, Bennett, & Fiese, 1992).

Recent studies of family rituals by Imber-Black and Roberts (1992) in *Rituals for Our Times* describe the pattern of making, keeping, breaking, and remaking rituals as they occur in middle class families in several cultures. His research identifies many parallels between each family's intention for ritual, even while differences existed in the way they chose to express ancient and traditional rituals, whether expressed in word, symbol and/or action. These parallels indicate enduring qualities of ritual from antiquity to the present. Imber-Black and Roberts (1992) describe familiar rituals common to family life, and provide helpful suggestions for families to remake time-worn rituals. They suggest that thoughtful review of symbolic actions and symbolic objects and words involved in a particular ritual will help decide whether particular symbols carry the meanings you want to express. Examples are recognized in the questions Imber-Black, Roberts, and Whiting ask: "Does Mother do all of the food shopping, preparation, and cleanup for a holiday, while Father stands at the 'head' of the table and carves the turkey?" and then asks the meaning of this symbolic action. "Does it express the gender relationships you want?" "What does it mean for a bride to be 'given away' by her father to her husband?" (1988, p. 139). Imber-Black et al. gives evidence of many couples who question and alter this symbolic action, creating a wedding ceremony where both sets of parents escort their offspring to the altar, symbolizing the profound change in family relationships that is about to take place. Families are encouraged to consider these questions for re-creating ritual in their lives. Similar questions can be asked about nursing actions, being mindful of the profession's social mandate from society to provide knowledgeable, compassionate service (Rogers, 1970).

For example, the cultural, religious, ethnic backgrounds of people seeking health care are very diverse, and without question, individuals will find different meanings in the same words or gestures presented to them by the nurse caring for them. What symbolic actions in the ritual greetings between nurse and patient convey the intentions to be caring and hospitable? These symbolic actions have different levels of meaning to both the nurse and patient. It is important to determine whether these symbolic actions help or prevent you from creating a caring relationship. The beauty of ritual is that dynamic dialogue is required to "create" the shared meaning that can be counted on between nurse and patient. Symbolic actions in nursing cannot be "delivered prepackaged." Modifications and changes are always indicated at some level to meet the dynamic, unique processes between people. Critical self-awareness of the nurse is necessary to recognize when actions lack a caring presence in tandem with the other's presence. It seems that symbolic actions (rituals) in nursing today ought to be actions that are at least non-invasive offerings that respect human dignity and choice. Rituals are qualitatively more like invitations to another to gather together one's life resources for moments of healing. Both nurse and patient are recipients of rituals of healing. In effect, as Marilyn Stiles (1988) indicates, in moments of spiritual relationship clients and nurses are "Shining Strangers" for one another.

Such qualities of ritual invitation and participation can be called mindful actions. Together they provide a critical lens for nursing in the recognition of practice as healing ritual, an example of which is presented later in this chapter.

RITUALS OF HEALING AND ALTERNATIVE MEDICINE

Recently, an increasing trend in alternative medicine in North America has been cited. The *New England Journal of Medicine* (Eisenberg et al., 1993) documents that more than 67 percent of the population studied seek out resources in alternative medicine, either while continuing to see their physician, or as a replacement. Examples of alternatives being used include approaches variously identified as life-style, botanical remedies, manipulative/hands-on treatments, and mind-over-matter sessions (Wallis, 1991). McGuire (1988) conducted research on *Ritual Healing in Suburban America*, and the results present the current needs expressed by people in the United States for adequate health care. The stories are testimonies! What has been taken for granted is now made public. That is, health care, which has always been a function of the family is now, McGuire (1988) asserts, being reclaimed by a large number of people who are already operating out of a different paradigm of health than the one espoused by health professionals. For example, in the population studied by McGuire, health "has cosmic meaning to adherents of alternative medicine. . . . They also spiritualize rather than medicalize moral concerns" (p. 47).

These trends mirror back to the profession of nursing a challenge of relevance to a new society which cannot be ignored. A new opportunity for nursing to shape health care for the 21st century comes into view. Fortuitously, the recent development of a new branch in the National Institutes of Health on unconventional medicine is very promising. Dr. Joseph Jacobs, a Native American of Mohawk descent, is head of this new branch and has knowledge of both western and Native American medicine values. Dr. Jacobs supports research on alternative approaches to healing, and $2 million has been allocated for the coming year. An overwhelming response to the initial call for research proposals bodes well for continuation and expansion of this new branch in NIH.

Nonetheless, the trend toward research support is still not firm, and will require persistent, well-designed studies to off-set the opposition from strong lobbying bodies well known in the health care industry. Pragmatism and utilitarianism are the major American philosophies of the twentieth century. They affect values and policies in society, including those of the ministrations of health care. The influence of the mechanistic, dualistic world view on the historic development of the scientific community and medical society is well documented. This same influence has also affected the nature of ritual in daily life by placing more emphasis on the external form. Charles Peirce (1905), an early moral pragmatist of Harvard University, expressed his concern with this country's prevailing rationality by emphasizing external behaviors and the consequences of human action. His concern was that more importance and attention be given to the intentionality of human action in the creation of a new society. Without this emphasis, ritual becomes an endangered species, and meaningless action cannot sustain the community.

Nevertheless, a sign of hope exists in the health-seeking individuals identified by McGuire (1988) and others in North America who now form a critical mass, providing critical evaluation of the rituals of western medicine. They are in pursuit of alternatives that restore the inner life of rituals of healing and ask for respect in what is meaningful to them, to the larger society, and to the cosmos (McGuire, 1988). Their lives represent the underside of ritual now being made public, lives rich in meaning and transformative for our times.

HEALING RITUAL AND NURSING

The discipline of nursing has avoided use of the word "ritual" for many years, particularly during the era of seeking to be recognized as a science by the scientific community. Having achieved a degree of success in this effort, like many other social science professions, nursing is in a stronger position to reclaim its imaginative, creative powers, and express the dynamic ritual nature of the art of healing. A history fraught with oppression of spiritual powers of women, evident in such writings as *Witches, Midwives, and Nurses: A History of Women Healers*

(Ehrenreich & English, 1973) in tandem with the feminist movement, provides a backdrop against which to understand nursing's avoidance of terms that can be used against its reason to exist. An atmosphere of positivism could not tolerate uncertainty; and certainly, the acknowledgment of spiritual healing abilities could not be admitted into a scientific profession. However, today science itself acknowledges the present era of uncertainty, and the professions recognize that the source of truth cannot be limited to one paradigm, no matter what its claim.

Several nursing theories have provided knowledgeable bases for the practice of nursing expressed in rituals of healing. I will discuss the mindful way of being present in actions that are by nature rituals of healing, and illuminate the role the imagination has had in recreating the meaning of ritual for nursing, particularly as it effectively bridges tradition and creativity for healing. The emphasis on *mindful action* is selected instead of the cultural contributions to ritual because I believe it is the most easily forgotten, or taken for granted feature of rituals of healing. The context of ritual and the physical expressions of culture are well documented in the works of scholars in transcultural nursing (Leininger, 1985; Ray, 1989) which assume the presence of meaning created from the mindfulness of a culture's individuals. The focus on mindfulness also is made with an encouragement to walk with other cultures from a position of mindfulness so as to avoid a one-sided positivistic interpretation of their cultural expressions.

Illustrations of Mindful Action in Nursing   For purposes of awakening the imagination I have shown slides in my discussions which depict places of healing ritual, nurse-patient interactions of healing through centering sessions, therapeutic touch experiences, scenes of waterfalls, balancing rocks, and multicolored etchings by Alex Grey (Wilber & McCormick, 1990) of the human energy auras expressive of the diverse paths along which the human spirit may journey from darkness to light.

Close to home, the Integral Life Patterning Project, which I direct at the University of Colorado School of Nursing Center for Human Caring, is housed in a comfortable, furnished room with signs of beauty, light, quiet, and support. Before clients arrive, a ritual of centering (intentional breathing, taking in the universe of order, healing, compassion, and finding my place of integrity and peacefulness) is thoughtfully engaged. The mindful presence to my own integrity opens me to listen attentively to each person, to be present to their newness and fresh perspective on their own lives and experiences. The dance of energy fields begins and ends in unique ways of healing as long as the attitude of mutual participation is the guiding cue to the process. The rituals are dynamically created in the dance of awareness I have of the other as a whole person. The dance of healing presence has its own time and rhythm. The enactment of the ritual of therapeutic touch requires a centered, mindful attention to the whole person rather than to problems isolated from clients' awareness of them. The manifestation of intentions, expressions, perceptions, and insights sets its own priorities, and as nurse-healer, I follow my partner's lead to a balance and synchrony of being that indicates the person has participated in a transforming experience recognizable to both of us (Reeder, 1990).

The nursing theories that inform the rituals of healing are multiple. Building upon a phenomenological awareness and presence, Rogers' Science of Unitary Human Beings (1970), energy field theory, and openness to the pandimensional nature of human relating, the mutual dance of healing ritual is then inspired by Watson's caring moment (1988). This reminds the ritual healer that healing is beyond time and space, inclusive of living and dying, beyond curing but always animated with caring. The intent to help or to heal are continuous attitudes informed by the work of Delores Krieger (1979) and Dora Kunz (1985), who developed the foundational work on therapeutic touch, and by the research of Janet Quinn (1992, 1993) and Janet Macrae (1988) who continue the practice and research of therapeutic touch. The key to rituals of healing is found in mindful action. Actions without mindfulness are like an empty gong and clanging cymbal, to borrow from the scriptural reference to love.

A quote from Jeanne Achterberg (1992) expresses well the caring moment and dance of ritual healing in nursing. "The dual face of healing ritual is that all members of the participating community benefit by receiving and by giving, by caring for others, and surrendering to receive care. The other duality of healing ritual is that in transcendent moments one is reminded both of the grounded, unitive connection in the flow of all life and, at the same time, one can perceive revelatory visions that are far beyond the life experience itself" (p. 158). Rather than being nonscientific, the practice of ritual healing encompasses the most attentive, elegant faculties of knowing capable to human beings, and expresses this knowledge through the fine art of caring. What society would reject such a response to its mandate for knowledgeable, compassionate service?

REFERENCES

Achterberg, J. (1992) Ritual: The foundation for transpersonal medicine. *Revision*, *14*(3), 158–164.

Brencato, H. D. (1990). *Women and Peacemaking Calendar*. Erie, PA: Pax Christie USA, August.

Cohen, D. (Ed.). (1991). *The circle of life: Rituals from the human family album*. San Francisco: Harper & Row.

Ehrenreich, B., & English, D. (1973). *Witches, midwives, and nurses: A history of women healers*. Old Westbury, NY: Feminist Press.

Eisenberg, D. M., Kessler, R. C., Foster, C., Norlock, F. E., Calkins, D. R., & Delbanco, T. E. (1993). Unconventional medicine in the United States: Prevalence, cost, and patterns of use. *New England Journal of Medicine*, *328*(4), 246–252.

Fox, M. (1985). *Illuminations of Hildegard of Bingen*. Santa Fe: Bean & Co.

Imber-Black, E., & Roberts, J. (1992). *Rituals for our times: Celebrating, healing, and changing our lives and our relationships*. New York: HarperCollins Publishers.

Imber-Black, E., Roberts, J., & Whiting, R. (Eds.). (1988). *Rituals in families and family therapy*. New York: HarperCollins Publishers.

Krieger, D. (1979). *The therapeutic touch: How to use your hands to help or heal*. New York: Prentice-Hall.

Kunz, D. (1985). *Spiritual aspects of the healing arts*. Wheaton, IL: Theosophical Publishing House.

Leininger, M. M. (1985, April). Transcultural care diversity and universality: A theory of nursing. *Nursing & Health Care*, *6*, 209–212.

Macrae, J. (1988). *Therapeutic touch: A practical guide*. New York: Alfred Knopf.

McGuire, M. B. (1988). *Ritual healing in suburban America: Sociological research*. Montclair, NJ: Rutgers, The State University.

Mead, M. (1972). *Twentieth-century faith: Hope and survival*. New York: Harper & Row.

Peirce, C. S. (1905). What is pragmatism. *The Monist*, *15*, 411–437.

Quinn, J. (1992). Holding sacred space: The nurse as healing environment. *Holistic Nursing Practice, 6*(4), 26–36.

Quinn, J. (1993). *Therapeutic touch: Healing through human energy fields* [Video]. (A new three-part short course produced by the Center for Human Caring, University of Colorado School of Nursing.) New York: National League for Nursing.

Ray, M. A. (1989). Transcultural caring: Political and economic visions. *Journal of Transcultural Nursing, 1*(1), 17–21.

Reeder, F. (1990). *Integrity of self in action: Grounded in phenomenological awareness.* Paper presented at the Center for Human Caring Series, University of Colorado School of Nursing. Audiotape available.

Rogers, M. (1970). An introduction to the theoretical basis of nursing. Philadelphia: F. A. Davis.

Stiles, M. K. (1988). *Shining Strangers: A phenomenological investigation of the nurse family spiritual relationship.* Denver: University of Colorado School of Nursing.

VanBiema, D. (1991, October). The journey of our lives [Special Issue]. *Life, 7.* New York: Time, Inc., Magazines.

Wallis, C. (1991). Why new age medicine is catching on. *Time, 138*(18), 68–72.

Watson, J. (1988). *The philosophy and science of caring.* Boulder: Associated University Press.

Wilber, K., & McCormick, C. (1990). *Sacred mirrors: The visionary art of Alex Grey.* Rochester, VT: Inner Traditions International.

Wolin, S. J., Bennett, L., & Fiese, B. (1992). The importance of ritual: Family strength, healing take hold. *Journal of Family Process,* George Washington University.

OTHER RESOURCES

Achterberg, J. (1990). *Woman as healer.* (First Edition). Boston: Shambhala, distributed by Random House.

Barrett, E. A. (1990). *Visions of Rogers' science-based nursing*. New York: National League for Nursing Press.

Campion, E. W. (1993). Editorial: Why unconventional medicine? *New England Journal of Medicine, 328*, 282–283.

Carlson, R., & Shield, B. (1989). *Healers on healing*. Los Angeles: Jeremy P. Tarcher.

Chia, M. (1983). *Awaken healing energy through the Tao*. New York: Aurora Press.

Corday, R. (1991). *Ode to the psychiatric nurse*. Number Five in the Common Loon Voice Essay Series on Major Mental Illness. Denver: Common Loon Productions.

Csordas, T. (1983). The rhetoric of transformation in ritual healing. *Culture, Medicine and Psychiatry, 7*, 333–375.

Dossey, L. (1989). *Recovering the soul*. New York: Bantam Books.

Dow, J. (1986). *The shaman's touch: Otomi Indian symbolic healing*. Salt Lake City: University of Utah Press.

Gaut, D., & Leininger, M. (1991). *Caring: The compassionate healer*. Center for Human Caring. New York: National League for Nursing Press.

Gill, S. D. (1977). Prayer as person: The performative force in Navajo prayer acts. *History of Religions, 17*, 143–157.

Harris, M. (1989). *Dance of the spirit: The seven steps of women's spirituality*. New York: Bantam Books.

Kaptchuk, T. J. (1983). *The web that has no weaver: Understanding Chinese medicine*. New York: Congdon & Weed.

Kan, Yue-Sai. (1990). *Mystical healing of Qigong—Doing business in Asia*. [Video]. A four-part series with study guide available for corporate use. For information contact: *Doing Business in Asia*, P.O. Box 68618, Indianapolis, IN 46268.

Kemp, T. P., & Rasmussen, D. (Eds.). (1992). *The narrative path*. Cambridge, MA: The MIT Press.

Lock, S., & Calligan, D. (1986). *The healer within: The new medicine of mind and body*. New York: Penguin Books, USA.

Moyers, B. (1993). *Healing and the mind*. New York: Doubleday.

Newman, M. (1986). *Health as expanding consciousness*. St. Louis: Mosby.

Nouwen, H. J. (1972). *The wounded healer*. New York: Image Books, Doubleday.

Ornstein, R., & Sobel, D. (1987). *The healing brain: Breakthrough discoveries about how the brain keeps us healthy*. New York: Simon & Schuster.

Richards, M. C. (1989). *Centering: Pottery, poetry and the person*. Twenty-fifth anniversary edition. Middletown, CT: Wesleyan University Press.

Rider, M. (1992). Mental shifts and resonance: Necessities for healing: Foundations for a homeodynamic theory of psychoneuro-immunology. *Revision, 14*(3), 149–157.

3

Voices of Healing: Elements of Caring

Joan C. Engebretson

Currently, there is a resurgence of interest in and popularity of alternative healing, particularly among the well-educated middle class (Eisenberg, 1993; English-Lueck, 1990; Hufford, 1986; McGuire, 1988). Many healers are using modalities that have their origins in cross-cultural, historical, and New Age ideologies (Engebretson, 1992). A parallel movement exists within the health care professions which seeks to expand the disease-focused perspective of biomedicine. The interest among professional and lay communities suggests a cultural shift in underlying beliefs about health and healing in the United States. This raises questions regarding the concept of healing and what elements are central to the practice of healing. The insights of the healers may unveil important wisdom for all practitioners of the healing arts. The six elements described in the following ethnographic report represent both collective views of the healers, as well as life themes of individual healers.

Ethnographic methodologies were used to explore the concepts of health and healing among three groups of healers in a large urban setting. More than 100 hours of participant observation were logged, as were long interviews with healers. The healers selected for long interviews and described in this report were between 35- and 75-years-of-age; five females and one male. Three had full-time jobs that were unrelated to the healing profession, and three were full-time healers.

The narratives were collected over a period of six months, categories were identified, and maps of the domains were described.

In addition to the collective findings of the study, a striking picture emerged as the investigator thanked each of the principle informants individually for teaching her a unique lesson. Narratives from these healers reflected a personal theme that defined her or his life experience in healing. While these concepts were identified by all of the participants, healers defined their life lesson as one of the six themes. They each described one of the themes as the lesson they needed to learn for their life work in healing. The six themes are forgiveness, love, surrender, protection, permission, and self-trust. The life themes have important messages for anyone in the healing professions.

FORGIVENESS—THEME OF HEALER ONE

Forgiveness is linked to love of others and particularly of oneself. It is especially difficult to forgive one's close friends and family. Forgiveness involves full understanding of all of the circumstances and the context of the actions. The triggering factors often stem back to childhood. Families may give a message to children that they are "no good." A child's fears of abandonment and separation fuel activities designed to get and keep those connections with others. "This creates an emotion that rules a response of anger which eats at them and eats at them." Build-up of that anger and fear is unhealthy and is often the base of many serious diseases.

Twelve-step programs or other healing environments facilitate forgiveness when they create an atmosphere in which "it is okay not to be okay." This atmosphere allows one to accept one's most "horrid and rotten parts," and to forgive oneself. Then one can forgive others and love others. Therefore, one is able to reweave the tapestry of one's life. If one believes that all is part of a universal plan, and everyone is working out his karma, it becomes easier to forgive. Issue was taken at Sunday school dictums of loving and forgiving everyone without an understanding of the basic fear and anger.

Forgiveness is necessary for self-love, a requisite for loving another. Forgiveness is also the foundation of being non-judgmental, which is the basis of unconditional love. The ability to accept another in a non-judgmental fashion is fundamental to healing. This is not as superficial as giving professional care; it involves truly accepting one's imperfections and forgiving oneself. Then, and only then, can one truly accept another person in a non-judgmental fashion.

LOVE—THEME OF HEALER TWO

The "heart" or love is the critical element in healing that informs and enhances all other aspects. It acts as a transformer or amplifier for all other aspects of healing. A reference to Eastern philosophies describes the heart chakra as the point "that the energy coming in from above and the energy coming in from below is merged and balanced in the heart chakra, so it has a very particular function of its own." "If any healing activity such as massage, diet, touch, etc. are done in love, the healing is enhanced." "This is what brings about some of the spectacular miracles of healing. If the healer can create an 'atmosphere of love' or use the 'current of unconditional love,' the most profound healings can take place."

This healer's personal experience with love was related to a spiritual phenomena called "the dark night of the soul," which is when the soul learns about and experiences love. St. John of the Cross and other spiritual writers have described this phenomena. At age 21 this healer had a stunning realization that she had no idea what love meant or what the experience was. She had grown up in a large, loving family with many friends, but she realized that she had no depth of experience with love. She prayed for lessons about love and spent the next 20 years trying to discriminate between love, clinging, bargaining or manipulating, and how to love an enemy. Working on self-forgiveness for several years, she received a more complete answer which comprised forgiveness, compassion, acceptance, and service.

Forgiveness

It is imperative to forgive oneself first. In personal experience, there is always an underlying illusion that there was blame involved. Until that blame is released, one is focused on where to direct it. The release of blame is often directed externally in an attempt to avoid the inner feelings of self-blame. Once one forgives oneself, it is irrelevant what the other person does. A lot of physical malfunctions and dysfunctions with aging stem from this unconscious habit of judging self and others.

Compassion

This is the emotional side of love which allows the heart to feel. Love has emotion but is not limited to emotion. Caring for another comes from this concept. This is the feeling that fuels and motivates one to involvement.

Acceptance

Acceptance stems from the release of fault-finding and judgmental ideas about the self and others and involves total acceptance. ". . . they are simply okay where they are and who they are." In applying this to healing, many healers work out of compassion but can't accept that the recipient may have decided to die or may not accept the healing being offered. Working out of acceptance, one has to:

> *Totally accept another person; accept the person, wherever that person is and know that wherever that is, it is sacred and that it is perfect in God's eyes. God doesn't judge . . . service comes last and becomes the natural expression of love; and that unfolds out of your living in a state of forgiveness with yourself, a state of compassion for yourself, and a state of acceptance of oneself. And then, out of that center extends forgiveness and compassion and acceptance to other people.*

Service

For a long time, this healer kept forgetting this fourth aspect of love. The aspect is poorly understood and is premature if one gets into service before working on the other three aspects. Once the other three are mastered, service comes and does not need to be solicited.

> *Many people will take on service and it may be very satisfying or rewarding, but if it's not fueled by the other three, there's not much energy to sustain it and it may be done in a way that is self-serving and not really service.*

SURRENDER—THEME OF HEALER THREE

The attitude of surrender was combined with the shift of the locus of responsibility to the individual, where the individual takes responsibility for his own healing. This, at first glance, appears contradictory; however, the healers felt that the healee needed to surrender to the healing. To surrender means to allow oneself to learn the lessons from the illness.

Surrender to the Healing Process

One of the healers who had a series of serious accidents necessitating hospitalizations, surgeries, and a long and involved period of therapy, described her rehabilitation process as learning to surrender to the illness in order to learn its lessons. This particular healer became acutely aware of her dislike of orthodox medicine. She realized she needed to surrender her will to enable herself to work with various biomedical treatments. It was only when she stopped fighting them or trying to overcome them, that she began to progress. "I have been blessed to have these accidents."

An attitude of trust was necessary to make the decision to seek help in the healing process and to allow the healing or the healers to work with her. Trust needed to precede faith, as trust is involved in the initial connection with any healer. Then the healing process can progress, and "it is faith that includes the desire and energy to work toward the future."

Surrender to Unite Body and Spirit

These accidents allowed this healer to respect her body and recognize the needs and limitations of the physical body. Previously she stated that she had been focusing on the spiritual aspects, and elevating that part of her to the denial of the more mundane physical aspects. She viewed the body as a cumbersome vehicle for the spirit; she would have preferred to jettison it, thus allowing the spirit to fly. The process of surrendering to the physical healing of the body allowed her to know her body and respect the physical needs for rest, exercise, good food, and nurturing.

PERMISSION—THEME OF HEALER FOUR

In keeping with the individual's locus of responsibility, the healers all agreed that it was imperative that they had the permission of the healee prior to any intervention. Permission was granted on two levels, the conscious level and the level of the higher self. The higher self was ultimately where the permission needed to be. The higher self might require that the individual may need to experience the illness longer for the growth of the soul's growth. In this case, it would appear to those who look for only physical manifestations of healing, that nothing was happening. Indeed, a great deal of healing could be occurring on other levels. Conversely, someone could be skeptical and reject the healing on a conscious level, but accept it on a higher conscious level and experience a healing.

The healer must be detached from outcomes. If the higher self rejected the healing, "the healing would not be accepted and the healer should let it go." If the healing was requested by someone, the healers feel obligated to work on them. Healing energy is very powerful, and the power of the mind or the intent is so powerful that the issues of control were vitally important to the healer. The healer should exert no control over the healing.

A healer who had worked on the concept of control for most of her adult life, believed that in the process of laying-on of hands, the healer should not exert any pre-meditated ideas of a preferred outcome. She also believed that one should not even consciously place one's hands in certain positions, but rather let them be directed totally by intuition, which would be more in tune to the individual's higher self.

She often talked and distracted her students during the laying-on of hands, so they would get their thoughts out of the way and not get involved with trying to control or direct the healing energy. She expressed concern that if the healing energy were directed against the wishes of the higher self, it would interfere with the healee's karma, and the healer would bear responsibility or karmic debt for interfering with another soul's path.

Prior to using the healing energies, the healer must say that "it is completely without bias whether that person gets well or not . . ." She was also concerned that, with the popularity of New Age ideas, some people would be attracted to the healing modalities because of their association with the occult. These people could be attracted by the potential of using these energies and techniques to gain control and power over others. Many people had developed their intuitive sense so they could detect the needs and the vulnerabilities of people seeking healing.

Without a concern for eliciting their permission, they could intrude their power and exert control over others. She cited an example of a person who had gotten involved in *Wicca*, a white magic group, so he could learn white magic and control people to do what he wanted.

She also discriminated between spiritual healing and magic. "Magic is magic whether it is black or white, it is directing energy without permission, knowledge or consent . . . it's manipulation." This related to some of the Hermetic universal laws of healing: one is forbidden to use any of the healing powers for the enhancement of the personal ego, which includes using the powers to build prestige, personal wealth or gain. Healing energies should never be used to exert power or control or manipulate another for sexual gratification.

She recommended that "the beginning of healing is the absolute alignment of the healer and the recipient regarding the goal of the healing." Options can be explored, and after the healing recipient has determined a goal, she would make a commitment to follow through on that agreement.

PROTECTION—THEME OF HEALER FIVE

One of the teachers stressed that healers always protect themselves during the healing. This would safeguard them from picking up any negativity from the recipient and also would protect the recipient from any negativity the healer might inadvertently project during the healing. Several healers also felt that the recipient was vulnerable during the healing sessions. Vulnerability was an important part of the healing, in that healers worked to "open up the healee to the healing energy." This rendered the healee vulnerable to all energies. Therefore, she advocated that the healers also use protection for the healee.

Protection could be obtained by visualizing white light surrounding oneself or the healee. This white light energy served to be a cleansing protective energy barrier. It served to protect both the healer and recipient from inadvertently getting one's ego involved. It also helped protect the healer from any depletion of energy. She noted that some healers claim that they are very run down and get sick easily after doing healing work. She felt that with proper protection, one is energized rather than depleted.

One healer, who did much of her work in an altered state of consciousness, stressed the importance of protection in doing healing work, especially if one were to work with the spiritual energies. She did not advocate the use of drugs, diet, or special activities to enter the trance state.

She entered the healing state by starting with a prayer and meditation. She then "leaves her body and the spirits work through her body." During this period, she has no conscious recall of what occurs. Spirit healers, angels, or spiritual guides are highly evolved entities that facilitate enlightenment and may evoke healing. In this altered state, the healer can channel messages from these entities. These messages often help the recipients understand the spiritual nature of their condition and have added insight related to healing.

Little was known about the state of consciousness of the healee, although several described a trance-like state occurring while the healer worked on them. "Some of the most powerful healings occur when the healer and the recipient are both in an altered state." In this state many of the psychological barriers were lowered; this allowed effective healings to take place. Reports of healings indicated that healings occurred whether or not the recipient was in an altered state—and even if the healer was unaware of the healing activities.

In working with spiritual entities, one can contact many types of spirits, and not all are spiritually evolved or motivated to work for healing and enlightenment. Therefore, it was important for healers to be very cautious and protect themselves and others when working in this realm.

This healer outlined specific steps to take to afford protection. First, one must know oneself and one's own energy before working with other energies. Next, one needs to be familiar with different energies and learn to know them. In working with these other entities, it is imperative that one be in control, not only of when and where one goes into an altered state, but also of who or what energy one works with and the time one works with that energy. The healer always made an agreement with the energies before contact; "I am going into a trance for X number of minutes and when that time is up we are going to sever our connections." Maintaining control of one's body and one's consciousness was imperative to working with energies.

This particular healer taught other healers a strategy she used to discriminate between positive and negative energies. She advocated asking "the entity to face the white light of Christ." "If the entity could not, it would have to leave; and if it could, she could safely work with it."

TRUST IN ONESELF—THEME OF HEALER SIX

This was the foundation for an individual's self-healing. References were made to Plato's dictum of "know thyself" as the highest goal and the pinnacle of knowledge. Healing work was a form of learning about oneself. Self-knowing was akin to self-love. Trusting oneself involved taking responsibility for oneself. This led to active choice-making about healing and trying to understand the illness from the perspective of the soul's journey.

As illness was not considered bad or as a sign of weakness or punishment, no blame was attached.

> *Do not blame yourself for your illness. Acknowledge that stress or persistent obsession with illness can contribute to your (disease) and then move on. Once illness is present, realize you can play a large role in correcting the problem.*
>
> *Self healing, I think, is a belief system . . . where it says trust yourself, that you are doing the right thing at the right time and that you are in the right place at the right time, and you're with whom you're supposed to be.*

One healer, who came from a mainstream Christian background, was concerned about the cultural influences that encourage us to not know or trust ourselves. She was concerned that children were not encouraged to think and know themselves. She felt that this upbringing discouraged children from trusting their own feelings or thoughts. She was also concerned about the church's emphasis on interpreting all spiritual matters and discouraging individual experience and thinking.

This healer quoted a Buddhist master who stated that "spiritual issues should also fit logic and, if something wasn't logical in any system, to seriously question it." She was concerned that so few people in Western society really take responsibility for themselves and how the medical system discourages anyone from taking responsibility for their health.

She cited several examples where prescriptions have been written or other intrusive interventions prescribed without even discussing lifestyle changes that individuals could make to greatly improve their health.

DISCUSSION

These healers emphasized the centrality of the spiritual aspect of healing. Healers working from this perspective have learned the importance and complexities of love and forgiveness. This perspective defies the efficiency that permeates the technological and procedural orientation of the biomedical approach. The conservativeness and caution of healers in approaching others in the act of healing, reflected in their comments on permission and protection, are antithetical to the aggressive, intrusive, and mechanistic culture of modern medicine. The issues of surrender and self-trust which place much of the locus of the responsiblity of healing with the client is again in opposition to the medical model which absolves the patient of responsibility in causation or correction of the problem. These controversies need to be addressed by health care providers moving from a curing to a healing model. From the voices of these healers and their individual life lessons in healing, come messages for all who bring care to cure, hope to suffering, and seek to hold the possibility of healing and wholeness.

REFERENCES

Eisenberg, D. M., Kessler, R. C., Forster, C., Norlock, F. E., Calkins, D. R., & Delbanco, T. L. (1993). Unconventional medicine in the United States; Prevalence, costs and patterns of use. *The New England Journal of Medicine, 328*(4), 246–252.

English-Lueck, J. A. (1990). *Health in the New Age: A Study in California Holistic Practices*. Albuquerque: University of New Mexico Press.

Engebretson, J. (1992). Conceptual models of healing and health: An ethnography of healers and nurses. (Doctoral dissertation, The University of Texas, School of Public Health, 1992.) *University Microfilms International-Dissertation Information Service*, Order No. 9302792.

Hufford, D. J. (1986). Contemporary folk medicine. In N. Gevits (Ed.) *Other Healers*. Baltimore: Johns Hopkins University Press.

McGuire, M. B. (1988). *Ritual healing in suburban America*. New Brunswick: Rutgers University Press.

4

Living Nursing's Values in Nursing Practice

Marilyn E. Parker

No one ever asked me about my nursing values. I've never had to think about my values. Now I have and now I want to know about my values and the values held by other nurses. And, I want to help other nurses reflect on what is important to them about nursing.

Values are enduring beliefs that motivate and guide actions (Lewis, 1990; Rokeach, 1973). Nursing values are enduring beliefs that guide nursing actions. The quotation above reflects the importance to nurses and nursing of nursing's values and encourages opportunity to examine and define values guiding nursing practice. This quotation supports assertions in the nursing literature of the need to affirm and share nursing's values (Boykin & Schoenhofer, 1989; Christensen, 1988; Elfrink & Lutz, 1991; Gadow, 1989; Gortner, 1990; Kerfoot, 1991; Manthey, 1989; Maraldo, 1989; Nyberg, 1990). This comment from a research participant reflects the significance of study of nursing's values as well as the meaning such research can have for nurses engaged in the research.

---

*The author and many co-researchers gratefully acknowledge financial support for this research from the following Florida hospitals: Boca Raton Community Hospital; Delray Community Hospital, Delray Beach; Good Samaritan Medical Center, West Palm Beach; and HCA Northwest Regional Hospital, Margate.

The emphasis of this chapter is on a survey of findings about nursing's values, related conflicts in nursing practice, and conceptions of nursing based on nursing's values. These findings emerged from data within the context of a larger study of nursing values, economic factors, and practice strategies. The philosophy of inquiry that grounded conduct of the research is presented and includes a discussion of essential concepts of clinical scholarship, co-researcher, and transition points. The chapter begins with a brief literature review, an overview of the larger research project and philosophy of inquiry, and concludes with current, ongoing and future directions of research into nursing's values.

LITERATURE ON VALUES AND NURSING'S VALUES

There is little evidence of study of nursing's values in the nursing literature prior to the 1990s. Extensive literature reviews during this research project identified ideas and research about values presented by nursing scholars. The literature review included study of works of nursing scholars for identification of implicit values grounding their research and writing. This section will introduce the classic work of Rokeach and present an overview of literature on nursing's values.

Rokeach (1973), a social scientist, provided the classic and often-used conception of values from his 1960s research on Americans' values. Values are described as enduring beliefs that specific modes of conduct, or outcomes, are preferable to opposite modes or outcomes (Rokeach, 1973). Further, values can be divided into terminal values of purposes and goals, and instrumental values related to the means to help one achieve those goals. A contribution to researching values was offered in the suggestion that such inquiry study persons in action in order to fully understand their values (Rokeach, 1973). It was concluded that direct observation or field study would provide a deeper understanding of values.

Fry (1989) proposes that nursing's values are grounded in caring and covenant, lived by the nurse in truth-telling, fidelity, and promise-keeping. Gortner (1990) states that nursing's values of equity and respect are expressed in caring, health promotion, illness prevention, professional competence and ethics. Schoenhofer (1989) asserts that nursing's fundamental value is caring which illuminates spiritual values of love, truth and beauty. Gadow (1980, 1984, 1985, 1989) discusses nurses' values from a philosophical perspective as aiming at protecting and enhancing human dignity. In addition, Watson (1988) describes nursing's moral ideal or value as caring committed to the protection and enhancement of human dignity.

Shank and Weis (1989) studied nursing's values by use of a questionnaire answered by 191 nursing students and graduate nurses. Results of data analysis were compared to the ANA Code for Nurses (1976). The values most often stated were dignity, worth, care, respect for the individual and client's self-determination. These were correlated to the first statement of the Code which states the nurse provides services with respect for the dignity of the client. These authors conclude that a value system is not fully developed in students and beginning practitioners and that more emphasis should be placed on values education to help new nursing practitioners develop the profession's values as expressed in the ANA Code (1976).

Elfrink and Lutz (1991) surveyed 679 nurse educators to determine agreement with values identified by the American Association of Colleges of Nursing. Seven values were determined to be the basis for nursing care: altruism, esthetics, human dignity, justice, freedom, equality, and truth. The researchers assert that nurse educators have responsibility to assist students to acquire practice competencies, including moral decision making based on nursing values (Elfrink & Lutz, 1991, p. 244).

Creation of a nursing practice environment consistent with expressed nursing values was the goal of a nursing research project reported by Parker, Gordon and Brannon (1992). Values identified by nursing staff were: respect for the patient as a whole, unique person; respect for family members; and respect for the complexities of nursing practice. The researchers conclude: "outcomes grounded in shared values can change practice environments in ways more powerful than outcomes attempted by actions of administrators, researchers, or nursing staff alone" (Parker, Gordon, & Brannon, 1992, p. 63).

CONTEXT OF THE STUDY

The study reported in this chapter is part of a larger research project titled "Valuing and Financing Selected Nursing Practice Strategies" (Parker, 1990). The major goal of the larger study is the development of pathways of communication, cooperation and sharing of resources to develop clinical scholarship among nurses in practice, education, administration, and research. This project was proposed by the author as principal investigator and was funded for two years by four participating acute care community hospitals in Southeast Florida.

The larger project is extensive and complex, with activities involving over 300 nurses. Outcomes include models of cooperative research endeavors, concepts of clinical scholarship, and nursing practice and administrative strategies balancing nursing's values and economic realities. Major activities of the larger project through which these models and strategies were developed and studied were courses, conferences, and consultations. Brief descriptions of each follow:

- **Conferences** Nurses throughout Southeast Florida participated in annual one-day regional conferences on nursing economics, nursing's values, and practice strategies. These conferences featured keynote addresses by and dialogues with Dr. Tim Porter-O'Grady (1991, 1992) and annual updates to the nursing community about the research methods and processes, and possible meaning of the study to the future of nursing practice and administration (Parker, 1991, 1992). Activities at each participating hospital was highlighted at the conferences.

- **Courses** Two elective graduate courses were designed and taught focusing on nursing's values, methods of nursing inquiry, creation of innovative nursing practice and administrative strategies, community building and the development of the nursing consultant role. During the courses, nursing students were full participants in the research and the conferences. Students participated with nurses in each hospital setting to develop nursing practice and administrative strategies. Two graduate students studied evaluation strategies during the project as independent study opportunities.

- **Consultation** Consultation in each of the four hospitals was a feature of the project throughout the two years as the researcher, graduate research assistant, and nursing students interacted with nurses during the phases and activities of the research project. Dr. Tim Porter-O'Grady joined the students for consultation in each hospital during one week each year.

Working with data from the project is ongoing and new studies building on the initial research are underway. Work with the nursing literature is extensive. Two nursing students have completed master's thesis research as part of the project (Barry, 1993; Strews, 1992). Six master's students are currently studying aspects of nursing's values and nursing practice within the larger research project for their thesis research.

OVERVIEW OF THE PHILOSOPHY OF INQUIRY

The research approach for this study is a synthesis of participatory, action, and cooperative methods (Parker, Gordon, & Brannon, 1992; Reason, 1988; Reason & Rowan, 1981). The conduct of the study included rich dialogue about values and belief essential to collaboration and full participation in researching nursing's values. The need to articulate and share these values and beliefs about nursing research was recognized. Following are major concepts that formed the philosophy of inquiry that unfolded during the larger study and influenced each aspect of this research.

Clinical Scholarship in Nursing

Clinical scholarship in nursing recognizes that the purpose of nursing research is to serve nurses and patients in nursing situations. Research processes must include questions as well as openness to other queries that may emerge during the course of the planned inquiry. Clinical scholarship is experiential and practical, always intending to be helpful. The persons involved in the research are not viewed as objects to be managed for research purposes but as experts who possess knowledge, and are central to the research. This lack of control, in the usual research sense, means the researcher has no agenda for what will be learned but is willing to be present with each participant as knower, being open to experience and learning with each one (Parker, Gordon, & Brannon, 1992). Processes and outcomes are equally important and are inseparable throughout the research.

The Concept of Co-researcher

All involved in the research are named co-researcher (Parker, Gordon, & Brannon, 1992; Reason, 1988). All are co-participants in the research work and share in building the knowledge of nursing through this work. Each contributes that which is theirs to give to the exploration.

All bring expertise to the process and are acknowledged and respected for unique contributions to the work. Creativity is mobilized.

Actualizing the concept of co-researcher encourages sharing authentic experiences and connecting with the world of nursing through this sharing. There is often a sense of genuine searching. The inner world of nursing is explored, working from the "inside" of experiences of nurses and seeking knowing from that central place. There is a sense of intimacy and personal knowing, acknowledging shared love for nursing with all its beautiful and painful realities. There is a spiral shape of growth, decision making, and action to the process of inquiry.

Transition Points

The nature of the research process is that it is dynamic and ongoing. There are transition points rather than conclusions. Transition points are experiences in the inquiry process of the need to move forward with the research work rather than continue to study the material at hand. This concept recognizes the complexity of the study of nursing and the need to be aware when appraisal of data or its analysis seems adequate for the time being. Transition points occur when it seems reasonable rather than when there is an answer. It is important that the co-researcher seek concurrence with co-researchers that a transition point has been experienced.

The concept of transition points is an important aspect of recognizing the wholeness of inquiry and extended participation as research processes continue in new ways. The process of inquiry in nursing is extensive, inclusive, and complex and calls for us to recognize its wide-ranging effects. The involvement as a co-researcher often has an impact on other nurses and practice settings. The data have continuing usefulness when they can be shared for the study of related research questions. Extended participation is a way to describe the ongoing nature of the research process as the work is shared and experienced anew.

PURPOSE OF THE PRESENT STUDY

The study reported in this chapter was designed to explore and describe nursing's values expressed by practicing nurses in four acute care hospitals in Southeast Florida. The major research question asked of nurses was, "What values do you hold most dear about nursing practice?" Participating nurses were also invited to share written and oral accounts of nursing situations to illustrate their most important nursing values.

METHOD

This research was a collaborative effort to discover, through reflection, open dialogue, and nurse's stories, the nursing values that guide nursing practice. The research methods, including data generation and analysis, are a synthesis of participatory, action, and cooperative methods (Parker, Gordon, & Brannon, 1992; Reason, 1988; Reason & Rowan, 1981), which evolved during the course of the research, and are grounded in the philosophy of inquiry described earlier in this chapter. The methods of this study include values and beliefs about nursing research as clinical scholarship, ways to consider participants in the research process, and the impact of nursing inquiry. The inclusive method of inquiry is inseparable from the purpose and findings of the study; all must be considered together.

Data Generation

The setting for the study was four acute care community hospitals in Southeast Florida. Bed capacity ranged from 150 to 450 beds. Two of the hospitals were not-for-profit institutions and two were owned by for-profit corporations. The proposal for research was approved by a university Institutional Review Board and by review boards or administrators at each hospital. A signed agreement for funding and conduct of the research was obtained from each institution. Participation of nurses in the study was voluntary, and informed consent with permission to tape record interviews and take field notes was obtained prior to data generation. Identity of participants and individual hospitals was protected.

In the context of reflective, guided group interviews, the research question, "What values do you hold most dear about nursing practice?" was asked of 45 staff nurses and middle managers in the four hospitals. Two group interviews, about two weeks apart, were scheduled at each hospital as a means of data generation. Nurses volunteered to participate as co-researchers and were all permitted time away from their work to be present at the interviews.

Each group interview began with a period of silence for thought and reflection guided by the research question. During the first interview nurses were asked to write their values on pieces of paper as reminders so nothing would be lost during the group dialogue. Full participation through sharing and discussion of each person's values was encouraged during the interviews. Each interview concluded with responses to a request for additional thoughts to share. The co-researchers were then asked to reflect on a story of nursing practice in which they had lived their values and to bring the story to the next interview. Many stories were then presented in writing and offered for dialogue by the group. Most interviews were an hour in length. Data were generated over a six-month period.

Interviews were audiotaped and transcribed into text. Field notes were transcribed, including notations of impressions, interruptions, and any incidents noted by the principle investigator and research assistant. Transcripts, along with demographic surveys and original field notes, were organized and secured in a binder specified by the name of each of the hospitals. The binders were kept in a locked file cabinet.

Data Analysis

A form of content analysis was selected as the method of data analysis that would be most useful in uncovering the essences of the rich material generated by interviews and stories provided by nurses in the study. The works of Woods and Catanzaro (1988) and Stern (1989) assisted in forming a structure and process for the method of data analysis. The process included immersing in the data, deciding on units of analysis, identifying these units in the text, extracting units from the text, grouping the units into categories, and describing the results.

The research question guided the search for values stated in a word or description. Following the identification of these expressed values, it was clear that other values held by the nurse participants were also present, although not explicitly expressed. These "lived" or latent values were uncovered from the data by a reflective process that unfolded as the data were read and re-read. It was discovered that values were often described within a context of conflict, a situation in which a value had been challenged. The conflicts became part of the analysis.

The values of each group of nurses were compared for common meanings and were synthesized. The expressed values, the lived, or latent values, and the conflicts of values were compared to the original texts for content and assurance of inclusion of all expressions of values and conflicts. Notes about the process of data analysis were kept and reviewed along with the results of the content analysis. Findings were shared with the participants at each hospital for further discussion and clarification of the values guiding their nursing practice.

Rigor

Research standards assist to verify findings of qualitative research. Beck (1993) has described three criteria of rigor for use in nursing research: credibility, fittingness, and auditability. The descriptions of findings that are easily recognized by participants in this study, as well as other nurses, speak for the credibility of the research. Fittingness is concerned with adherence to research procedures; the findings of this study reflect the purpose of the study and the data generated. The purposes, processes, data and results of this study have been widely shared and the decision trail can be followed. The standard of auditability has been met.

RESULTS

Results of the research process revealed nursing's values that guide nursing practice. Conceptions of nursing describing nursing practice at each hospital were developed based on values expressed by nurses at each hospital. Conflicts in which nursing's values were challenged were analyzed and described. These results were used to develop other aspects of the research project, such as nursing practice and administrative strategies. Results are presented in this section.

Nursing's Values

Nursing's values were divided into two categories: expressed values and lived values. The expressed values, those articulated in a word or expression, were: Caring, Respect, Compassion, Competence, Excellence in Practice, Inner Harmony, and Accountability. The lived values, embedded in transcripts of the dialogue or field notes, were: Commitment, Honesty, Humility, Sisterhood/Brotherhood, Courage,

Sense of Humor, and Autonomy. Expressed values, with examples from data offering illustrations of the dialogue, follow..

Caring

"I think nursing is caring."

"I find if you can't treat the person in a caring way you will never reach them, you will never help them."

"It's caring for the whole; knowing you are responsible. Not only do we deal with the patient, but with the family, the physician and everything. It's sympathy, empathy, and everything you could have and we keep it all in a neat little package and pull from it when something is needed."

Respect

"I think of modesty and maintaining privacy for the patient. Nobody knocks. The gown just gets lifted up. And the gowns don't go around and we don't have many pajama bottoms."

"We changed visiting hours and it worked out real well. We thought it would be advantageous for the grandparents particularly to have their grandchildren and families come in at any time of the day or evening."

"The person has the right to know, to be a person. The doctor is treating the disease and does not know what is going on with the person as a human being."

Compassion

"I think about how the patient feels. I feel for them, I give 110%."

"There was this little old patient who was the worst outlier this hospital ever had—he was here for about a month and a half. Well, the Utilization Review (UR) Director persisted and finally he was discharged to a nursing home and his wife was crying . . . and he was dead the next morning. I was devastated and so was everybody on the floor. We should have kept him and maybe he would have survived longer. His wife came back to see us and was crying."

"It hurts to see a 92-year-old put through this. Every time I went in to her she would cry, and I cried with her."

Competence

"He had pain when he moved but pain shots were ordered. He needed physical therapy, not a pain shot every four hours. I would hate to give him a shot, he would become disoriented. I didn't know any nurse who would give him the shot. Now he's oriented and strong."

"You just can't take orders, you have to fight for the patient. We don't have to jump in and do whatever is ordered, we can use our judgment."

Excellence in Practice

"At the bedside the patients trust us and it's important we give them our best."

"When you have a patient for a couple of days and you walk in and his numbers are okay but you know something is wrong you have a responsibility to call the doctor. You ask him to come in and sit down and talk about the patient—they don't always like it but it is our responsibility to the patient."

Inner Harmony

"Knowing that at the end of the day I've done all I could do for the patient . . . is a good feeling."

"It's hard to deal with death and dying and the death of a child. I prayed with her. And I guarantee I didn't get all my nursing recorded on those notes! What I didn't get done was my charting, but I really got my nursing done."

Accountability

"The most important thing is knowledgeable care. We have to be informed, up-to-date, be a resource to the community. If you don't know, ask someone or find out somehow."

"The most important value is to consider the patient's welfare and well being at all times regardless of the circumstances."

Conflicts in Nursing Practice

Analysis of data generated during this study, including transcripts of interviews and stories about nursing situations, revealed conflicts of nursing values. Stories of conflict were often shared to illustrate or highlight nursing's values. The conflicts that emerged from the data were Disrespect, Dishonesty, Disconnectedness, Distance, and Distrust. The conflicts, with examples from data offering illustrations of the dialogue, follow.

Disrespect

"I think it is crazy to think we can care for the patients and are not capable of calling a physician after 11 p.m."

"We have a patient who is made a no code and then the doctor comes in and orders all these tests and we feel guilty because we are the ones who have to do them and at the same time appease the family and make it seem all right."

Dishonesty

"It's hard trying to be honest when you can't be. You're in constant turmoil. When someone asks 'how's it going?' you try to be honest and then the physician paints a different picture."

Disconnected

"There are days I drive home thinking I did absolutely nothing and things are in utter chaos. I wonder what I forgot to do, the promise I made to get someone a cup of coffee. But I have done all my charting, all my assessments, and all my paper work. But I didn't do any nursing. It's more than not having a sense of accomplishment, it's not doing what I came here to do."

". . . sometimes I say just let me be a nurse."

"This is Burger King nursing: You only get the pieces you ask for—Burger, Burger, Fries, Fries."

Distanced

"Time moves nurses from doing the nursing we'd like to do."

"It's hard to give dignity in the ER to someone who is passed out and wouldn't understand. We get dignity from about 70 percent of the people and it's hard to give it back. It's amazing to me the number of women who bring their children in and don't know how to take a temperature, don't know how to help themselves, don't know how not to get infections, and how not to get pregnant."

Distrust

"You go along with treatments you don't believe in—doing things that are not in the best interest of the patient."

"Are we doing things in the best interest of the patient or to serve somebody's pockets?"

"I want the patient to trust me."

Conceptions of Nursing

Conceptions of nursing can be thought of as expressions of living nursing's values in particular nursing practice settings. Conceptions of nursing describing nursing practice at each hospital were developed based on values expressed by nurses at each hospital. Participating nurses who reviewed the conception of nursing revealed by analysis of data provided at their hospital embraced the unique conception that reflected their values.

- Hospital #1: Nursing is caring for the patient in such a way that dignity (recognition of personhood) is supported and nurtured until each is on his/her own.

- Hospital #2: Nursing is caring for the patient as a whole being, with individual needs, not only while hospitalized but also as the person grows toward well being or toward a peaceful death.

- Hospital #3: Nursing is caring for the patient holistically, providing comfort while the patient progresses from sickness to health.

- Hospital #4: Nursing is caring for the patient: mind, body and soul; treating the person with respect and advocating for his/her rights in the hospital while preparing for return home or for a peaceful death.

TRANSITION POINTS AND DISCUSSION

A response to the research question about what values nurses hold most dear about nursing practice is: Caring and respect are essential values guiding nursing in a practice that honors compassion and competence as necessary components of excellence in practice and encourages hope for inner harmony. This response was developed at a transition point in the study, a time requiring that co-researchers move forward the work of the larger project.

The research question, the process of inquiry, and the results of this study inform us that nursing's values are enhanced as these values are lived in nursing practice. Further, nursing's values energize the nursing situation with a creative drive to care for the other. Bringing nursing values to increased awareness enhances these values and encourages continuing refinement and development of nursing's values in practice. There is a sense that both nurse and patient become more of who they are through the process of living nursing's values. The circle continues as nurses experience increased fulfillment from the enriching of their values in their practice.

In this research, statements about conflict in the context of nursing situations are clearly connected with nursing's values. One group of co-researchers described conflict as inevitable, and as a source for creativity and growth (Barry, 1992). The conflicts described by nurses often led to creative nursing practice strategies, as nurses continued to live their values in their practice.

Data in this study revealed that economics and financial realities are not the driving force against values we might have expected to find. Financial realities are part of the "soup" or context of nursing practice. In fact, strategies of nursing practice and administration that balance nursing values and economic realities often came out in the data generation interviews as assumed sets of actions clearly in place. Many nurses who were co-researchers in this study were so immersed in the life work of nursing that financial aspects were often obscured and ways of dealing with these realities in nursing practice did not require usual articulation.

It is also clear from the data that nursing's values can be expressed and experienced in nursing practice in brief periods of time. It may take a few seconds or a minute to share acts of compassion, respect and sisterhood. These acts may not be talked about among nurses and are usually not even recognized in many settings. For example, the form for nursing notes often requires only checks in boxes instead of narratives about the unique, mutually gratifying nursing that has taken place. This form of reporting nursing is not conducive to sharing and rewarding excellent nursing and does not support nursing's values in practice.

The method of inquiry developed during this study has been presented in several forums and discussed among many nurses in research, practice, and education. Use of the data generation methods set the stage for open dialogue about enduring beliefs. No value or idea was suppressed and each was appreciated and honored, leading to generation of other ideas. The philosophy of the method also fit the many dimensions of the larger study. The results of the study of nursing's values have been useful in developing nursing practice and administrative strategies.

Current and Ongoing Research

The methods and values of inquiry presented in this chapter guide current and ongoing studies that contribute to the larger study of nursing's values, economics, and nursing practice strategies. The purposes of ongoing studies include identifying and describing expressed and unarticulated nursing practice and administrative strategies that balance nursing's values and financial constraints. Nursing's values held by nursing administrators and managers are being analyzed for identification of nursing's values that guide the practice of nursing administration as well as nursing administration strategies that support value-directed nursing practice. The nursing practice and nursing administration strategies developed during this study may be examined using more traditional means of nursing inquiry.

One study is being conducted using the Guba and Lincoln (1989) approach to evaluation research to inquire about the meaning of this project to nurses at one of the participating hospitals. Another study has been proposed to explore the notion that nursing's values, emphasizing compassion and respect for the person, are central to the practice of nurses who successfully anticipate the need for and take leadership in productive change. Use of photography as a method of inquiry, with photo essays developed by practicing nurses, is being used to explore nursing values and nursing practice (Gordon, 1993). In Chapter Five, Charlotte Barry presents one of the studies related to the study reported in this chapter.

REFERENCES

American Nurses Association (1976). *Code for nursing with interpretative statements*. Kansas City, MO: American Nurses Association.

Barry, C. (1992, April). Expressing nursing values in nursing practice strategies. M. Parker (Chair), *Nursing in the twenty-first century: Dreams and designs.* Conference conducted at Florida Atlantic University, Boca Raton.

Barry, C. (1993). *The values lived in the day-to-day practice of nursing.* Unpublished master's thesis, Florida Atlantic University, Boca Raton.

Beck, C. T. (1993). Qualitative research: The evaluation of its credibility, fittingness and auditability. *Western Journal of Nursing Research, 15*(2), 263–266.

Boykin, A., & Schoenhofer, S. (1989). Caring in nursing: Analysis of extant theory. *Nursing Science Quarterly, 3*(4), 149–155.

Christensen, P. J. (1988). An ethical framework for nursing service administration. *Advances in Nursing Science, 10*(3), 46–55.

Elfrink, V., & Lutz, E. (1991). American Association of Colleges of Nursing essential values: National study of faculty perceptions, practices and plans. *Journal of Professional Nursing, 7*(4), 239–245.

Fry, S. (1989). Toward a theory of nursing ethics. *Advances in Nursing Science, 13*(3), 9–22.

Gadow, S. (1980). Existential advocacy: Philosophical foundation of nursing. In S. Specher & S. Gadow (Eds.), *Nursing: Images and ideals.* New York: Springer.

Gadow, S. (1984). Touch and technology: Two paradigms of patient care. *Journal of Religion and Health, 23*(1), 63–69.

Gadow, S. (1985). Nurse and patient: The caring relationship. In A. Bishop, & J. Scudder (Eds.), *Caring, curing and coping.* University of Alabama: University of Alabama Press.

Gadow, S. (1989). Clinical subjectivity. *Nursing Clinics of North America, 24*(2), 83–89.

Guba, E., & Lincoln, Y. (1989). *Fourth generation evaluation.* Newbury Park, CA: Sage.

Gordon, S. (1993). Using photographs to explore values underlying rituals of care. D. Gaut (Chair), *Caring as healing: Renewal through hope.* Conference conducted by the International Association of Human Caring, Portland, OR.

Gortner, S. (1990). Nursing values and science: Toward a science philosophy. *Image*, 22(2), 101–105.

Kerfoot, K. (1991). Managing by values: The nurse manager's challenge. *Nursing Economics*, 9(3), 205–214.

Lewis, H. (1990). *A question of values*. New York: Harper & Row.

Manthey, M. (1989). What nurses value. *Nursing Management*, 20(12), 12–13.

Maraldo, P. (1989). The nineties: A decade in search of meaning. *Nursing & Health Care*, 11(1), 11–14.

Nyberg, J. (1990). Theoretical exploration of human care and economics. *Advances in Nursing Science*, 13(1), 74–84.

Parker, M. E. (1990). *Valuing and financing selected nursing practice strategies*. Unpublished proposal, Florida Atlantic University, Boca Raton.

Parker, M. E. (1991, March). Expressing nursing's values. M. Parker (Chair), *Economics and nursing practice*. Conference conducted at Florida Atlantic University, Boca Raton.

Parker, M., Gordon, S., & Brannon, P. (1992). Involving nursing staff in research: A non-traditional approach. *Journal of Nursing Administration*, 22(4), 58–63.

Parker, M. E. (1992, April). Research design for valuing and financing nursing practice strategies. M. Parker (Chair), *Nursing in the Twenty-first Century: Dreams and Designs*. Conference conducted at Florida Atlantic University, Boca Raton.

Porter-O'Grady, T. (1991, March). Nursing Economics. M. Parker (Chair), *Economics and Nursing Practice*. Conference conducted at Florida Atlantic University, Boca Raton.

Porter-O'Grady, T. (1992, April). Nursing in the twenty-first century: A community of clinical scholars. M. Parker (Chair), *Nursing in the Twenty-first Century: Dreams and Designs*. Conference conducted by Florida Atlantic University, Boca Raton.

Reason, P. (1988). *Human inquiry in action*. Newbury Park, CA: Sage.

Reason, P., & Rowan, J. (1981). *Human inquiry: A source book of new paradigm research*. New York: Wiley and Sons.

Rokeach, M. (1973). *The meaning of human values*. New York: Free Press.

Schoenhofer, S. (1989). Love, beauty and truth: Fundamental nursing values. *Journal of Nursing Education, 28*(8), 282–284.

Shank, J., & Weis, D. (1989). A study of values of baccalaureate nursing students and graduate nurses from a secular and non-secular program. *Journal of Professional Nursing, 5*(1), 17–22.

Stern, P. (1989). Are counting and coding a cappella appropriate in qualitative research? In J. Morse (Ed.), *Qualitative nursing research: A contemporary dialogue*, 135–148. Rockville, MD: Aspen.

Strews, W. (1992). *The structure of values from the lived experiences of agency nurses*. Unpublished master's thesis, Florida Atlantic University, Boca Raton.

Woods, M., & Catanzaro, M. (1988). *Nursing research: Theory and practice*. St. Louis: Mosby.

Watson, J. (1988). New dimensions of human caring theory. *Nursing Science Quarterly, 1*(4), 175–181.

5

Nursing's Values Expressed in Caring Rituals

Charlotte D. Barry

The present and future of nursing, as a profession and discipline, resides in the discipline's ability to know more about what it means "to nurse." Reflecting on the nature of nursing by examining and defining its beliefs is a natural beginning point of the process. Reeder (1988) states "it seems crucial . . . to illuminate the persistent enduring values and goals of our discipline which empower, emancipate, and impassion human caring and awaken sensitivity to our shared human condition/situation" (p. 229).

Authors from both social science and nursing (Benner, 1991; Leonard, 1989; Lewis, 1990; Rokeach, 1973), state the importance of studying persons in context, for it is in actions and words that values are made known. The context of nursing is in the nursing situation and it is in milieu that nursing is known in its fullest (Boykin, Parker, & Schoenhofer, 1991). Reflective storytelling of nursing situations communicates the meaning of the nursing experience and gives voice to the content of nursing.

PURPOSE

The purpose of this study was to examine nursing's values as they are lived day-to-day in caring rituals of nursing practice. A nurse's story describing a situation in which nursing's values were lived was explored for caring rituals and for the values guiding those rituals. The question that guided this investigation was "What are nursing's values lived in the day-to-day practice of nursing's caring rituals?"

DEFINITION OF TERMS

Nursing's values are enduring beliefs that guide nursing actions and energize the nursing situation. Day-to-day nursing practice encompasses "the all at once, ordinary, unique, profound, intentional, and thoughtful service activities of the nurse" (Barry, 1993, p. 2). Nursing practice takes place in the nursing situation described as "a shared lived experience in which the caring between nurse and nursed enhances personhood" (Boykin & Schoenhofer, 1993, p. 33). Story is a reflected description of a nursing situation. Rituals are stylized routines done in a particular way that carry meaning (Elsbree, 1982). Caring rituals of nursing are thoughtful, purposeful, stylized, routines that preserve and enhance the personhood of the other and symbolize the knowing of the connectedness to the other.

RESEARCHER'S PERSPECTIVE

Interest in this work developed out of an experience as research assistant in a nursing research project that explored nursing's values and nursing practice strategies. The project is described in Chapter Four by Parker in this volume. One particular part of the data, texts of nurses' stories, presented beautiful descriptions from practice and called for closer scrutiny to understand all that was said and all that was left unsaid. The importance of nursing's caring rituals, described in nurses' stories, became clearer to this investigator after watching two films this past year.

The first film, *A Midnight Clear* (Pollack, Bader, & Gordon, 1992) reaffirmed for this researcher the sacredness of rituals in our lives. The film documents the story of several men, both ally and enemy, who met during World War II. The setting was a forest in Europe and the time was late December. On Christmas Eve fears and arms were laid down for the rituals of singing Christmas carols and gift giving. The story unfolded in turmoil but for a short period of time a sense of order and tranquility was restored as one by one the American soldiers bathed in a footed bath tub in an abandoned chateau that had been established as their headquarters. The viewers participated in this ritualistic bathing, a symbolic washing away of the horrors and a preparation for the antici-pated proceedings of war. The most poignant scene followed as the men, together bathed their friend, a fellow soldier, who had been killed acci-dentally in a chaotic misunderstanding.

The second film, *A Woman's Tale* (Cox & Naidu, 1992) reaffirmed the sacred responsibility nurses have as they are called to participate in the rituals of another's life. It tells the story of Martha, a woman suffering with cancer and living her life fully in each moment. Her life is inter-twined with many others but particularly with her neighbor Billy and her home health nurse Malenka. Four scenes in particular depicted the significance of the nurse's response to be with the other, to do with the other, and to do for the other in the thoughtful, stylized actions of nursing's caring rituals.

In the first scene the viewers share in the sacred ritual of bathing as Martha submerges herself in a tub of hot water. We can vicariously feel the hot water against our skin and begin to relax along with Martha. As the water buoys Martha she becomes transformed into a younger woman caught in a terrifying scene of war. Martha is called from this dream or reverie by her elderly, frail neighbor, Billy. Struggling to take care of his toileting needs he uses a common bathroom on the floor below; after climbing the stairs he finds himself locked out of his apart-ment. Martha helps him into his apartment and suggests it would be easier for him if he used a jar in the night. In the next scene Martha responds to Billy's knocking on the common wall of their apartments and finds him wet in his bed. She changes his bed, wraps up his soiled pajamas and conspires with him to keep it a secret so he can continue living in his own place alone. The next two scenes focus on Malenka's visits to Billy. Malenka promotes Billy's personhood as she participates with him as his life unfolds in increasing complexity and compromise. While visiting Billy one day Malenka puts on his favorite old record and stands back as Billy struggles with shaving himself. His eyes call for Malenka to understand he can't manage shaving and Malenka re-sponds by helping him shave. In the final scene Malenka sits on Billy's bed and washes his face. He reaches out to her and she gently takes his hand and cuddles it to her face. The beauty of Malenka'a practice of nursing is vividly portrayed throughout the film but these clips in par-ticular seem to depict the profound connections of nurse to nursed in the performance of caring rituals.

LITERATURE REVIEW

Nursing Values

Most of the literature on values is written from a philosophic framework, and little research of nursing's values has been reported in the literature until recently. Gadow (1980, 1984, 1985, 1989) describes the values of nursing from a philosophical framework and identifies care as nursing's core value that aims at protecting and enhancing human dignity. Embedded in Watson's (1988) work on caring is a description of nursing's moral ideal or value as caring committed to the protection and enhancement of human dignity. Caring, health promotion, illness prevention, professional competence and ethics, are expressions of nursing's values of equity and respect (Gortner, 1990). Nursing's fundamental value of caring is illuminated in the spiritual values of love, beauty, and truth (Schoenhofer, 1989).

Wolf (1989) studied the relationship of nursing to medicine and asked expert nurses to define nursing and to describe the values of the profession. The same questions were asked of physicians. The data were analyzed using phenomenological hermeneutics, and the results were compared to seek patterns among the relationships. Nursing's core values included viewing persons as individuals and safeguarding the wholeness of life as manifested through caring. The caring purpose of each profession was different, with the nurse promoting possibilities from within the person while the physician promotes the possibilities from outside the person.

Nursing's values—honesty, respect for life, and responsibility were uncovered in a research study on the meaning of excellence in nursing practice (Scelsi, 1992). Seven nurses participated in this study and described how they experienced excellence, how they saw themselves when engaging in excellent practice, and what this meant to them. Phenomenology was used to analyze data which included stories and descriptions of practice.

Strews (1992) described values of agency nurses in a qualitative research study. Six nurses participated and offered a story of practice which reflected their nursing values. Giorgi's method (1985) was used to analyze and synthesize the data into a specific description of values. Caring was described as the fundamental value in nursing, unfolding in the unpretentious presence of the nurse. The nurse was impelled by caring in the lived experience of nursing to learn through unpretentious presence the compassionate actions of listening, touching, and truth telling. This research study affirmed caring as the core value in nursing and further described the usefulness of storytelling as method.

Storytelling as Inquiry

Stories can illuminate meanings and values, transmit values, and generate knowledge. Finding meaning in the context of a person's life is described by many authors in social science and nursing (Benner, 1991; Coles, 1989; Lee, 1988; Leonard, 1989; Reeder, 1988; Rokeach, 1973). Stories as recounted narratives of persons' lives provide the context for the study of actions and conduct.

Coles (1989) used fictional stories in novels to provide models for moral development of medical students. The characters of the novel can become models for goodness or evil, can inform readers how to live their lives more fully, and can demonstrate ways to avoid actions that distance one person from the other. Younger (1990) reflected this work and further espouses the "Great Books" as a source of wisdom for students of nursing. Novels allow the student to experience suffering vicariously and help move the reader to compassion.

Polkinghorne (1988) proposes human research focused on the narrative of one's life. Narrative is described as "any spoken or written presentation" and story as "the narrating or relating of an event or series of events" (Polkinghorne, 1988, p. 13). The terms story and narrative are equivalent in Polkinghorne's work. Storytelling allows persons to share beliefs and to transmit these beliefs or values.

Storytelling as a means to relate the liveliness and passion of one's experience is described by Reason and Hawkins (1988). As a mode of inquiry, storytelling is multidimensional and can work to explain or express, to analyze or understand" (p. 79). "The best stories stir peoples' minds, hearts and souls and by doing so, give insights into themselves, their problems and the human condition" (Mitroff, in Reason & Hawkins, 1988, p. 83).

Story as a method of organizing and communicating nursing knowledge is offered by Boykin and Schoenhofer (1991, p. 245). The authors believe nursing takes place in the nursing situation and it is in the situation that nursing is known. The reflective story of the situation creates anew, illuminates the essence of nursing, and allows it to be known to others. In addition, Sandelowski (1991) states that lives can be understood, transformed, or revealed in stories (p. 163). The author describes storytelling as a qualitative research method and offers a framework for generating nursing knowledge.

Benner (1984, 1991) has written extensively about the use of exemplars and paradigm cases, stories, and reflected accounts from practice, to learn about the practice of nursing. Narrative accounts of clinical examples of practice provide texts for intrepretive studies which can "uncover meanings and feelings in ways that shed light on the contextual, relational, and configurational knowledge lived out in the practice" (Benner, 1991, p. 3).

Embedded in stories are keys to understanding nursing (Parker, 1990). Nurse's stories provide a resource for studying dilemmas and revealing concepts of ethical theorizing built on connectedness: engaged listening, authentic responsiveness, mutual disclosures, and negotiation.

Rituals

Rituals are described by Elsbree (1982) as stylized routines done in a particular way. They are a form of symbolic action over technical. Rituals are purposeful and the actors or agents are active participants. Often associated with life's passages, rituals can create order out of chaos, allow for reflection on the situation and for the laying on of hands. The purer the action the stronger the hold on us as ritual.

Imber-Black and Roberts (1992) assert that every culture in the world has created rituals to celebrate, guide, and ease the way through life's passages. Rituals are built around common symbols and symbolic actions and can provide us with a sense of personal identity and family connections. They help heal losses, express our deepest beliefs, and celebrate our existence. Rituals not only announce change but they create change.

Family rituals within the family paradigm theory are described by Campbell (1991) as windows to view the family's efforts to maintain its shared beliefs and identity. Rituals are classified as regulating mechanisms through which the family can express its being. Assessment of rituals provides information about the family's being and can provide clues for other possibilities. Maintaining rituals can be a source of conflict as family structures change. Helping families create new rituals symbolizing transformation reflects the notion of rituals announcing change as well as creating change.

The bath is described as a nursing ritual by Wolf (1993). The author traces the roots of this ritual to the 1800s and to nursing's association with hygiene. As a therapeutic nursing ritual, the bath symbolizes the essential character of nursing and is grounded in its beliefs, art and science. Carrying many meanings beyond hygiene the bath may be looked upon as a healing or purification rite. It also provides a sense of community, connectedness, and continuity for nurses as they practice in different settings.

METHOD

This study unfolded within the context of a larger nursing research project (Parker, 1990, 1991, 1992; see Chapter Four) which explored nursing values and nursing practice strategies. The research method was a synthesis of participatory, action, and cooperative methods (Brown & Tandon, 1983; Parker, Gordon, & Brannon, 1992; Reason, 1988; Reason & Rowan, 1981) and unfolded in a milieu of collaboration and mutual respect for values. Participation in this larger project, as research assistant, was full and collegial in all phases of data generation and analysis.

Data Generation

The notion of storytelling as inquiry was explored as a valuable method of the larger study to generate nursing knowledge and was included with two reflective, guided, group interviews. The principal investigator, in a spirit of mentorship and collegiality, shared the raw data (Sieber, 1991) with this researcher to analyze for this study.

The data for the present study were presented by a nurse participating in the larger research project. At the end of the first interview the participating nurse was invited to reflect on a story in which she/he felt nursing's values were lived, to write the story, and bring it to the next interview. The second interview began with a reflective exercise during which the participating nurse was asked to quietly reflect on nursing's values. At the end of the exercise, the nurse was asked to share her/his story. The nurse read the story and it was audiotaped. Field notes were also recorded. The nurse typed the story and gave a copy to the principal investigator. This researcher was present during the interview when the nurse read the story into the tape recorder. The edited story is presented in the following section.

The Nurse's Story

It was an unusually quiet night at work when the phone rang and we were told that a patient on the surgical floor, who I will call Mrs. C., needed to be transferred to the Surgical Intensive Care Unit (SICU) for overnight observation. As Mrs. C. was wheeled through the doors of SICU it was quite evident to me that Mrs. C. was very ill. Her initial vital signs were okay but just looking at her you could tell something was very wrong. The surgeon on her case was immediately notified and stated he was on his way in. The family of three children were, needless to say, very anxious and scared. After explaining Mrs. C.'s condition to the family, I assured them I would keep them updated but would have to ask them to step outside for awhile. They were very understanding and cooperative. Within the next hour Mrs. C. had crashed and the doctor spoke with the family. We proceeded to intubate Mrs. C., started Dopamine, inserted a Swan-Ganz, started pushing fluids at over 1000 cc an hour, obtained X-rays and lab work. Unfortunately none of our efforts were helping Mrs. C. As soon as possible, I had the family come in and the doctor explained Mrs. C.'s condition to them. I then gave report to the 11-7 shift, feeling badly that Mrs. C. was not responding well but knowing she had received the best possible care.

The next day at 3 p.m. I reported to work and was assigned Mrs. C. In report I was told by the off-going nurse that Mrs. C. had not improved and, after a conference between the family and the doctor, that Mrs. C. had been made a No-Code and the ventilator, Dopamine, and Swan had been discontinued. Mrs. C.'s blood pressure was very low and the family was very hostile. My initial response was dreading having to deal with this 'hostile' family. I immediately re-introduced myself to the family and they were indeed agitated and hostile. After speaking with them for a few minutes I turned to check Mrs. C. She was lying in a blood-filled bed with dried, crusty blood on her mouth. I touched her hand and turned to the family. I asked them if they would mind stepping outside for a few minutes so I could try and make Mrs. C. more comfortable. They were hesitant to leave the bedside and angrily said they would leave but only for a few moments. I thanked them and assured them I would get them as soon as I was finished or sooner if Mrs. C.'s condition changed. I then proceeded to quickly bathe Mrs. C., change her bed, clean her mouth, and reposition her. I also taped the two rosary beads that were lying in the bed to her hands. I then immediately went to get the family. I gave them a few minutes and then went to see how the family and Mrs. C. were doing. When I entered the room the family was all crying. The son saw me first and grasped my hand and just kept saying 'thank you.' The family was no longer angry and hostile. The door was now open to talk and listen to them. Their mother had a living

*will and often talked about never wanting to be kept temporarily alive
on life support. This was the hardest decision of their lives and they
were trying to deal with their feelings of stopping life support of their
mother. They also felt they had been judged for their decision by the
hospital staff. I'm not sure this is true but it's how they felt. I sat with
them for a long time letting them ventilate their feelings. The rest of the
night I would inform them every hour what Mrs. C.'s condition was
and every two hours I asked them to step outside while I repositioned
and cleaned her. The fact that Mrs. C. was kept cleaned and comfortable
made the family feel Mrs. C. was at peace. Unfortunately, the family
decided to go home for a short break around 9:00 p.m. that night and
Mrs. C. expired 10 minutes later. I spoke with the family twice after
Mrs. C.'s death. When they returned to the hospital one-half hour after Mrs. C.'s death they were grief stricken but kept saying 'thank-you
for everything you did.' The last time I spoke with them was about a
month later when they showed up at the hospital and asked to speak
with me outside the unit. When I walked outside the unit the entire
family was there including Mrs. C.'s 10-year-old granddaughter. They
wanted to give me a lovely present and thank me again. They stated the
thing they remembered most was my keeping her clean and comfortable,
and the taping of the rosary beads to her hands so they would be with
her always. The little girl started to cry and her mother stated 'She's
okay, she just insisted on meeting the lovely nurse who took such good
care of her grandmother.'*

Anonymous, 1990

Analysis

In a spirit of intense concentration the text as data was read and re-
read within the context of the whole and its parts. A reverence for the
story developed; the story seemed to have a spiritual presence. The
researcher became part of the story and was able to place herself in the
unit watching the story unfold, like the narrator in *The Twilight Zone*
series. Reason and Hawkins (1988) warn the researcher about stories
". . . not to jump immediately to analyze but to take time to deepen
them" (p. 100).

The text was analyzed for content and organized into words or
phrases that described a caring ritual. This entailed a four-step process
synthesized from several processes (Parker, in Chapter Four of this
book; Polit & Hungler, 1987; Stern, 1989; Woods & Catanzaro, 1988).

The steps included: becoming fully immersed in the data; deciding on the unit of analysis—which was a word, phrase or sentence that described a caring ritual; identifying these significant statements; and extracting these statements from the data. This was an intentional and intuitive process which emerged from reading and re-reading the text. Bateson (cited in Reason & Hawkins, 1988, p. 80) states all boundaries are arbitrary and it is a matter of choice where the inquirer applies the scissors. The choices made by this researcher derived from the literature on rituals and from a deep knowing of nursing. Eleven caring rituals were identified.

The rituals were then analyzed for an understanding of the value or values embedded in each. A similar process of analysis was then employed—the text was read and re-read concentrating on the rituals extracted from the text and the rituals as part of the whole. The second step was to establish the unit of analysis which was values. The third step was to identify the values embedded in the rituals. The fourth step was to extract the values from the text. A fifth step included grouping the values into categories. This analysis was done in a spirit of intense concentration allowing for the transformation of text into units of analysis (Stern, 1989, p. 143). The definition of values as enduring beliefs guiding actions directed this analysis. The process of uncovering the values was a creative one that required ". . . carefully considered judgments" (Woods & Catanzaro, 1988, p. 443). There were 11 values identified, informed by the extensive literature review of values and nursing's values, and by nursing's values identified by Parker in Chapter Four.

FINDINGS

Caring Rituals of Nursing Care

Caring rituals of nursing are thoughtful, purposeful, stylized routines that preserve and enhance the personhood of the other and symbolize the knowing of the connectedness to the other.

The rituals that emerged from the data by this process of inquiry were: the admission to the SICU; the explanations of Mrs. C.'s condition to the family; the technological interventions (intubation, infusion of Dopamine, insertion of the Swan-Ganz, infusion of IV fluids, obtaining lab and X-ray data); giving report; touching Mrs.'s C.'s hand;

bathing Mrs. C.; providing mouth care; changing the linens; repositioning Mrs. C.; taping the two rosary beads to her hands; and accepting the gift.

Nursing's Values

Nursing's values are enduring beliefs that guide nursing actions and energize the nursing situation. The values embedded in the rituals were: compassion, honesty, courage, trust, humility, commitment, hope, competence, caring, respect for the personhood of the other and inner harmony.

Nursing's Values in Caring Rituals

By wandering through and dwelling with this nurse's story the values embedded in the text were uncovered and described. The complexity of each caring ritual revealed one or more values lived all at once. Although the most profound value in a ritual was chosen, there were always others present. Nursing's values guide nursing's actions and take priority over each other in the living of each unique moment. The nurse and Mrs. C. became known through the analysis.

The admission of Mrs. C. to the SICU that night was energized by the values of compassion, courage, and respect for the personhood of the other as the nurse all at once feels the urgency in the presence of Mrs. C., as person, and responds with courage to the rapidly unfolding events.

The explanations of Mrs. C.'s condition to the family, immediately and all through the situation were guided by the value of honesty as the nurse was present for the family with the reports of their mother's condition.

The technological interventions: insertion of the Swan, infusion of IV fluids, etc. were guided by the value competence. This empirical knowing was purposefully learned so the nurse would be available to the other with a deep understanding of technical skills.

The ritual of giving report was guided by the value trust as the nurse informed the next shift about Mrs. C. and her family, knowing the next nurse would care for them in her/his own way.

The nurse touched Mrs. C.'s hand and was guided by the value of humility. Humility in nursing grounds the nurse to nursed in a shared humanness as the nurse remains open to know all that can be known of Mrs. C.

The rituals of bathing, providing mouth care, changing the linens and repositioning were guided by the value of hope. Hope energized the situation with the possibilities of making Mrs. C.'s moments the best they could be for her.

The caring ritual of taping the rosary beads to Mrs. C.'s hands was guided also by the value of hope. The rosary beads are a powerful symbol of hope for Catholics: a transcendence to a higher plane and a transformation to a higher form of being. The nurse participated with Mrs. C. in hope.

The caring ritual of accepting the gift was guided by the value of humility. The family wanted to show gratitude and the nurse responded by gracious acceptance of the praise and gift.

The values of caring, respect for the dignity of the personhood of the other, commitment and inner harmony apparent in each ritual. Each ritual symbolized the nurse's respect for Mrs. C.'s personhood, the promotion of Mrs. C.'s process of being and becoming, the nurse's commitment to be all she/he could be as nurse in the moment, and inner harmony. Inner harmony expresses living a congruence between values and behaviors (Mayeroff, 1971, p. 72) and provides a sense of peace with oneself for living the values of the community of nursing.

IMPLICATIONS FOR NURSING

Nursing's values exist even though the nurse may not have a sensitivity to them. Reflective storytelling allows nurses to journey to their souls to find meaning in the experience of the nursing situation by examining the values that awakened and energized the unfolding possibilities of the moment. Nursing stories can illuminate caring rituals and allow the profound beliefs of nursing to be communicated and understood.

As the nurse participated with Mrs. C. in these rituals of caring a deeper knowing of Mrs. C. evolved and the nurse became embodied with Mrs. C. The nurse knew Mrs. C. would have washed away her own blood if she had been able; she would not have lain in a pool of blood if she had been able to change her own sheets. The nurse knew Mrs. C. would have comforted her own children and protected them from her suffering if she had been able. The nurse knew Mrs. C. would have wrapped her own rosary beads around her fingers and prayed to Mary for transformation if she had been able to pray.

What would inquiry of this story reveal if the researcher wandered into the story? Reason and Hawkins (1988) suggest the nature of a story should be personified and treated as *thou*. Taking on the roles of persons or objects in a story reveal a deeper knowing of the story.

What would be known of Mrs. C. if I had become her blood? How would the blood have described this situation? What would the blood have to say about this nurse? What would the water have to say about this nursing situation—Mrs. C. and the nurse? Would the water describe how the nurse worked to get the temperature just right or how the water facilitated the touching of nurse and nursed? What would the pillow say? Or the hospital bed? Or Mrs. C.? What would Mrs. C. tell us about this nurse and how the nurse nurtured her and her children? How did the nurse, guided by nursing's values, lovingly lay on hands and perform the caring rituals of nursing?

What would we know of nursing if we created a ritual of storytelling, reflected on the story for caring rituals and values and gave voice to the beauty of nursing in the most sacred place, the nursing situation?

Nurses' stories of living nursing's values, illuminate nursing's caring rituals and allow the profound beliefs of nursing to be communicated and understood. Common rituals of bathing a patient, changing soiled sheets or wrapping rosary beads around a patient's limp fingers come alive with possibilities in the nursing situation, by symbolically expressing nursing's values. As nurses accompany others through the most intimate, the most beautiful, the most shattering and the most ordinary experiences of their lives, rituals provide comfort in the shared knowing of our connectedness to patients, family members, and the discipline of nursing.

REFERENCES

Anonymous, 1990. The nurse's story. Palm Beach County, FL.

Barry, C. D. (1993). *The values lived in the day-to-day practice of nursing.* Unpublished master's thesis, Florida Atlantic University, Boca Raton, FL.

Beck, C. T. (1993). Qualitative research: The evaluation of its credibility, fittingness and auditability. *Western Journal of Nursing Research, 15*(2), 263–266.

Benner, P. (1984). *From novice to expert.* Redwood, CA: Addison-Wesley.

Benner, P. (1985). Quality of life: A phenomenological perspective of explanation, prediction, and understanding in nursing science. *Advances in Nursing Science, 8*(1), 1–14.

Benner, P. (1991). The role of experience, narrative, and community in skilled ethical comportment. *Advances in Nursing Science, 14*(2), 1–21.

Boykin, A., & Schoenhofer, S. (1991). Story as link. *Image, 23*(4), 245–248.

Boykin, A., & Schoenhofer, S. (1993). *Nursing as Caring: A model for transforming nursing practice.* New York: National League for Nursing Press.

Boykin, A., Parker, M., & Schoenhofer, S. (1991, August). *Beyond Carper: Aesthetic knowing an explicit conception of nursing as caring.* Paper presented at Aesthetic Expressions in Nursing Conference, Gainesville, Florida.

Brown, L., & Tandon, R. (1983). Ideology and political economy in inquiry: Action research and participatory research. *Journal of Applied Behavioral Science, 19*(3), 277–294.

Campbell, D. W. (1991). Family paradigm theory and family rituals: Implications for child and family health. *Nurse Practitioner, 16*(2), 22–31.

Coles, R. (1989). *The call of stories.* Boston: Houghton Mifflin Co.

Cox, P., & Naidu, S. (Producers), & Cox, P. (Director). (1992). *A Woman's Tale* [Film]. Burbank, California: Orion Home Video.

Elsbree, L. (1982). *The rituals of life: Patterns in narration.* Port Washington, New York: Kennikat Press.

Gadow, S. (1980). Existential advocacy: Philosophical foundation of nursing. In Specher, S., & Gadow, S. (Eds.), *Nursing: Images and ideals.* New York: Springer.

Gadow, S. (1984). Touch and technology: Two paradigms of patient care. *Journal of Religion and Health*, 23(1), 63–69.

Gadow, S. (1985). Nurse and Patient: The caring relationship. In A. Bishop & J. Scudder (Eds.), *Caring, curing and coping* (pp. 31–43). University of Alabama, University of Alabama Press.

Gadow, S. (1989). Clinical subjectivity. *Nursing Clinics of North America*, 24(2), 83–89.

Giorgi, A. (1985). *Phenomenology and psychological research*. Pittsburgh: Duquesne University Press.

Gortner, S. (1990). Nursing values and science: Toward a science philosophy. *Image*, 22(2), 101–105.

Imber-Black, E., & Roberts, J. (1992, September/October). Rituals for our times. *New Age Journal*, 70–73.

Lee, P. (1988). Hermeneutics and vitalism. *Revision*, 10(3), 3–13.

Leonard, V. (1989). A Heideggerian phenomenological perspective on the concept of the person. *Advances in Nursing Science*, 11(4), 40–55.

Lewis, H. (1990). *A question of values*. New York: Harper & Row.

Mayeroff, M. (1971). *On caring*. New York: Harper & Row.

Parker, M. (1990). Valuing and financing nursing practice strategies. (Unpublished proposal). Boca Raton: Florida Atlantic University.

Parker, M. (1991). Research design for valuing and financing nursing practice strategies. M. Parker (Chair), *Nursing in the Twenty-first Century: Dreams and Designs*. Conference conducted at Florida Atlantic University, Boca Raton, FL.

Parker, M. (1992, April). *Nursing in the Twenty-first Century: Dreams and designs*. Presentation at seminar, Boca Raton, FL.

Parker, M., Gordon, S., & Brannon, P. (1992). Involving nursing staff in research: A non-traditional approach. *Journal of Nursing Administration*, 22(4), 58–63.

Parker, R. (1990). Nurses' stories: The search for a relational ethic of care. *Advances in Nursing Science*, 13(12), 31–40.

Polit, D. F., & Hungler, B. P. (1987). *Nursing research: Principles and methods*. New York: Lippincott Co.

Polkinghorne, P. (1983). *Methodology for the human sciences: Systems of inquiry*. Albany: State University of New York Press.

Polkinghorne, P. (1988). *Narrative knowing and the human sciences*. New York: State University of New York Press.

Pollack, D., & Bader, B. (Producers). Gordon, K. (Director). (1992). *A Midnight Clear* [Film]. Burbank, California: Columbia Tristar Home Video.

Reason, P. (Ed.). (1988). *Human inquiry in action: Development in new paradigm research*. Newbury Park, CA: Sage.

Reason, P., & Hawkins, P. (1988). Storytelling as inquiry. In Peter Reason (Ed.), *Human inquiry in action: Development in new paradigm research*, 79–101. Newbury Park, CA: Sage.

Reason, P., & Rowan, J. (Eds.). (1981). *Human inquiry: A sourcebook of new paradigm research*. New York: Wiley.

Reeder, F. (1988). Hermeneutics, in B. Sarter (Ed.), *Paths to knowledge: Innovative research methods for nursing*, pp. 193–238. New York: National League for Nursing Press.

Rokeach, M. (1973). *The meaning of human values*. New York: Free Press.

Sandelowski, M. (1991). Telling stories: Narrative approaches in qualitative research. *Image, 23*(33), 161–166.

Scelsi, D. B. (1992). *Forgotten moments: The paradox of excellence in nursing practice*. Unpublished master's thesis, Florida Atlantic University, Boca Raton, FL.

Schoenhofer, S. (1989). Love, beauty and truth: Fundamental nursing values. *Journal of Nursing Education, 28*(8), 282–284.

Sieber, J. E. (1991). *Sharing social science data*. Newbury Park, CA: Sage.

Stern, P. (1989). Are counting and coding a capella appropriate in qualitative research? In J. Morse (Ed.), *Qualitative Nursing Research: A Contemporary Dialogue*, 135–148. Salem, MA: Aspen.

Strews, W. (1992). The structure of values from the lived experiences of agency nurses. Unpublished master's thesis, Florida Atlantic University, Boca Raton, FL.

Watson, J. (1988). New dimensions of human caring theory. *Nursing Science Quarterly*, 175–181.

Wolf, B. (1989). *Nursing identity: The nursing-medicine relationship.* (Doctoral Dissertation, University of Colorado Health Sciences Center.)

Wolf, Z. (1993). The bath: A nursing ritual. *Journal of Holistic Nursing*, *11*(2), 135–148.

Woods, M., & Catanzaro, M. (1988). *Nursing research: Theory and practice.* St. Louis: C. V. Mosby.

Younger, J. (1990). Literacy works as a mode of knowing. *Image*, *22*(1), 39–43.

Part III

Healing Modalities

6

Healing Through Therapeutic Touch: One Person's Perspective

Monica Nebauer

People say that what we're all seeking is a meaning for life. I don't think that's what we're really seeking. I think that what we're seeking is an experience of being alive, so that our life experiences on the purely physical plane will have resonances within our own innermost being and reality, so that we actually feel the rapture of being alive.

Joseph Campbell, 1988

This paper is a case study approach to understanding the experiences of a person receiving therapeutic touch over time. The person is Mary, aged fifty-eight, who was rather tense, controlled, and anxious to have me "give" her "some Therapeutic Touch" (TT) for her high blood pressure, for which she had received medication for the past six years. She had heard that I was a practitioner and teacher of TT and was very anxious to experience the modality.

Mary had been prescribed a number of different medications, and had suffered side effects from them all. She was somewhat anxious about recently having her blood pressure medication increased to the maximum dosage possible, despite her healthy lifestyle. There was no family history of hypertension and Mary was angry that she was having this trouble despite a good diet, daily meditation and exercise, and taking her prescribed medication over a number of years. Her medical practitioner was aware that she was seeking out this new treatment, and was very much in favor of her actions. She begged to be given an opportunity for the treatment, although aware it could be prolonged because of the chronicity of her problem.

Mary was widowed, with four grown children and eight grandchildren. She had worked in the same organization for approximately twelve years, in a position of seniority and influence. In the last couple of years, the organization had undergone considerable growth and restructuring. As a result, Mary now found herself in a position of less power and influence, and answerable to a supervisor who appeared to have somewhat different ideas from Mary.

Perhaps Mary sensed a need to search for a deeper experience of life when she came to see me. In her deep knowingness, she realized the need to reach out beyond her present place of being for answers to many issues that had been with her for a long time. The old solutions were not working.

During our initial discussion, it soon became clear that Mary thought Therapeutic Touch (TT) was a massage technique. We discussed Macrae's (1988) definition and explanation of TT, based on Krieger's (1975 and 1979) pioneering studies. Macrae (1988) claims that TT is derived from the ancient practice of the laying-on of hands, and is based on the fundamental assumption that there is a universal life force or energy that sustains all living organisms. This life force, or energy, has been generally defined in the physical sciences as "a continuous quality or condition throughout space" which "permeates space, becoming more concentrated within and around living organisms" (Macrae, 1988, p. 4). In this way all living things share a "generalized life-energy field, in the same way that all physical objects in space are subject to gravity" (Macrae, 1988, p. 4).

The idea of all living organisms sharing a life-energy field has been further expanded by Quinn (1992), who has developed a conceptual framework which originates in nursing in works by Rogers (1970) and Newman (1979). This framework further developed the works of Bohm (in Weber, 1978), Pribram (1976), Grof (1985), Watson (1988) and others. Quinn's (1992) view is not just that human beings have an energy field that is in and around the person, but that the human being *is* an energy field. Her conceptual framework and underlying assumptions, which are the basis for TT are as follows:

1. The fundamental unit of the living system is an energy field, coextensive with the environmental energy field.

2. There is an interconnectedness of all life.

3. The human being is a nonmaterial, multidimensional field integral with the environment/universal field.

4. Consciousness is nonlocal, unbounded by physical structure and function.

5. Separateness of the individual from all other individuals is an illusion.

(Quinn, 1992, pp. 27–28)

Mary was interested in the explanation about TT, and volunteered to be part of a research project. We agreed that when possible, she would come to my office three times each week. I was concerned about a request that Mary made to have her blood pressure taken and recorded before and after each treatment. I was aware of the multidimensional healing that could occur, and I knew that there may not be immediate changes purely on a physical level. I was also aware that, with healing, one should not be attached to the outcomes. Because of the complex and mystical nature of human spirituality, as practitioners we cannot predict what the outcome of healing will be. The nurse's role in healing is best explained as follows: "As nurses assist clients to illumine their patterns, the insight and synchrony the client achieves in the process is healing. Ultimately, it is not our role to control or to fix anything for another" (Joseph, 1991, p. 54). All healing is self-healing. The nurse is not the healer (Quinn, 1989). The nurse is, in fact, the "midwife" to healing—"to assist in the birth of healing" in the recipient, who, in fact, self-heals (Quinn, 1989, p. 555). The recipients who self-heal do so because of their innate human potential for wholeness and healing, rather than because of any control of the healing process. In fact, healing occurs when the recipient lets go of control; lets go of whatever blocks the path to healing and wholeness (Levine, 1987). Healing can not be forced, but occurs naturally when the person lets go of the "personal separatism, the self-images, the resistance to change, the fear and anger, the confusion that form the opaque armoring around the heart" (Levine, 1987, p. 6). Despite my misgivings, I decided to go along with Mary's request, and our sessions started.

We always commenced with a short dialogue about how Mary was feeling and coping with her day-to-day life, in order to give her the opportunity to relax before her blood pressure was recorded. Following the blood pressure recording, TT was given for approximately twenty minutes, or whenever I felt it was sufficient. The method consists of:

- a nurse "centering,"

- making an intention to help the subject,

- moving the hands four-to-six inches from the participant's body from head to foot without physical contact, in order to assess the energy field,

- helping the participant to re-establish an open, balanced energy flow—
    —clearing congestion,
    —transferring life energy into depleted areas,
    —balancing the energy flow.

(Macrae, 1988)

Immediately after the IT session, Mary's blood pressure was recorded again, followed by a dialogue about her experiences during the TT, which often included intriguing accounts of imagery. This imagery provided us with rich material for discussion and Mary's interpretation and later reflection.

I had decided on a case study approach as a way of providing an in-depth study over time of the experiences of a person receiving TT. I began note taking after each session, while Mary commenced regular reflective journaling. We also decided on regular audiotaped open, but focused, interviews of Mary's experiences. Mary gave consent unhesitatingly. All the data were transcribed using the software program "Ethnograph," coded, and analyzed using thematic analysis. For validation, the themes, interpretations and final summary were all given to Mary to read, and were later discussed. She agreed that the interpretation and summary represented her healing experience accurately.

RESULTS

There were a number of themes that emerged and appeared to fall into two main categories—the experience of TT, and how the TT experience helped (see Table 6.1). Each category and theme will be discussed in turn.

Table 6.1   Categories and Themes

Category	Themes
The experience of Therapeutic Touch	Sense of a holistic self
	Sense of being protected
	Sense of space and freedom
	Sense of timelessness
	Sense of openness
	Sense of child-likeness
How the Therapeutic Touch experience helped	Healing of multi-dimensional self
	Deepening of awareness of spirituality
	Ongoing effects

The themes and categories were reflected upon to once again get a sense of the whole experience, a description of which follows.

Therapeutic Touch (TT) was a freeing experience. It gave Mary a sense of space and timelessness in which she was able to leave her usual concerns and responsibilities and move into a different kind of time dimension, one in which the focus could be more truly her self. She discovered a re-emergence of joyful, mystical symbols of a child-like world which she enjoyed immensely. She was aware of a deep, relaxed, calmness and tranquillity, and as she allowed herself to fully experience the moment, she became open to the true nature of her multidimensional self, with the integrating factor being her spiritual self. As her openness to the experience increased, she was aware of an ever-deepening sense of healing occurring at all levels of her being. She was especially aware of a new, intimate, spiritual relationship with her personally-perceived God and with the cosmos. The ongoing effects for Mary are that as her sense of wholeness and newly-established life changes persist, she continues to tap into the child-like symbols of the imagery discovered during her healing sessions with Therapeutic Touch.

THE EXPERIENCE OF THERAPEUTIC TOUCH

Sense of a Holistic Self

The relaying of universal life energy to Mary produced change on multi-dimensional levels of which she was aware. When Mary was open to receiving healing energy, she experienced a deep awareness in the very essence of her being. She explains this awareness as follows:

> . . . *sometimes I've noticed that, deep into or a longer time into the TT experience, and when I'm particularly relaxed, that sometimes I can feel it right within, right down at my gut level, if you want to put it that way* . . .

She was aware of a synchronicity between the actual relaying of energy through my hands and her experience of something happening at various levels of her being. It was as though, at this moment, Mary realized the fullness of her own nature, which is to be whole. This sense of all levels of her being coming together as a unified whole is in her following words:

> . . . *(during TT) your whole self is being addressed at the same time . . . sometimes it is very difficult I believe to talk about psychological and spiritual because I really think that they interface somewhere at some point* . . .

Each one of us has a wholeness deep down within, which beckons us (Nasr, 1985). We have become separated from that wholeness by our externalized existence. We talk about and yearn for wholeness, because each of us has a reminiscence in our being of wholeness at some time in our existence. Mary may have experienced this sense of wholeness deep within herself which had been beckoning her "to live in such a way as to fulfill the innate need for wholeness" (Nasr, 1985, p. 29).

Sense of Being Protected

During TT, Mary experienced a feeling of being protected and invulnerable. She described it as "almost as if (I was) being cuddled." Mary described this sense of security:

> *Sometimes I almost felt when you were doing TT on me that, it's almost like being in a cocoon. . . . I guess it was almost like a baby being wrapped up in something that gave it a sense of security, and I think that's the word I'm looking for. So that there was a sense of security there in that feeling of being enveloped in something* . . .

Thus, TT was seen as an embrace or caress which was perceived by her consciousness as a pleasant, comforting feeling. The movement of my hands through her energy field created a sense of her being, extending beyond her skin into a diffuse, unknown, but safe area. The gentle, flowing hand movements provided a sense of boundary and safety for Mary. My presence of "being with" Mary totally in the moment further reassured her and provided a feeling of security. It could be described as a life-giving mode of being with another. According to Halldorsdottir, 1991, p. 39:

> One affirms the personhood of the other by connecting with the true center of the other in a life-giving way . . . (which) relieves the vulnerability of the other and makes the other stronger and enhances growth, restores, reforms, and potentiates learning and healing.

This presencing of myself with Mary occurred as the transpersonal caring expanded the "limits of openness" and accessed the "higher human spirit or field consciousness," thus expanding our human consciousness, transcending the moment, and potentiating healing for Mary (Watson, 1988, p. 176). It is this human caring-healing consciousness that can facilitate healing and release personal "inner power and resources by creating (an) expanded energy field (Watson, 1988, p. 177).

Sense of Space and Freedom

The TT experience provided a sense of space and freedom and, simultaneously, a sense of security.

> I think perhaps it gave me that sense of freedom and space—that your hands were there—but I could still move within that ambit . . . so that there was a sense of security there in that feeling of being enveloped in something, but there was also a tremendous sense of freedom at the same time . . .

Her sense of freedom was experienced as a disconnection from her everyday duties and responsibilities. She experienced a lifting of her usual sense of having something to do within a specific time frame. The time available was totally free for Mary to use as she wished for her healing. Mary explains this freedom:

. . . perhaps because, for that period of time, I would always feel that I had no responsibilities, that almost as if you're claiming that time just for yourself, so that that gave you a sense of freedom within that time.

The freedom allowed Mary the space to do whatever was necessary for her to heal on all levels—just to enjoy feeling relaxed, occasionally to enjoy a deep sleep, or to be available to fully experience and focus on images that came effortlessly to her mind.

Sense of Timelessness

Time is nothing else than an extendedness . . . of the soul itself.

(St. Augustine in Casey, 1991, p. 271)

During TT, Mary sensed a calmness and tranquillity which had a timeless and lasting quality, and was in itself a healing experience. It was as though she experienced a different time dimension. In this time dimension, freedom and space existed to be used as she saw fit.

I don't know whether your hands were moving or not or whether you're holding your hands very still at a certain point or a certain position— but I could just sense a tremendous sense of stillness there, almost as if you were just being held in time, at that particular point. And I found it a very healing experience, a very beautiful, healing experience.

According to Quinn (1992), one of the indices of expanded consciousness is thought to be an alteration in time perception, in which the intentionality of the nurse through the "centering" process provides a shift in consciousness of the recipient. It is thought that this phenomenon occurs in TT because of the nurse's interconnectedness with the client, and his/her knowing participation in human field patterning which is possible in a "four-dimensional universe of open (energy) fields" (Cowling, 1990; in Quinn, 1992, p. 28). In the meditative, centered state, the nurse provides a type of template upon which the client may repattern. Quinn (1992) likens the nurse's consciousness to that of a tuning fork, which resonates at a healing frequency, while the client tunes or resonates to that frequency. Thus, Mary's experience of timelessness may have been an indication of the shared, expanded consciousness that we shared, which provided the freedom and space for her to heal.

Sense of Openness

Initially, Mary wanted to have control over the healing process—she placed demands on herself and looked for changes in her blood pressure readings.

> *And when we started this program you will recall that we were doing the blood pressure readings and they were coming down. But the moment I started to think 'Oh, I must relax,' or 'I must do something,' then we didn't achieve anything, so that, in that way the healing there came when I was able to let go and be open. And so the blood pressure came down as a by-product of what the other, the other dynamic thing that was happening. So, it's either a very subtle shift or a very subtle difference in approach.*

When Mary detached herself from the outcomes of our healing sessions by relinquishing her need to control and have power over the healing situation, healing occurred spontaneously, because of her openness to change at all levels of her being. When she let go and became open to the healing that was occurring, her systolic and diastolic blood pressure reduced, almost, as Mary said, "as a by-product" of the "dynamic" healing that was occurring. Initially, Mary was quite anxious to see changes in her blood pressure readings, but as she became aware of the multi-dimensional nature of her healing, the blood pressure readings became less important to her.

The healing journey to wholeness requires that a person sacrifice the will to achieve and control. The time comes when the person has to let go—let go of the ego and experience the whole self (Luke, 1985). Wholeness occurs when a person experiences the difference between the ego and the self, which is the whole self. It is at this point that the person is able to begin letting go of the ego, a process which may take many years. Healing and wholeness occur as the person lets go of the need for achievement and power (Luke, 1985). Mary explains her "letting go" of her own ego and her need to control and influence situations, as follows:

> *. . . but in addressing them (tensions or problems in everyday life), sometimes it was very spiritual. . . . It was a giving over of your own*

ego, your own—your own power base or whatever, and that's where I
think that the spiritual comes into it.

Thus, for Mary, her healing started when she was able to allow an
openness to the universal life energy without any demands or attach-
ment to the outcomes of healing. As she relaxed more and more, she
became more aware of her spirituality and the integrating nature of it.
For this integration or healing to occur, Mary had to not only recognize
her own need to hold onto her own ego and powerbase, but also to be
prepared to give over her powerbase to a greater integrating spirituality, both within and outside of her self.

Sense of Child-Likeness

Mary experienced a wonderful sense of returning to childhood through
her spontaneous imagery during TT. The imagery was a very powerful
experience for Mary, who was never quite sure if it came during sleep
or deep relaxation. The images in our dreams contain a healing power
by presenting us with a picture of what is needed to be dealt with in
our subconscious (Sanford, 1978). The imagery or dreaming that Mary
experienced shows that she was making a link to a much deeper connection with her true self. Amiotte (1986, p. 32) stated in his beautiful
description of the Lakota Indian dream experience, that dreaming "is
an alternative avenue to knowing" for the Lakota, who realize that one
is "more than mere physical being (and that there is) the possibility for
interaction, transaction and intercourse within other dimensions of
time, place and being."

Mary's imagery included a dolphin, a unicorn, country scenes, the
color blue, which was the color I was visualizing for healing, and blue
water. One of her almost constant companions was a friendly dolphin
which swam with her endlessly through blue waters. He found her on
an underwater ledge and gently encouraged her to swim with him. For
Mary, a non-swimmer, this was a little frightening. Eventually, she
was able to leave the ledge and swim with the dolphin in free, untram-
melled joy. Later, she reflected on this image, and realized that her
dolphin was gently asking her to free herself to take more risks with
her life. Mary's joy is expressed in the following:

And I was at the seaside just recently and I saw some dolphins, and I
thought, 'Oh, how wonderful!' So there's a great sense of fun in all this

too. It's lovely! It's almost like going back to being able to become child-like again, not childish but child-like, you know—just being able to hear the old fairy tales again, and imagery, and let your mind go and feel very comfortable doing it; not feel as if you . . . 'I'm too old for this' . . . I was going to use the word 'silly' but that's nonsense. I suppose it is too, it's 'no-sense' stuff, isn't it?

Mary experienced a freedom to be comfortable with a sense of fun and child-likeness which unexpectedly emerged from the TT experience. Perhaps for Mary, the second half of life provides an opportunity to discover "that level which makes all the other levels distinct, yet one in the whole" (Luke, 1985, p. 23). As the person ages, experiences from childhood are remembered vividly, while, at the same time, an event that occurred yesterday may be forgotten. The aging person can allow the memories from childhood to become nostalgia or senility, or the person can choose to have those memories—

acquire an enormously enhanced meaning in the whole of . . . life. You begin to see your life as a circle instead of as a straight line. That's just one place where you begin to find that level where everything is a circle. But we have to walk on the straight lines, and we have to experience fully the horizontal and the vertical, the earth and the spirit, and the meeting point at the center before that can happen.

(Luke, 1985, p. 23)

According to Luke's (1985) Jungian approach, this later part of life is a time for new growth, which comes by gradually letting go of unimportant things and focusing on the importance of the present and the smallest things in the present. Also inherent in this new growth is the appreciation of childhood joy and the sense of the circularity of life. Jung argued that the challenge of later life is to reclaim the forgotten aspects of childhood. "If the individual succeeds, the outcome is psychological balance and inner wholeness" (Chinen, 1989, p. 69).

Mary was surprised by this re-emergence of childhood images. She obviously found it a wonderful, light-hearted experience, but was also aware that she needed to reflect on the symbols and their deeper meanings for her healing process.

HOW THE THERAPEUTIC TOUCH EXPERIENCE HELPED

Healing of the Multidimensional Self

One of Mary's images was not so light-hearted, but was the basis for a deep healing experience which she describes as follows:

Another set of images, not at all friendly, provided me with tools to handle a most difficult situation in my working life. During this meditation I found myself in the Antarctic. I was standing on a ledge with my back against an ice cliff. In front of me was a deep crevasse and on the other side of the crevasse was a group of Alsatian-type dogs, yelping and snarling at me. I was very frightened and knew that one move would find me either in the crevasse or at the mercy of the dogs. I also knew instinctively that no harm would come to me if I remained exactly where I was and stood perfectly still. I remained in this position for most of this particular meditation period. As time passed the dogs eventually quieted although they were continually watchful. While always remaining attentive to the dogs, I nevertheless found myself gazing at the beauty around me. . . . Toward the end of this meditation I found myself sitting on clouds far above the dogs, which I could still see quite clearly.

In discussing this scene later with me Mary realized it was a reflection of a volatile situation in her working environment. While only being a junior player in a particular set of circumstances she was, also, a key player. Because the situation had not developed as the senior players had wanted, and because individual powerbases and egos were at stake, it seemed to Mary that she could become a scapegoat for any recriminations that were likely to follow. Her imagery during TT had told her to be perfectly quiet and still and she would be safe. She applied this to her role in the situation and this is exactly what happened. Any suggestions or invitations made to her to offer more than the most basic objective assessments were either bypassed or ignored, nor did she comment on the behavior of any of the other key players in the situation.

For Mary, this image was significant in understanding not only the best way to handle this particular incident but also in understanding what would have been her normal responses to such a situation. Usually she would have seen it as her duty to step into the role of rescuer and trouble shooter. Mary came to see that the current crisis confronting her was not a problem she had created or over which she had any control. She was shown by the scene in her imagery to let go any desire to move outside certain obvious boundaries, and to become no more than an observant bystander.

During the ensuing weeks Mary called upon the image of the dogs whenever this particular event was under discussion and it has become a reflecting point for many other confrontational or tense situations in her everyday life. She could see that her job was not the most important aspect of her life, and as a result, she was able to distance herself and remain calm when tensions and crises occurred. Mary explains the process that was occurring at this time:

> (I was) being forced to prioritize my values . . . I think the best way to describe the healing would be that I could say exactly what I thought about something and that I could prioritize—what is important and what is not important. The things that aren't important, you're able to give away, or see through, or not worry about. But the things that are important, you are able to name them and then act on them, and that's where I see the spiritual and the psychological coming together . . . I was able to address issues that were affecting my day-to-day life and it gave me a new sense of perspective about them.

Quinn (1989, p. 553) states that the root of the word "heal" is an Anglo-Saxon word, "haelan," which means "to be or to become whole." Wholeness is "a dynamic process of being in right relationship . . . when true healing occurs, relationship is reestablished—relationship to and within self, to others, with one's purpose" (Quinn, 1989). The prioritizing that Mary did caused her to re-evaluate her whole life and her relationship with herself, her family, her colleagues, and her work itself. Mary was becoming healed.

Deepening of Awareness of Spirituality

Through Mary's healing and awareness of the integrating nature of her spirituality, came an increased sense of cosmic consciousness and awareness of a personal God. She realized that she had retained a childhood image of God as being remote from her, but that was replaced by an image of God as being a deep and integrating part of her.

(During TT) my own identity still appeared to remain intact, but I was also aware of becoming an integral part of a much wider reality. I can only liken this to what my idea of God or the Holy One had become, an idea far removed from my childhood image of a kindly bearded old man in the sky. On these occasions, there was a great sense of awe at my place in the cosmos.

This image of God was of a life force which she shared with all other creation. The life force suffused her very being and provided a sense of connection to all other humans and life forms in the cosmos. This realization was a totally unexpected change that occurred in her, and increased her motivation to explore this personal deity more fully in her daily meditations.

Through TT, the imagery that came with it, and her personal reflections and journaling, she was able to re-prioritize the importance of concerns and relationships in her life. She was able to dissociate herself from much of the organizational stress that occurred around her, and focus much more on her relationships with her aging parents, her children, grandchildren, and friends.

Ongoing Effects

The TT sessions continued for six months. By the end of this time, Mary's antihypertension medication was reduced from the maximum to a very low "holding" dose, with her doctor considering ceasing it altogether. Two months later Mary explained:

I certainly haven't gone back to where I was before I started—nothing like it. . . . I tend to find, if I am getting stressed again that I do some meditation and images that came up during the TT—I can recall those now fairly quickly. . . . No, it wasn't something that you do, it's great, and then next week you do something else . . . it has had long-term effects."

The ongoing effects are that Mary is much more aware of her priorities. She is able to invest herself in what is important in her life, and separate herself from what is not. She remains in touch with her spirituality, her personal God, and the imagery that arose from her TT. She has continued to explore her spirituality, her interconnectedness, and her place in the cosmos. When necessary, she is able to once again tap into the wonderful images of the dolphin, the unicorn, country scenes, blue water and so on, and remind herself of the healing that occurred and continues to occur through TT. The ongoing effects could best be summed up by Mary herself, in the conclusion of her personal journal:

> *In conclusion I believe it would, however, be simplistic to attribute the now very satisfactory blood pressure readings solely to the visualization techniques. I had been down similar paths before, 'seeing' and 'affirming' my blood pressure as normal without achieving the results that had now been obtained through TT. Something else was also happening, and I can only suggest a combination of factors, both spiritual and psychological; and however that particular dynamism or force might be named, it opened to me a new and beautiful dimension to my life journey. For this reason Therapeutic Touch is much more than the 'new' massage technique I had initially expected. It has provided me with the tools to explore my unique place in the universe.*

CONCLUSION

This case study is exploratory and it is not possible to make any generalizations about the findings. There are many opportunities for further qualitative studies into the potential of this gentle, non-invasive nursing intervention, to ascertain whether the themes that emerged from Mary's experience are common to others receiving TT. The multidimensional healing experienced by Mary points to many possibilities for further qualitative research in healing of people of all ages with problems such as chronic pain, anxiety, and spiritual distress.

Mary's journey of healing is just one person's journey, but it is unique. Her story provides insight into the richness and beauty of an in-depth exploration over time of Therapeutic Touch as a healing modality in nursing. For Mary at her life stage, healing and wholeness meant re-evaluating her life and her priorities, and re-investing in her relationships. Her healing also meant returning to a circular, rather than a linear concept of the life span, in which she was able to fully experience the Divine and the integrating nature of her spirituality. Mary's healing experience is best summed up in the following words:

> *The mature adult moves backwards, later in life, returning to the earliest stage of psychological development. But that stage then becomes*

something 'higher.' The elder embraces the past, not to regress, but to illuminate all of life. The end is the beginning, transfigured.

(Chinen, A., 1989, pp. 136–137)

REFERENCES

Amiotte, A. (1986). Our other selves: The Lakota dream experience. *Parabola: The Magazine of Myth and Tradition*, Spring, *VII*(2), 26–32.

Campbell, J. (1988). In B. Flowers (Ed.), *The power of myth*, p. 1. New York: Doubleday.

Casey, E. (1991). *Spirit and soul: Essays in philosophical psychology*. Dallas: Spring Publications.

Chinen, A. (1989). *In the ever after*. Wilmette, IL: Chiron.

Grof, S. (1985). Modern consciousness research and human survival. *ReVision*, *8*(1), 27–39.

Halldorsdottir, S. (1991). Five basic modes of being with another. In D. Gaut & M. Leininger (Eds.), *Caring: The compassionate healer*. New York: National League for Nursing Press.

Joseph, L. (1991). The energetics of conscious caring for the compassionate healer. In D. Gaut & M. Leininger (Eds.), *Caring: the compassionate healer*. New York: National League for Nursing Press.

Krieger, D. (1975). Therapeutic Touch: The imprimatur of nursing. *American Journal of Nursing*, *75*, 784–787.

Krieger, D. (1979). *The Therapeutic Touch: How to use your hands to help or to heal*. New York: Prentice-Hall.

Levine, S. (1987). *Healing into life and death*. Bath: Gateway Books.

Luke, H. (1985). Letting go—an interview with Helen M. Luke. *Parabola: The Magazine of Myth and Tradition*, Spring, *X*(1), 20–27.

Macrae, J. (1988). *Therapeutic touch—A practical guide*. New York: Alfred A. Knopf.

Nasr, S. (1985). The long journey—An interview with Seyyed Hossein

Nasr. *Parabola: The Magazine of Myth and Tradition*, Spring, X(1), 28–41.

Newman, M. (1979) *Theory development in nursing*. Philadelphia: F. A. Davis.

Pribram, K. (1976). Problems concerning the structure of consciousness. In G. Globus (Ed.), *Consciousness and the brain*. New York: Plenum Press.

Quinn, J. (1989). On healing, wholeness, and the haelan effect. *Nursing & Health Care*, 10(10), 553–556.

Quinn, J. (1992). Holding sacred space: the nurse as healing environment. *Holistic Nursing Practice*, 6(4), 26–36.

Rogers, M. (1970). *An introduction to the theoretical basis for nursing*. Philadelphia: F. A. Davis.

Sanford, J. (1978). *Dreams and healing—A succinct and lively interpretation of dreams*. New York: Paulist Press.

Seidel, J. (1988). The ethnograph: Version 3.0 (computer program). Littleton, CO: Qualis Research Associates.

Watson, J. (1988). New dimensions of human caring theory. *Nursing Science Quarterly*, 1(4), 175–181.

Weber, R. (1978). The enfolding-unfolding universe: A conversation with David Bohm. *ReVision*, Summer/Fall, 24–51.

7

Art and Beauty as Healing Modalities

Lynette C. Sheppard

Where do we go when we want to re-create ourselves, when we want to heal ourselves? Often, we go to places of great beauty. A few years ago, I was lying on a beach and wondered, "Is beauty a healing force?" I knew that it was healing for me, but what about others? Was this a unique experience? What about the arts? If art and beauty are healing forces, how do they heal? As an artist and a nurse, I was haunted by these questions.

Many times I have wished that I lived long ago when wisdom was passed along through the sharing of stories in the tribal circle. I wished for wise women and men to pass on their experiences, thoughts, and ideas to me. I knew instinctively that these stories would give lessons and meanings beyond the literal and disperse wisdom over time.

Then I realized that we can have these stories today. We simply have to ask for them. Qualitative research offers us an avenue for eliciting stories and extracting the themes of wisdom to further our growth as healers. When we hear stories, and when we tell our own stories, we find common experience, validation, and deep resonance. We learn to apply the themes of wisdom and may ultimately become forces for change in our caring profession and in our lives.

Are art and beauty healing forces? With these and 34 other open-ended questions on healing, Cathie Haynes, MS, RN and I asked 35 nurses across the United States for their stories and their answers. The questions in this phenomenological study were administered through taped interviews and written questionnaires. Content was analyzed for themes. It is useful to know that all respondents defined healing as "being whole" or "harmony of body, mind, and spirit" and differentiated healing from merely curing. Curing was felt to be "just physical," dealing with symptoms or fixing disease.

ART AS A HEALING FORCE

Respondents unanimously felt that art was a healing force. Art was inclusive of all the arts: music, writing, theater, the visual arts, and storytelling. The nurse healers talked about the healing power of art in their own lives as much as in their practices with clients.

Art heals by empowering the individual. The creative process involves bringing forth something from nothing. When we create, we find that we are not helpless. We are in touch with our own power through the artistic act. One healer said it so eloquently, "I've learned to turn my suffering into song—my pain into poetry. *Magic!*"

Art heals by offering us a way to understand our deeper selves. The respondents felt that knowing ourselves is a path to healing. As one healer shared with us, art provides a way "to contact the beauty inside us." Another healer expanded on this writing, "Art is expression of our inner natures, it both describes our process (diagnoses) and facilitates the process, acting as a catalyst to healing." When we connect to our inner wisdom, our intuition, our soul, we may find what we need for healing.

Art heals in a direct fashion when used as a therapeutic tool. Art therapy and imagery are modern-day uses of symbolic healing. Symbolic healing has been around for eons. It operates on the premise that there is something greater or more powerful than our ego-selves that can be accessed in the service of healing. Whether this power is the Muse, spirits, or our own inner healer/wisdom, there is an assumption that symbolic healing can enact physical healing. In some cases, symbolic healing can even diagnose physical/emotional ailments before overt recognizable symptoms are found.

Let's look at a concrete example. A client visited me to explore some art and imagery for relaxation. She had been having aching pain in her ovarian region for some months. As a nurse, she assumed the worst— thinking she had ovarian cancer. She was scheduled for an abdominal ultrasound and wanted to work on her anxiety. After imaging a trip through her body and visiting her reproductive organs, she drew the work shown in Figure 7.1.

Her original drawing showed her ovaries as pink rosebuds. There were several green vinelike structures over her entire reproductive system and a blue uterus. The uterus contained a tiny figure, "desperately pushing against the walls." After viewing the drawing, she expressed the strong intuitive sense that there was nothing seriously wrong with her. She called me after her ultrasound and exam to report that all was normal, except that her vaginal smear had revealed an overgrowth of normal flora, presumably due to stress. We were both struck by the accuracy of her inner wisdom.

All the healers in the study felt that images and symbols have the power to heal us. Music, theater, all the arts "have a language of their own; symbols are like a secret language." Most believed that art allows us to access our own subconscious material; our own symbols. "One day of creative arts play moves me toward greater growth and healing than a year of talk."

Barbara Dossey, PhD, RN, used crayons and paper with patients in the critical care unit, combining relaxation and imagery with patients'

Figure 7.1   The healing imagery of art.

drawings (Dossey, Guzzetta, & Kenner, 1985). Patients were able to contact their right brain and communicate to themselves and their care-givers through images. They naturally went on to create therapeutic images using their own symbology for healing imagery. They became active partners in their own healing processes.

As an artist, I've found that art has been a pathway in to beauty. I have found myself paying more attention to the world around me, seeing everything as a work of art with my new eyes. Once your eyes are opened, you don't close them again. Your vision only becomes stronger.

BEAUTY AS A HEALING FORCE

Unlike the active processes of art, beauty requires no action. There is nothing to do except to notice and appreciate. Often it catches us by surprise and we are moved to the aesthetic gasp. We are overwhelmed by the contemplation of this moment of beauty.

The predominant theme extracted from the healer's responses on the role of beauty in healing was the power of *awe*. Webster's defines awe as "an overwhelming feeling of reverence in the face of something greater or more powerful than ourselves" (Webster's, 1989).

One respondent put it very simply, writing, "the beauty of nature puts us in touch with something bigger than ourselves."

That beauty need not be the grandeur of Hawaii or Yosemite. One healer described an experience working in the garden to heal herself at a time of considerable emotional distress. "The only way I can describe it is that I became aware that there is nothing real except goodness. At the onset of this awareness I felt guided in the earthy work I was do-ing, as some force wordlessly indicated the places to dig for roots or rocks. The awareness of good persisted for some hours after I had con-cluded my gardening for the day, and I just felt happy and peaceful."

Most of us were taught that beauty is in the eye of the beholder. But this old adage is not completely true. Certainly, personal taste in-fluences our preferences in decorating, or clothing, and these choices vary from person to person. However, in the natural world in particu-lar, there are those moments and sights of beauty that evoke a univer-sal *ooh*—the awe response. A rainbow, a beautiful sunset, the sound of a loon quavering across a northern lake all engender awe within us.

Even the most jaded human being may be moved momentarily by these encounters with beauty to utter the aesthetic gasp.

One healer wrote "Man is a multidimensional being, interconnected with the environment and fields. Beauty, particularly nature, activates our awareness of our connection to the whole. It takes us outside of ourselves lifting us up and out. We can see more" (Anonymous subject response).

Awe is a transcendent experience in which we recognize a power, force, or order greater than ourselves. It is a momentary peak experience. It inspires hope. Hope is the feeling that what is desired is also possible; or that events may turn out for the best. If magic exists, if something greater than ourselves in this moment exists, then there is always hope. There is hope, if not necessarily for the cure, that all will turn out for the best, regardless of the outcome. Perhaps, healing in some form will take place.

What about false hope? Hope by its very nature cannot be false. Healing is still in the realm of great mystery and despite all our knowledge, we never really know how or when it will take place. Our sense of some power greater than ourselves inspires hope in that power. Albert Einstein was asked what the most important question science could study was and he replied, "Is the universe friendly?" (Noetic Sciences Bulletin, 1990). Beauty evokes the response that not only is there something greater than ourselves, but that it is benevolent, even loving. Robinson Jeffers wrote, "Is it not by his high superfluousness that we know our God? For to meet a need is natural, animal, mineral, but to fling rainbows over the rain" (Jeffers, 1965). For what is the purpose of a rainbow, save to fill our souls with awe and wonder? Beauty reminds and encourages us to hope every day.

APPLICATIONS

We can begin to incorporate the arts into our practices. Dossey, Guzzetta, and Kenner (1985) relate how providing simple crayons and paper for critical care patients enabled them to draw their disease processes. They combined art with relaxation and imagery. Patients then drew their healing images. Guzzetta researched music and relaxation with coronary care patients. Not only did they feel better but they had fewer complications than the control group or relaxation alone group. We can explore other arts such as storytelling, theater, writing, movement and dance. We can continue to research the effects of the arts on healing to offer validation for our colleagues. We can use the arts to heal ourselves as well as to heal others. As one of the healers in our study stated, "The healers must constantly be working to heal themselves. We cannot lead where we have not been."

We can begin to recognize the need for beauty, and provide it. Hospital rooms should have windows that look out upon nature. Bird feeders can hang outside amid the flowers and greenery. If the hospital has multiple floors, then central atriums can be the locus around which rooms are built. Some hospitals are planting healing gardens for patients, families, and visitors to enjoy. Others, such as the Planetree model hospital unit at Pacific Medical Center in San Francisco, have redecorated rooms to look more like home. Patients can choose their artwork for their room. (Planetree has also incorporated the arts in their everyday healing program.)

Even simple photographs of nature can evoke the "awe response." I was flying on Alaska Airlines recently. They brought me my standard airline meal. The first thing I noticed on the tray was a small card with a lovely photograph of nature and an inspirational saying. Ooh! I looked over at my husband's tray to find a different scene and words. I saw how little it takes to bring beauty into our lives. I don't remember what I ate, but I remember how that small glimpse of beauty touched me.

I recalled a former patient I had followed as a student nurse. Mr. S. was a lovely man and I felt a special connection to him. He had a malignant brain tumor, but the doctor and family had decided not to tell him. Like most terminally ill patients however, he knew he was dying. He told me and his private duty nurse, Ms. M., that the one thing he regretted was not having gone to the ocean. He had wanted to see it his whole life, but just had never gotten around to it. Acting on our instincts, we brought the beauty of the sea to Mr. S. Together we looked at a book of exquisite photographs of the ocean while Ms. M. held shells up to his nose so he could smell the hints of salty tang. We described the ocean as we knew it to Mr. S. He oohed and aahed and told us that he felt he had been there, at last. He died shortly thereafter. Those simple photographs of nature brought him healing.

A PERSONAL JOURNEY

It is important to elicit stories to gain knowledge and wisdom, it is equally important that we each tell our own story. Stories told are no longer owned, they belong to each one of us. We extract our own meanings from stories and pass on what we've learned through our words and actions.

I invite you to join me on my personal healing journey, where discovering beauty and awe forever changed me. Perhaps some of this story will resonate within you. Take from it what you like and make it your own.

I had effectively left nursing after my fourth episode of burnout. I worked in a critical care unit part-time merely to finance my art education. Somehow, art school gave me back nursing. Becoming an artist changed nursing forever for me—it became healing.

I learned an important lesson from the conceptual artists. There is no end product when they complete their art. The process of making art *is* the art. Through their example, I realized that the process of healing *is* the healing. If I'm wedded to the outcome, I may miss out on the healing, and my opportunity for caring and connection. There is no pot of gold at the end of the rainbow. The rainbow *is* the pot of gold. Facilitating and allowing healing, rather than striving for a predetermined bodily outcome, is the essence of caring.

I learned what the shamans knew for centuries—that caring means being open to other realities. Healing takes place in the invisible realms. Yet, no review of historical healers and their beliefs had really moved me. I could understand it as an intellectual concept, but it had no real bearing on my day-to-day practice. Surprisingly, it was my camera that captured these realms for me.

I'd taken dozens of pictures of clouds that were easily recognizable. But one lovely dawn, I pointed my lens upward to photograph God's vermillion paintbrush strokes across the sky. I watched crashing waves turn to soft cotton when I slowed the shutter speed far below my eye's normal detection. I found flickering flames deep inside a bird-of-paradise blossom. These realities are no less real for my not having seen them at the time. Now I see it in my mind's eye more and more often. Is a psychotic patient's reality less real than mine? Contrary to everything I learned in nursing school, sometimes accompanying patients in their delusion is the most caring thing that I can do.

I've seen rainbows in the filaments of spiderwebs. They look like nature's musical compact discs. If music exists in spiderwebs, then surely there is music in my patients. I have only to listen for it. I've found angels lurking deep in the hearts of white orchids. Might they not be everywhere I look, if I am aware of them? As I look deeply into another human's eyes, I begin to see the mystery in each one and to hold them in my heart as the magical beings they are.

I found that there is beauty in everything, especially if I stopped naming what I saw. People that I had labeled noncompliant or alcoholic had beauty that the names prevented me from seeing. I have only to remember to pay attention, to see their beauty.

Photographing the land gave me moments of connectedness when everything merged: the camera, the photographer, that being photographed. In these moments, I was beyond my feelings of separateness, beyond clock time, present in, yet transcending, the present moment. These were experiences of profound awe that brought a sense of peace, hope, and joy.

Sometimes, not often, I touch these moments with another person—when patient and self boundaries blur and we are both caring and cared for in a moment of being human beings together. These times give my life great joy and meaning. And yes, hope.

The cultivation of awe and wonder begins as a solitary pursuit. Then we naturally share it with another. Soon we are all participating in a glorious dance of wonder, striving to understand the symbols and language of ourselves and a friendly universe.

Plato said "Beauty is certainly a soft, smooth slippery thing, and therefore of a nature which easily slips in and permeates our souls. For I affirm that the good is the beautiful" (Plato, 1986). We all know it. We can seek out beauty, cultivate the experiences of awe and wonder, and heal our own lives. Then we cannot help but pass it on to our patients, clients, and loved ones. I wish every one of us as much healing beauty as our hearts can take in.

REFERENCES

Dillard, A. (1974). *Pilgrim at Tinker Creek.* New York: Harper & Row.

Dossey, B., Guzzetta, C., & Kenner, C. V. (1985). *Critical care nursing: Body-mind-spirit.* Boston: Little, Brown, and Co.

Jeffers, R. (1965). *Not man apart.* San Francisco: Sierra Club Books.

Noetic Sciences Bulletin. (1990). No. 17, Winter, 32.

Plato. (1986). *The Dialogues of Plato.* New York: Bantam Books.

Webster's Encyclopedic Unabridged Dictionary of the English Language. (1989). New York: Gramercy Books.

OTHER SOURCES

Achterberg, J. (1985). *Imagery in healing: Shamanism and modern medicine.* Boston: Shambala.

Epstein, A. H. (1989). *Mind, fantasy, and healing: One woman's journey from conflict and illness to wholeness and health.* New York: Delacorte Press.

Jung, C. G. (1959, 1969). *The archetypes and the collective unconscious.* Princeton: Princeton University Press.

Lauck, M. S., & Koff-Chapin, D. (1989). *At the pool of wonder.* Santa Fe: Bear and Co.

Leininger, M. (1985). *Qualitative research methods in nursing.* Philadelphia: W. B. Saunders.

May, R. (1985). *My quest for beauty.* San Francisco: Saybrook.

McMurray, M. (1988). *Illuminations: The healing image.* Berkeley, CA: Wingbow Press.

McNiff, S. (1992). *Art as medicine, creating a therapy of the imagination.* Boston: Shambala.

Rogers, P. (1987). *A painter's quest: Art as a way of revelation.* Santa Fe: Bear and Co.

Samuels, M., & Samuels, N. (1990). *Healing with the mind's eye, a guide for using imagery and visions for personal growth and healing.* New York: Summit Books.

Schuman, S. G. (1989). *Source imagery, releasing the power of your creativity.* New York: Doubleday.

8

Care Recipients' Voices: Elders' Dependency Work

Cynthia K. Russell

Literature from the social sciences and health sciences is replete with articles about caregivers of older adults, primarily discussing their burdens, stresses, needs, and concerns. Another significant portion of this literature describes the demographics of caregivers and care recipients. Virtually non-existent, however, is research which focuses on elders' perspectives of their care experiences. The lack of attention to elder care recipients is substantiated by Barer and Johnson's (1990) literature review of the years 1983 to 1987. Their findings revealed the care recipient has rarely been interviewed, leaving caregivers, researchers, and policy makers with little understanding about the characteristics of care recipients, their subjective experiences, and the extent to which the care given meets their needs or creates stress. Other researchers (Dunkle, 1983; Lee, 1976; Parsons, Cox, & Kimboko, 1989; Thomas, 1987) similarly reinforce the lack of knowledge of elder care recipients' perspectives of their care relationships.

Mitteness and Barker's (1991) research on elders' chronic illness hierarchies, however, demonstrated the value of research focused on care recipients' perspectives. These researchers found elders organized multiple chronic illnesses into hierarchies which differed across individuals. The particular hierarchical ordering of specific chronic illnesses affected whether care was sought as well as elders' satisfaction with the care they received. Yet, unless elders are asked about their perspectives this information remains unknown to health care providers. The research reported in this chapter is one step undertaken in addressing the disparity between the plethora of information focused on caregivers' experiences and the glaring lack of information about elder care recipients' experiences. This is a necessary and logical progression at this time since the care relationship is, at the least, a dyadic one, comprised of the care recipient and caregiver.

The questions which guided the research were: (1) What are the care-seeking strategies elders use? and (2) How do individual, interpersonal, and structural processes and characteristics interact to affect elders' care seeking? The conceptual framework which guided the research arose from the synthesized symbolic interactionist and life span developmental perspectives undergirding the inquiry. Processes and characteristics of individual, interpersonal, and structural levels were expected to be of most empirical and theoretical interest in their effects as facilitators or constraints to elders' care seeking. At an individual level, biological and psychological processes or characteristics of elders were of interest. On an interpersonal level, the processes and characteristics of relationships were of concern. Administrative, institutional, and organizational issues were relevant on the structural level. The concern with the interaction of the levels as they affected elders' care seeking was of importance, since the processes and characteristics of each level were assumed to be embedded within and affect the processes and characteristics of the other levels.

RESEARCH PROCEDURES

The methods used in this study were carefully selected for their abilities to privilege elders' voices and elders' care experiences. Qualitative methods were deemed the most appropriate for focusing on these areas, as well as most appropriate for the research questions and the conceptual framework. The research adopted the stance of Benoliel (1984), who eloquently stated:

> . . . qualitative approaches in science are distinct modes of inquiry oriented toward understanding the unique nature of human thoughts, behaviors, negotiations, and institutions under different sets of historical and environmental circumstances. These approaches to inquiry are built on a world view and paradigm that take account of the symbol-produc-

ing nature of the human species, the act of interpretation as a basic human characteristic, and intentional or goal-directed behavior as a complicated human activity affecting individual and group endeavors (p. 7).

Since very little is known about elders' care-seeking strategies and the processes and characteristics which interact to affect elders' care seeking, qualitative research which could begin to build a body of knowledge about these phenomena was required.

The setting of this research was a life care retirement community in the greater Phoenix metropolitan area. The use of a life care retirement community ensured that under one administrative and governing umbrella were several types of care (formal and informal) which would be most illuminating to the inquiry. Access to the community was granted by its administrator. The administrator introduced the researcher to the facility's social service director who served as the contact person throughout the research.

After receiving human subjects' approval by using a purposive sampling strategy, individuals were identified who were, or had been, receiving care from the primary sources of care at the facility. The social service director sent a personal letter to each of these residents which briefly described the researcher's background and the research and asked them to indicate to her if they would be interested in participating. Once replies were received the researcher contacted the elders who agreed to participate, setting a mutually convenient day, time, and location to meet and conduct an interview.

Three primary methods of data collection were employed: semistructured interviews, participant observation, and a focus group. A total of 15 interviews were conducted with elders who were representative of the different types of care, for a total of 27 hours. The focus and content of the interviews changed over time as dictated by the emergent patterns in the data obtained from other interviews and the participant observation component of the research. The participant observation component involved 14 different visits to the facility's adult day care center for a total of 61 hours. Incorporation of a participant observation component into the research assisted in more fully securing "perspectives *in* action" as well as "perspectives *of* action" (Snow & Anderson, 1987), thereby facilitating a broader understanding of the day-to-day life of care recipients. The focus group, conducted with four elders, lasted one and three-quarter hours. During the focus group elders described their care experiences, feelings, and beliefs with a minimum of direction from the researcher, as elders made comparisons between their own experiences and those of others.

The research protocol established at the outset of the research determined the strategy for data collection. Some interviews were tape recorded and transcribed in their entirety, while for others copious notes were taken during the interview and typed into more detailed notes upon return from the field. The interviews not audiotaped were those with elders who had moderately severe dementia who repeated their stories.

Field notes and detailed memos were written after every excursion into the research setting. Analysis proceeded concurrently with data collection, in keeping with the sage advice of grounded theory, ethnographic, and naturalistic inquiry researchers (Glaser & Strauss, 1967; Lincoln & Guba, 1985; Spradley, 1980). A constant comparative method of analysis, whereby the bits of information gathered from each method of inquiry and different individuals was compared with other information already gathered, was useful in generating new questions and issues. The search throughout this research was for both the nomothetic and the idiosyncratic.

FINDINGS: THE CARE-SEEKING PROCESS

The initial concern of the research with elders' care-seeking strategies provided an orienting frame of reference to the data which emerged in relation to the care-seeking process. Care seeking was defined as a process whereby an elder engaged help or assistance from another person. The sequence of activities that took place when an elder sought care from someone was composed of four stages. Interview and participant observation data supported the taxonomy of the sequence of activities in the care-seeking process outlined in Table 8.1. This section of the chapter contains a very brief overview of the care-seeking process.

In order to receive assistance with meeting their needs, elders sought care from others. Care eliciting, the first phase in the care-seeking process, included two stages elders went through as they attempted to evoke assistance from other individuals. The first stage in the care-seeking process, initiating, began when elders made an initial determination that the assistance of others was, or might have been, required. Within the initiating stage, elders considered their preferences in terms of desires for independence and the origination of care

Table 8.1   Sequence of activities in the care-seeking process

Phase I: Care Eliciting

    Stage 1: Initiating
        1. preferences
            a. desires for independence
            b. expectations for origination of care initiation
        2. beliefs
            a. appropriate caregivers
            b. potential contingencies

    Stage 2: Alerting
        1. verbal
            a. statements
            b. complaints
            c. queries
            d. expressions of preferences
            e. directives
        2. nonverbal
            a. movements
                 a.1. musculoskeletal pinpoint movements
                 a.2. physical body relocation to a specific area
                 a.3. looking around
            b. volitional noises
                 b.1. sighing
                 b.2. choking
                 b.3. coughing
                 b.4. devices (alert systems)

Phase II: Care Negotiating

    Stage 3: Negotiating
        1. content
        2. history
        3. doing
            a. doing by self
            b. doing with
            c. others doing

    Stage 4: Evaluating
        1. feelings about care settings
        2. feelings about caregivers
        3. feelings about care

initiation. Beliefs about appropriate caregivers and potential contingencies which elders or their caregivers could face were also considered in the initiating stage. Elders could remain in the initiating stage for a period of time or, with an emergent situation such as a fall or a stroke, may have been moved abruptly to the next stage in the care-seeking process. Alerting was the second stage of the care-seeking process. In the alerting stage elders made it known to others that they required help or assistance. Signifying a need for care to others occurred through verbal or nonverbal means. Statements, complaints, queries, expressions of preferences, and directives were examples of verbal alerting strategies. Nonverbal alerting took place through physical body movements or volitional noises. Once elders made it known to others that they needed some form of care, the second phase in the care-seeking process commenced.

Care negotiating was the second phase in the care-seeking process. This phase represented the give and take of participants in care relationships which formed an understanding among the participants for the enactment of care. Negotiating was the third stage in the care-seeking process. Within the negotiating stage the give and take around issues of care receipt and care provision were primary. The content of the negotiations, the historical components of relationships, and doing (by self, with or for others), were significant characteristics of the negotiating stage. Finally, the last stage in the care-seeking process, evaluating, was the periodic appraisal elders engaged in to determine whether their care relationships should be continued, altered, or disbanded. The evaluating stage was comprised of elders' feelings about their care settings, caregivers, and care.

For an average care occasion, the typical transition through the care-seeking process occurred in the following manner. An elder identified whether she or he needed help or assistance from another person. The elder considered her or his preferences for independence and whether she or he expected to originate the call for assistance. Virtually simultaneously, the elder decided on an appropriate caregiver for the type of care required, which led the elder to consider potential contingencies that may be faced. After elders clarified their preferences and beliefs, they alerted potential caregivers to their desire for care. At that point in the process, phase two was initiated and the elders negotiated the care with a caregiver. Out of those negotiations came information used by the elders to evaluate that specific care occasion, as well as material which served to inform future care interactions.

While accurate in one sense, presentation of the care-seeking process as linear and consisting of discrete and sequential phases and stages belies the complexity of the process and interactiveness of the stages. When care was sought for a discrete need and elders were afforded the opportunity to progress through the stages as identified, the prior description was reflective of that particular care interaction. What the prior portrayal does not clearly indicate is the work which elders engaged in as they not only sought care for a specific need but also situated this specific care occasion within past experiences of care and future possibilities for care. Within care relationships a great deal of effort and energy was invested in initiating, maintaining, and evaluating these relationships. The term dependency work captures the essence of the activities engaged in by elders.

FINDINGS: DEPENDENCY WORK

Dependency work can rightly be thought of as agency in action (whether visible or invisible), since dependency work involved elders' active application of their cognitive or physical powers to initiate, maintain, and evaluate their care relationships. Insight arose from elders' dependency work, as a result of the learning which occurred as elders engaged in their dependency work over time. Dependency work was comprised of three facets: personal considerations, considerations of others, and managing obligations. Table 8.2 shows these facets and the remainder of the chapter documents the facets, providing examples from the elders' stories.

Personal Considerations

In the facet of personal considerations, an elder managed concerns of a primarily individual, intra-personal nature. The primary personal considerations included (1) self-care preferences, (2) integrating additional people or settings into one's life, and (3) covering (camouflaging a personal situation or aspect of life).

Self-Care Preferences   Self-care preferences were one type of personal consideration, wherein an elder considered her/his desires to do for self without assistance from others or with only the assistance the elder deemed necessary.

Table 8.2   Facets of Elders' Dependency Work

I. Personal Considerations

    A. Self Care Preferences
    B. Integrating Extras
    C. Covering

II. Considerations of Others
    A. Asking
    B. Considering Others' Abilities
    C. Expressing Gratitude

III. Managing Obligations

    A. Balancing the Exchange
    B. Expectations of Self
    C. Expectations of Others

Some elders verbalized their desires for self care directly, as captured in the following interchange of the focus group elders:

#1.   Well, I'm independent enough that I don't want people around all day.

#2.   It's more fun to be on the other side of the fence, isn't it?

#1.   You bet ya!

#3.   It sure is, you're right. Being able to do for yourself and for somebody else.

Even though self-care preferences were identified on an individual, intra-personal level, they affected an elder's interpersonal relationships, since a desire for self-reliance affected whether, or if, an elder would integrate others in her or his care. Elders' preferences for self care sometimes led them to alter their routines, patterns, or environments to accommodate these preferences, as the following example illustrates:

> *(The physician) let me come home after hearing that I didn't have steps. He said, 'Let your neighbors carry in your groceries.' But I would carry them in one by one instead of asking the neighbors.*

Integrating Extras   A second type of personal consideration was integrating extras. When elders sought care, it was with the realization that other individuals would enter into their lives, whether on a time-limited basis or for the remainder of their lives. In certain cases, as when elders sought care from specific caregivers or institutions, an additional setting became part of their lives.

Integrating people was one aspect of integrating extras. Costs were associated with bringing certain extra individuals into elders' lives. Monetary costs were the most obvious; for example, one woman paid $16 an hour, 16 hours a day, 5 days a week for a nurse's aide to be with her in her home. For some elders there were psychological costs to integrating extra people—as highlighted by a woman with Alzheimer's disease who described how she felt when her residential aide helped her with her shower, "It's hard to be denuded. I don't like that too well."

Elders similarly related difficulties with people taking over and doing things, either without waiting for the elder's agreement or without knowing the elder's situation. One woman, who was essentially blind, described her experiences with well-meaning caregivers who did not understand her situation.

> *If I find out that they are going to help and they don't know what to do, I just let them go ahead and do it their way. And then I wait (laugh) until they go and we sometimes have to undo it. You know, because they mean well, you see . . . some people are very aggressive about everything, about their helping and everything. And they, they don't wait to be told what to do, they do it. Now sometimes that works out beautifully. You see, sometimes they know what they're doing and they do it better than you had thought about doing it. Usually if I can't get control of the situation right away, . . . because I can't really see what they're doing and I don't really always know if they're doing things wrong, I just let them do it, and try and make the best of it, you know (laugh). And if they came along another time I'd find an excuse to not let them do it.*

An additional aspect of integrating extras was integrating settings. New settings brought with them new people and also other structures which were, generally, less open to change and adaptation to individuals' schedules. Several environments had a great deal of uncertainty associated with them as elders entered and tried to discover the operative rules and routines.

One of the greatest problems associated with integrating settings, particularly nursing homes and hospitals, were the roommates elders had. Issues associated with having roommates, who seemed to always be demented in the cases these elders described, were the need to protect their belongings, the need to attend to their safety, and (sometimes) the need to protect their roommates.

In some cases, having a demented roommate meant the elder had to remain alert to make certain her/his belongings were not tampered with. Other elders felt they had to remain on guard in order to assure their own safety. One elder had just such a memorable experience with one roommate.

> *And she was so mean to me. They wanted to move me out of that room because she was so mean to me. She didn't want my commode chair in the room at all. After I was finally able to start getting up, she'd take her cane and push my walker out of my reach; sometimes she would get up and push my walker out of the way. She complained of people being in the room all night and said to the nurses that I had visitors in my room having a party all night. They knew that wasn't true. . . . You know, it's dangerous to have people in with people who have Alzheimer's. She could have taken her cane and hit me in the head with it during the night.*

Still other elders described how they felt a sense of responsibility to look out for their roommates and intercede on their roommates' behalf when caregivers were not attending to them. An elder could never be certain, on admission to the hospital or care center, what type of roommate she or he would have, hence what was required was an immediate assessment of the situation with strategies developed to fit the specific circumstances.

Covering   Covering was the final personal consideration. Just as there was some information elders wanted their caregivers to know in order for their care encounters to be meaningful and address issues of concern, there was, likewise, certain information elders desired to keep from others. Covering involved elders' camouflaging aspects of their lives or beliefs to receive the level of care they desired or to maintain their relationships with others.

One elder described how she was rearranging her activities to make certain the facility would continue sending meal trays to her apartment, instead of going to eat in the congregate dining room. She was having dental problems and her partial plate of false teeth was quite loose. She did not want to eat in the presence of others because of her concern that her dentures might fall out, embarrassing her. She described the alteration she was making in her activities; an action she deemed necessary to continue receiving meals in her apartment.

> *I'm not going out too much right now either, because I have to call for them to bring me a tray and if they see me wandering around in the main part of the building they're going to think that I don't need that tray.*

Summary Managing personal considerations was stressful for elders, as they attempted to process information rapidly to respond to fluctuating individual, interpersonal, and structural processes and characteristics. Mentally managing considerations related to self-care preferences, integrating extras, and covering was challenging, yet elders did this and more. The next section delineates the second facet of elders' dependency work.

Considerations of Others

While personal considerations reflected elders' attempts to manage individual and structural level issues primarily, considerations of others related fundamentally to managing concerns of an interpersonal nature. The primary considerations of others were: (1) asking, (2) others' abilities, and (3) expressing gratitude.

Asking Asking was one consideration of others. For most elders a primary concern was not asking too much from their caregivers, anticipating if they asked too much their requests might have been turned down or ignored. As one woman said:

> *If you want to keep people saying to you, 'Now you call on me anytime you want,' you just don't call on them very much. And if you call on them, be careful how much you take.*

More often, elders carefully considered their potential requests, evaluating them in terms of how much they would be imposing on others if they asked for particular types of assistance. Looking out for one's family, friends, or the greater good of all as opposed to the good of oneself were themes described by the elders. One woman made sure she used what she called "business connections" instead of asking her friends to help her with things. Her friends would sometimes say to her, "Why don't you call on us to have us do that?" and her reply to them was, "I don't want to impose on you."

Using paid help instead of calling on one's friends, however, was identified as problematic by some elders. One woman described her efforts to make sure and accept help from friends occasionally as, "if you will accept their help once in awhile they like that. That makes them feel good. And it should, because they're being nice." The woman who was virtually blind related the following story about her neighbor.

> I just felt it that she got a little annoyed with me because I never did ask her for any help. You see, I never asked her for anything. And, so, one day I had a pair of slacks that needed a new hem . . . I had marked the hem then and I wanted her to cut it off even. . . . So I gave it to her. I had even marked it with, I had put a piece of cardboard on it and marked it, you know. But I couldn't cut it. So I took it over to her and I asked her, I said, 'Now you always said you wanted to do something for me. Would you cut these two legs?' And I was gonna hem them myself, because I could do that. It would take me a long time, but I could do it. And, ah, so, well she sent them back all done. And she was so tickled, you know, and she said, 'Well, I just told you that I wanted to do things for you. And I'm just not gonna ask ya anymore.' She's very frank, you know, when she said, 'I'm just not gonna ask you. If you won't ask me I can't do it for you.' So, ah, now someday I'll have another little job that I'll take over (laugh), you know, because she really means it and she wants to help me and, ah, you know, you can, you can tell.

Certainly, in the minds of most of these elders, weighing whether they had crossed the line and become too much of an imposition on friends, family, or caregivers was important. Equally important, perhaps, was making certain one had asked enough of those people who wanted to help so those people could feel useful.

Others' Abilities   In considering others' abilities, elders accumulated information about the physical and mental abilities of their caregivers, i.e., whether caregivers could perform certain activities and whether elders should ask them to perform certain activities. Elders drew upon their experience to make these determinations on an individual basis.

One elder described a recent encounter with a friend who had driven her to see another person. The elder, in relating this story, was quite distressed, feeling as if she may have caused her friend more problems than she expected. Even though her friend wanted to assist her, the elder perceived the friend's difficulty and felt badly about asking her for assistance in the first place. The elder's stressful feelings were compounded as she also thought she could have done for herself much of what her friend did for her, yet her friend would not permit it.

> *Well, like yesterday. But I'll never do that again. I just thought it was asking too much. Ah, she, the trouble is they want to do so much for you and I could have managed very well on my own if they'd have just, if they just would let me do it, but they want to do it for me. I have a walker that I use and, ah, my cane isn't enough for me anymore. . . . But, ah, I made arrangements to have this friend, since she was making a trip to the doctor, take me up to my old neighborhood, which is just north of here a couple of blocks. And, ah, she got out of the car, opened up, got my, ah, walker out and everything that I could have done myself and let her just sit there in the car; because she had a back problem that she was going to the doctor's to see about. And I preferred to do it myself. But she just* insisted. *(laugh) And so that kind of upset me, to think that I was taking up her time and her energy that she needed herself and so I, that taught me something right there. I thought, well, I'll find some way to get transportation without calling on my friends. So I hope I don't have to do it again. (laugh) . . . Well, I, in going out yesterday . . . I'm sure I won't ask, though this friend seems to be the kind of person that wants to do these things for you. But I can see the difficulty that she has and I just hesitate to and I, I don't think I'll ever ask her to do me a favor like that again.*

Some elders were concerned their caregivers might blame the *elders* if something happened to the caregivers while they were offering assistance—such as developing a back problem or hernia. Equally important to other elders was protecting caregivers from blaming *themselves* if something happened to the elders. One woman, who had never had any such problems with friends blaming themselves, believed strongly in that possibility.

I quit driving and sold my car, but I don't want to depend on friends. They feel like they're responsible for me. If I'd fall, they'd feel like they're responsible. So I very seldom depend on them.

Expressing Gratitude Expressing gratitude was the final element of elders' considerations of others. Elders made sure they demonstrated appreciation and thanks to their caregivers. In some instances, elders seemed to feel that mere words were insufficient to express their gratitude to caregivers. Even a woman who said thank you and had a gift for her friends was at a loss as to what more she could do to show her appreciation, though she wanted to. Yet, at some point, some elders felt as if they had gone above what was necessary in giving thanks. One elder's experience highlighted this aspect, as her cost to express her gratitude, in this case, was prohibitive in relation to what she received.

I would love to have a friend that enjoys to get out and go places. I had one and we'd go places together. She'd never let me pay for any gas or anything and I felt indebted to her all the time. She'd say, 'I'd love to have so and so, but I can't afford it.' She wouldn't take anything from me for gas, so I would buy her whatever she said she'd like to have but couldn't afford. That got expensive.

Summary Managing considerations of others was, perhaps, even more complex than managing personal considerations. Not only did elders need to manage the uncertainty related to their individual, intrapersonal issues and concerns, the addition of other individuals brought with it interpersonal and relational issues and concerns. Yet one additional facet of elders' dependency work remains.

Managing Obligations

In the area of managing obligations elders most clearly integrated individual, interpersonal, and structural information. Managing obligations reflected the work elders did in acting upon and evaluating their beliefs about their own, or their caregivers', sense of duty within care relationships. Balancing the exchange, expectations of self, and expectations of others were the three key issues of managing obligations.

Balancing the Exchange In balancing the exchange, elders' activities were directed toward maintaining, as much as possible, reciprocal relationships with their caregivers. It went beyond a mere thank you to actually giving something back to a caregiver. For something to count as balancing the exchange an elder had to perceive it as being helpful, useful, or desirable to her or his caregiver. How an elder determined whether a strategy met one of those criteria was unclear. It appeared that what elders valued themselves, or what elders were actually able to contribute, was judged an adequate contribution.

Physical activities were one means used by elders to assist their caregivers. In the adult day care several individuals helped to rearrange chairs, pass out or collect exercise equipment, and prepare lunch tables. Responding to caregiver requests for help, in terms of facilitating group activities (i.e., leading a game of trivia or being responsible for the table of elders playing dominos) was another way for elders to provide concrete assistance.

Different, non-physical strategies for balancing the exchange were provided by the elders interviewed. Some of these strategies included offering advice to a caregiver on how to be a good father, or giving a residential aide "a little push to make her decision" to go on to school, or getting caregivers additional work if they wanted it. One elder described her recent efforts to call the dining room staff by their names as, "I think they like to have their names called, you know," even though, when she was not so disabled, "I didn't bother calling their names or learning their names. Now I'm very meticulous about it, you see."

Self Expectations Self expectations were the actual, and sometimes ideal, beliefs elders held about their responsibilities within care relationships. Self expectations translated into "shoulds," ways elders *should* conduct themselves in care relationships. Responsibilities for having a proper attitude and prescriptions for planning for and maintaining care relationships were two self expectations described by elders.

Having a proper attitude was important for participants of care relationships. Proper attitudes translated, quite literally, into means for achieving more help or assistance. Focus group elders offered the following observation: "Attitude makes a whole lot of difference," in that, "to keep a sort of a happy attitude if you can is apt to get you more help. Absolutely!" Other useful attitudes identified were: (1) being patient, content, accepting, and outgoing, (2) appreciating what one had, and (3) not complaining all the time.

Elders also described self expectations related to planning for care relationships. One expectation was that people should plan for their future care relationships. Some elders had definite ideas about how early this pre-planning should start. Elders at the focus group had the following lively interchange:

#1. We can put an age limit. When you get to be 70.

#2. 39!

#1. Okay, 39, you should go over and take care of all these things alone, the things you have to take care of to make it easy for the people that are going to help you as much as they can.

#3. I made arrangements for my funeral, now I'd better take care of this! (laugh)

Acknowledging that an elder would need some type of care from others at some time was necessary, as was the second step of acting on this knowledge. Particularly, elders were expected to become aware of available resources.

Elders described several expectations of themselves that focused on their responsibilities for initiating their care relationships. One elder described how he sometimes needed to use his "very special words" to get caregivers to do what he deemed necessary. Stating expectations or needs firmly and with authority worked for some other elders but, as one elder pointed out, "well, sometimes you just have to be nasty, (laugh) and, ah, it is too bad if that has to happen." Elders also described a variety of self expectations related to maintaining care relationships with caregivers. At a basic level, most elders believed it was necessary to "get along with" their caregivers and make their caregivers feel good.

Expectations of Others Expectations of others were the actual, and sometimes ideal, beliefs elders held about the responsibilities of others within care relationships. Expectations of others translated into "oughts"; how caregivers *ought* to act and conduct themselves in care relationships. Elders recognized that caregivers were sometimes constrained by other individuals (i.e., family or other patients) or by structural conditions (such as a lack of staff and proper equipment or the need to follow rules and regulations). Even though elders articulated explanations for specific situations in which caregivers were unable to attend to them in the manner in which elders desired, elders held clear ideas about the actions and attitudes they expected of their caregivers.

First and foremost, elders expected their caregivers to be prompt, as the following interchange from the focus group highlighted:

#1. But you put your light on for the nurse to come and you could wait ten minutes before they got to you. That has never been my experience before. Well, I think we expect promptness. As John has mentioned, that, ah, you know, particularly if you're a bed patient and you need *help, you need it right then.* (laugh)

#2. That's right.

#1. And, ah, it is distressing to have to wait.

Caregivers were also expected to "look out for" elders, by keeping track of things such as medications or the need for shopping, which elders could forget. Overwhelmingly, however, elders expected their caregivers to: (1) include them in decisions, (2) keep them informed, (3) respond to their requests, and (4) perform activities in the manner, or within the time frame, which the elders preferred.

Summary   Managing obligations was, in many respects, the most difficult of the three facets of elders' dependency work. Elders were required to simultaneously manage issues and concerns related to individual, interpersonal, and structural processes and characteristics. The fact that caregivers were expected to live up to elders' expectations of them, without being told what these were, significantly increased the complexity of this facet of elders' dependency work. Given the description of the three facets of elders' dependency work, the conclusion of this chapter offers an example of one elder's dependency work, highlighting the complexity of this work.

DEPENDENCY WORK IN ACTION

Elders' dependency work was complicated, multi-faceted, and effortful. Because of its complexity there were many opportunities for breakdown, which caused elders great angst since, with a breakdown, they realized their efforts in the delicate dance of dependency with others went awry. Elders' feelings of inner distress were compounded by their perceptions of distress in others which, they perceived, occurred as a result of their mis-steps.

One woman's experience beautifully demonstrated the "work" involved in managing dependency. Her story reflected how she considered, and experienced the interactions of, individual, interpersonal, and structural processes and characteristics when attending to her dependency work. Early in the interview she described how she (nearly blind) and her husband (with a progressive neurological disease) used to work together to put his wheelchair on their golf cart.

> *You see, we put his wheelchair on the golf cart. And, I have these bungy cords that I fasten it on with. And we go off to dinner. And then, now we used to, for two years, the two of us together could lift that down and help ourselves completely and never get any help, even up there (at the dining room).*

She went on to talk about their general experiences with individuals offering to assist them with his wheelchair, and her general reaction to those offers of assistance.

> *I've had wonderful experiences with people in Amesville coming over. And it's mainly women. Little old ladies, you know, come over to help us lift that wheelchair on and off. They see, ah, I suppose, ah, it's sort of a pathetic picture (laugh) of this crippled man and this blind woman trying to lift a wheelchair. You see. It is. (laugh) I know it is, because people come over and they want to help you, you know. And, ah, sometimes they don't know I'm blind until they get there and then, 'Oh my!' And then they want to do everything. Well, of course, ah, I just tell them, 'Now we've been doing this for months and months. And don't worry about it. We're perfectly able to do it.' That was when we did it all the time.*

Later in the interview, the elder related a story which reflected a perceived breakdown in her dependency work. As she talked about her experience she clearly identified the point at which the difficulty in the care interaction occurred.

> *I know just the other day I had an instance, where were we? We were somewhere. And we had to lift that wheelchair up. Oh, we had to go in (to the physician's office) and they were all, it was past the time they had any service (van service which takes people to and from their appointments) from here. So we hadn't been able to take the van in, which*

they would help ya, and we had to come back from Hillcrest alone. And we had to lift the wheelchair up on the (golf cart), well, I knew for that one time we could do it if we exerted ourselves. Which we were trying to do. And immediately a man came up and just as he came up a, no, a woman came up first. And I could tell she was a little old woman, you know, perhaps about like me. And she had come up to help. And I said, to her, I said, 'Oh no!' I said, 'You're too old!' She was going to, you know. And in order to not get her to lift that cart, I didn't want her to lift it at all 'cause I could tell she was old. She was even a little stooped over, you know. And I said, 'Oh no! You're too old!' And I didn't mean it, you know, I was trying to get her to stop quickly. Because then this man came up and I said, I said, 'Oh, I'm sorry. I don't mean you're too old. But you should not be lifting things like this, you know.' And then, then I felt I had refused her terribly, don't you see? But I was trying to hurry and say it so she wouldn't lift it. And, ah, I don't know whether I hurt her feelings or not. And, 'cause she said to the man, 'She told me I was too old.' Now I don't know whether she was hurt, you know. But anyway, I said, 'No, no I didn't mean it that way. I just meant it that you shouldn't, you should not offer to lift a thing this heavy.' So, see, I make the same mistakes that other people make.

The elder had attempted to protect her unsolicited caregiver from physical problems she anticipated might occur as a result of the caregiver's assistance. The elder felt her attempt to protect her caregiver was in vain, since she was only able to protect the caregiver from potential physical problems but not the internal distress she perceived she had caused by her "terrible refusal." As a result of her experience, the elder made plans to make certain a similar experience did not happen in the future.

I do think a person that is on the receiving end has to learn how to receive gracefully so that you don't hurt. I, I felt in that case I could easily have hurt her feelings, you know. 'Cause some people would be very sensitive about being called old. It wouldn't bother me, but, ah, it wasn't, (laugh) I'll have to dream up something to say in a hurry that I don't make a mistake like that again.

The researcher's question to her was, "How would I know it as an outside person observing if you were to receive something gracefully?"

The elder's response showed her insight regarding how to "refuse" others' help in ways that were not alienating to them.

Well, I would thank you without saying to you something wrong, like 'You're too old.' That, that was wrong, you see. And I knew it the minute it came out but I was trying to keep her from lifting it and I didn't know just exactly what she was doing 'cause I couldn't see, you see. And so I said that. Well, that's an instance of what not to say. And, ah, instance I usually tell them, ah, if I don't want them to do it, I'll say, 'Well, you're so very kind for coming over here.' But, I said, 'We've been doing this for two years and we're strong and' you know, I go on at great length 'cause I don't want them to feel like I'm repulsing them. Because I think if they go to the trouble of coming over, which many people do, I think most of the time maybe I say the right thing. But that time I didn't. (laugh) And, ah, so that's how things can happen.

CONCLUSION

The care-seeking process is informed by elders' dependency work and is able to progress relatively smoothly because of elders' dependency work. While the care-seeking process itself is highly complex, with interactive stages, the effort required to navigate the stages of the care-seeking process pales in comparison to the energy elders invest in their dependency work. Elders' dependency work is complex, complicated, and multi-faceted. A great deal of learning is required, as elders face recurrent situations and make determinations related to issues such as what their roles are in care relationships, what others' roles are within care relationships, how they and their caregivers should enact these roles, and what to do when their care relationships are not progressing as desired.

This qualitative research aimed to uncover something "That's Interesting" (Davis, 1971) about elders who are care recipients. In so doing, the oft-unspoken (but real) assumption of older adults as passive care recipients was challenged. Elders, in this research, invested significant time and energy in their care seeking. Elders' dependency work required an even more intense investment of physical and cognitive activities on the part of care recipients. Truly, the elders' voices in this research resounded with the efforts of their work. Even the more physically and cognitively challenged elders actively initiated, maintained, and evaluated their care relationships.

It seems fitting to close with one elder's story which clearly illuminates the overwhelming nature of her dependency work:

> *You see, my time is occupied (laugh) trying to, trying to live. And, ah, so, there are those adjustments, I would call them adjustments that you have to make if you're going to cope with it at all. . . . Somehow things do work out. But, ah, to say they get easier, is far from the truth. They get harder. Because it's harder this year for me to even get around. . . . It's so tremendous a frustration that I don't even think of it as a frustration. I mean, ah, I can't explain it. . . . But I don't sit around saying I'm frustrated, I don't think. But I know life is one huge mountain of frustration. I mean, I think it's so big that you can't, you can't, ah, you just can't talk about it you know. . . . It's hard to know what is the worst part. (laugh) I don't know. Because it's, it's a lot. You see, it's from the time you open your eyes in the morning until you close them at night. That's, your frustration never stops. And I think that's what gets ya. . . . I can't sit and cry about it. Sometimes I wish I could. I wish I could just sit down and, you know, you get to the end of your tether some days and I wish sometimes I could just sit down and get a little release from it. But you can't. That's the worst part of it. It's omnipresent, you know. It never ceases.*

REFERENCES

Barer, B. M., & Johnson, C. L. (1990). A critique of the caregiving literature. *The Gerontologist, 30*(1), 26–29.

Benoliel, J. Q. (1984). Advancing nursing science: Qualitative approaches. Keynote address of the 17th Annual Communicating Nursing Research Conference, *Advancing nursing science: Qualitative and quantitative approaches.* San Francisco, CA.

Davis, M. S. (1971). That's interesting! Towards a phenomenology of sociology and a sociology of phenomenology. *Philosophy of Social Science, 1*, 309–344.

Dunkle, R. E. (1983). The effect of elders' household contributions on their depression. *Journal of Gerontology, 38*(6), 732–737.

Glaser, B. G., & Strauss, A. L. (1967). *The discovery of grounded theory.* Chicago: Aldine Publishing Company.

Lee, R. J. (1976). Self images of the elderly. *Nursing Clinics of North America, 11*(1), 119–124.

Lincoln, Y. S., & Guba, E. G. (1985). *Naturalistic inquiry.* Beverly Hills, CA: Sage.

Mitteness, L., & Barker, J. C. (November, 1991). Hierarchies of disorder in the management of chronic illness. Paper presented at the Annual Scientific Meeting of the Gerontological Society of America, *New knowledge: The key to meeting the challenges of aging.* San Francisco, CA.

Parsons, R. J., Cox, E. O., & Kimboko, P. J. (1989). Satisfaction, communication and affection in caregiving: A view from the elder's perspective. *Journal of Gerontological Social Work, 13*(3/4), 9–20.

Snow, D. A., & Anderson, L. (1987). Identity work among the homeless: The verbal construction and avowal of personal identities. *American Journal of Sociology, 92*(6), 1336–1371.

Spradley, J. P. (1980). *Participant observation.* New York: Holt, Rinehart and Winston.

Thomas, J. L. (1987). Adult children's assistance as a health care resource: The older parent's perspective. *Family and Community Health, 9*(4), 34–42.

Part IV

Workshop Sessions: Healing Expressions

9

The Healing Art of Clay:
A Workshop for Remembering Wholeness

Marilyn E. Parker

Five workshops were offered during one evening of the 1993 International Human Caring Research Conference. Each workshop was an invitation to explore rituals and arts. Each one was an opportunity for growth to fuller understanding of the title and themes of the Conference: Healing, Renewal, Ritual, Caring, Traditions, Art, Beauty, and Hope. There was a sense of anticipation of this special evening as conferees looked forward to one of the following workshop sessions on: The Healing Art of Clay, The Healing Art of Journaling, The Healing Expression of Dance, The Healing Ritual of Tai Chi, and Therapeutic Touch. This chapter presents a description of the workshop titled The Healing Art of Clay, from the viewpoint of the workshop facilitator. Described is the flow of our work together, including the sharing of reflections on healing and wholeness.

GATHERING

The clay workshop was designed as a collective quiet time for remembering our wholeness through individual experiences with clay and writing, as well as joining to share our experiences. Native American flute music, "Canyon Trilogy" (Nakai, 1989) contributed a background of soft, easy, solitary expression supporting rest and reflection. The group was invited to gather for the clay workshop with the reminder that each person is creative and the creative process is healing. Our personal growth takes place in safe, comfortable places that support and encourage reflection and contemplation. Creating art leads us into inner knowing places, into our creative connections with all beings. There is need to be mindful of our self, our body, and our wholeness that we bring to this joining with the clay.

Some ways of being with clay were briefly described: opening and circling, pinching, and use of elbows and knees. Some "primers" were recalled to promote reflection and remembering: children working with clay; the expression of our heritage in art; ways caring can be expressed in ceremony and rituals in life; making useful objects; and being with the earth, trees, and flowers. We talked briefly of ways of choosing the clay and selecting tools, and finding comfortable places for centering and work. I described a clay piece of my making that for me represents "The Source" of all nursing situations, and told of writing about my experiences with the clay (Parker, 1992). Several sources for further reading were offered in a handout for later discussion (Berensohn, 1972; Blom, 1977; Moore, 1992; Progoff, 1985; Richards, 1962; Rogers, 1993; Truitt, 1986).

AN ENTRANCE MEDITATION*

An entrance meditation was read to assist workshop participants to enter the realm of quiet and depth where inner knowing takes place. Progoff (1983) describes entrance meditations as a help to us to "go to that place within ourselves from which we can reach beyond ourselves . . . leaving us free to follow our own rhythms of inner experience and to move in whatever direction to explore whatever feels right to us" (p. 13). Meditations, according to Progoff, are used in the same way that a fish learns to swim: it finds itself in the water and does what comes naturally. The meditations in *The Star and the Cross* (1983) draw on the world of nature, and it was from this book that "Letting the Self

---

Note: Entrance Meditation is a servicemark of Ira Progoff. Dr. Progoff's *Intensive Journal*® writing programs are offered throughout the United States, Canada and overseas through Dialogue House Associates, 80 East 11th Street, Suite 305, New York, NY 10003-6008. They have been approved by the New York State Nurses Association's Council on Continuing Education.

Become Still" was chosen for reading at this workshop (Progoff, 1983, pp. 33–43). The meditation follows:

Letting the Self Become Still

1. We are sitting
   In a place of quietness
   Letting the Self become still,
   Letting the breath become slow,
   Letting our thoughts come to rest.

2. Letting the Self become still,
   Energies that were moving about
   Can go inward now,
   Can come to rest
   In the stillness
   Of our quiet being.

3. Breathing becomes quiet now,
   Not breathing
   By the tempo of outer things
   But by an inner tempo,
   Breathing at an inner pace,
   The breath moving in
   And out
   Of itself,
   Carried by its own rhythm
   Adjusting itself
   To itself.

4. Breathing at an inner pace,
   Our thoughts let go
   Of our breathing.
   Breathing at an inner pace,
   The breath is free
   To come and go
   In its own timing.
   The breath is slow
   And regular,

Moving in and out
By its inner tempo,
Carried by its own rhythm,
Adjusting itself
To itself.

5. Breathing at an inner pace
    Thoughts become quiet,
    Restless thoughts
    That have been moving about,
    Restless thoughts
    Dissipating their energies
    Can come to rest now,
    Can bring their energies together
    Into one place
    Resting
    On the steady breathing.

6. Excess thoughts drop away.
    We become still.
    Thinking becomes quiet,
    Thoughts fitting together
    And settling into one place
    By themselves
    Without our thinking them.
    Many mixed thoughts
    Become one whole thought
    Contained within itself,
    One whole thought
    In the mind at rest.

7. Letting the Self become still,
    Letting our thoughts come to rest,
    Letting our breath become slow.
    Breathing becomes slow,
    And slower;
    Breathing becomes regular,
    Regular.
    The unevenness
    Of nonessential thoughts

Drops out of the breathing.
It becomes
The breathing of the Self.

8. Breathing at an inner pace,
    The breath moves
    At the center of my Self,
    At the center of my Self
    In regular rhythms.
    My body is quiet,
    Holding its place.
    The breath is moving evenly,
    Inward,
    Outward,
    Evenly,
    In its own rhythm.
    The breath moves evenly
    At the center of my body,
    At the center of my Self.

9. The breath is moving
    At the center of my Self
    In a regular rhythm.
    The breath moves at the center,
    The breath moves at the center
    Breathing at an inner pace.
    As the breath moves at the center,
    Quietly,
    Evenly,
    The Self becomes still
    Like quiet water.

10. The Self becomes still
    Like quiet water.
    In the stillness of the Self,
    In the quiet of the water
    My inward ear hears,
    My inward eye sees
    Signs and words and visions
    Reflected in the quiet waters

In the stillness of the Self,
In the Silence. . . In the Silence.

EXPRESSING/KNOWING

We began our work with the clay with a reminder that each of us as clay artists would give, receive, and respond with the clay. Listen to the clay. Sense the spirit of the clay. Let our art flow.

We worked with the clay in solitary quiet for less than an hour. Some began to write or draw. Then there was an invitation for each one to share. We laughed, asked questions, told of our feelings, thoughts and observations, and knew a few quiet tears. We talked of ways to take our creations home and of hopes to dry and fire them.

One of the workshop participants offered her own description of this experience to me on the morning following the workshop and agreed this could be included in this chapter. Joanna's Story assures us there is no real conclusion to the experiences in this workshop. The accompanying figure is a photograph of the artist's sculpture of Spirit Woman (see p. 143) taken from a photograph of Joanna's creation and from the reading of her story.

Joanna's Story

As I sit here in my dark office at 10:30 this night, I have this deep sense of urgency to write, to not lose these feelings of excitement and wholeness, feelings of discovery, which scare me a lot really.

When I was thinking and talking with friends about which workshop I would take, my first thoughts were that I definitely wanted to learn Tai Chi. I had been thinking about Tai Chi for about six months or more as something I should learn. After all, it would make me whole, it would help me find myself in this current long gray abyss I have been traveling in. But when I got ready to fill out the registration slip, I marked clay.

Designating the clay workshop was right, it felt soooo right to me. I tried to convince my friends and colleagues that they needed to do clay too. It was all set. We were going as a group to the clay workshop. Well, my friends followed their hearts too in the end and we all went to different personal experiences.

I have been thinking about working with the clay on a meta level for weeks. I really can not describe this, but I know that I was excited about creating with clay. Something inside of me needed to be created, shared, articulated, and set free.

At the beginning of the workshop, Marilyn was talking and leading the group through a centering experience. Music was playing the whole time in the background. I personally did not hear what Marilyn said. The clay and the music were talking to me. They literally were pulling my mind, my thoughts away from the present interaction and into interaction with self and the clay.

I was colors, muted in hue. I remember yellows, purple, mint green. The colors were feather-like in texture. My mind said wings. I will create two wings in a free-standing context that represent being nurtured. I placed my hands on the clay and my physical body was not present. The clay and what was in it called to my hands and a symbolic being began to be molded.

I remember cutting away the clay. It was too bulky, too big. My hands were burdened with the amount. Quickly I put aside two-thirds of the clay. The remaining piece of clay felt warm, alive. I was working the piece: pushing and squeezing. I looked down into the clay and saw a face. The connection was immediate. I knew that I had to make an old woman with wings. The face came out of the clay. It created itself through my hands. I had a sense of urgency, a sense of rightness. I was not scared. I knew the woman in the clay would guide me. I would not make a mistake. I trusted wholly in the woman in the clay.

I worked on the fine details of her face first. Next, the clay woman's right arm and wing appeared. I molded the left arm and wing but did not spend detail on it. The body began to take shape. I spent much time on making her breasts sag. I had to show the fragile old, old breast bones. I spent considerable time on this aspect of the clay woman's creation. It was important to get it just right. I kept making the wings thinner. They had to have a sense of fragility, yet be strong against the winds.

I knew when the clay woman was completed. I experienced a sense of urgency again. I just absolutely had to write. I felt almost frantic about writing. I heard: 'See me, I am here, your spirit woman' as if the words were spoken to me and only me in acoustic space. The following message was sent to me from my spirit woman:

See me, I am here
your spirit woman.
I am old.
I have borne much.
To you, my gift
is love.

My arms are wings
to help you fly,
to help support your burdens.
My arms are wings
that I might embrace you
with compassion and warmth.
My arms are wings
that will let you soar
on your life
journey to becoming.

My hands are uplifted.
I send you on your way
with blessing and prayer.
My arms are wings
so I can fly home with you
to peace and self.

I am here . . .
your spirit . . . WOMAN.

As soon as I scribbled the message above, I was energized. I did it! I listened to me and found a part that was lost. I felt such a sense of wonder at what my soul and hands could do together. I thought: ah, this was meant to be!

I was reflecting on the meaning of my creation. Why this, a spirit woman? I knew that I needed protection and love. I have much love in my life from others, what has been missing is my own spirit. I have personally been on a vision quest for many months. I have been struggling with 'Where am I going? Who am I? What is my purpose in life? There must be more to life than this.' I do not have these answers even now. What I do have is my spirit woman. I have found my spirit connection. Now I will not travel my roads alone.

Figure 9.1 Spirit Woman.

FOCUSING ON HEALING AS WHOLENESS

Some of my personal reflections on healing and art were shared as we moved into our focus on work with the clay. This section is written from recalling and thinking about my many experiences of dialogue, reading, working with clay, and writing. Perhaps the most essential message I wanted to share with the group was that healing is remembering our wholeness. Art links the outer world and inner being of each of us, and supports connections among us. Through centering, reflecting, working with clay and sharing, we explore and express connections between our inner being and outer world. Perhaps through working with clay, writing, or some other form of art, we can make more real those connections or links that join us. Maybe we can discover ways to expand our awareness, helping us be more fully alive. In addition, clay art offers a special opportunity to join with the earth and sense our common source of creation.

Art is the making and doing, the creating of presence of our reflections, visions, inner experiences, recalled connections. Art is not a thing, but a re-presenting; a re-presentation of our discoveries, remembered awareness, source of grounding. A "piece" of art is also a making, a doing, as each viewer experiences the art anew, creating a new presence of reflections and connections. Our inner and outer worlds become more intense. We can focus more clearly, express ourselves more fully, and be nourished.

The clay is alive as we are alive, and the clay is willing to grow with us. We come to know the clay when we realize that, like us, it can move, stretch, take new forms, be acclaimed for its beauty and usefulness. And, we come to know the clay as we recognize that it seems to have limits. Like us, it can be pushed too far, stretched beyond its capacity to respond. Potters will advise to "let the clay rest"; its strength and flexibility is restored by resting. Like us, the clay has spirit, uniqueness, and connections with the larger whole. The clay is living. The clay will let you know what it is and what it will become.

Each of us is an artist when we live and experience wholly, fully, openly, and faithfully. We live as artists when we authentically live our story, offer genuine presence, overcome separateness, and remember our wholeness. Moore (1992) urges us to live artfully—letting ordinary activities invite us into contemplation. We have no need to be concerned about rules of art or concepts of aesthetics. Through art we express our knowing and gain insight. Then we listen and hear as our art speaks to us anew, and we reflect and learn from its messages.

REFERENCES

Berensohn, P. (1972). *Finding one's way with clay*. New York: Simon and Schuster.

Blom, D. (1977). *Art imagery and the mythic process*. Wallingford, PA: Pendle Hill Publications.

Moore, T. (1992). *Care of the soul*. New York: HarperCollins Publishers.

Nakai, R. C. (Flutist). (1989). *Canyon Trilogy*. (CR 610). Phoenix, AZ: Canyon Records Productions, Inc.

Parker, M. E. (1992). Exploring the aesthetic meaning of presence in nursing practice. In D. Gaut (Ed.), *The presence of caring in nursing* (pp. 25–37). New York: National League for Nursing Press.

Progoff, I. (1983). Letting the self become still. In I. Progoff, *The star and the cross: An entrance meditation* (pp. 33–43). New York: Dialogue House Library.

Progoff, I. (1983). *The star and the cross: An entrance meditation.* New York: Dialogue House Library.

Progoff, I. (1985). *The dynamics of hope: Perspectives on process in anxiety and creativity, imagery and dreams.* New York: Dialogue House Library.

Richards, M. C. (1962). *Centering in pottery, poetry and the person.* Middletown, CT: Wesleyan University Press.

Rogers, N. (1993). Person-centered expressive arts therapy. *Creation Spirituality, 9*(2), 28–30.

Truitt, A. (1986). *Turn: The journal of an artist.* New York: Viking.

10

The Healing Power of Dance

Carol Picard

Dance is more than movement. It is movement with the intent to create meaning. This meaning may be as simple as a graceful statement about the capacity of the human body to move beautifully through space or as powerful as using the body as an instrument to convey some universal aspect of the inner life of the dancer, the choreographer, and the audience. Martha Graham (1991) describes dance as the "outer space of the imagination." It is one of the oldest forms of public human expression. The healing power of dance for native peoples worldwide continues to this day. These dances help people create meaning in all lived experiences including illnesses of the body and mind. So why should modern-day nurses dance or participate as an audience in a dance?

DANCE AS LIVED BODY EXPERIENCE

Dance is not a cognitive exercise. As we dance, we experiment with movement which lies outside usual patterns used in daily life. We become very much aware of our bodies in space. Through dance we experience our body as unique (individual) in its abilities to use gesture, movement and posture, as well as notice how our bodies share ways of expression with other dancers (universal). Dance is a lived body experience. Human movement and human body are experienced as synonymous and inseparable, according to Fraleigh (1987). My body has unique possibilities and limitations. I experience both vulnerability and power through my body. It is a form of risk-taking as I move. The dancer must learn to trust the wisdom of her body and its ability to learn how to move and remember movements. Translating a dance from the stage of idea, to experimenting with its movements, to incorporating the movement into muscle memory requires this trust in one's body.

CONFERENCE AND WORKSHOP DANCE EXPERIENCES

Dance was a part of each day of the conference. The opening church service included a meditative dance interpretation of poetry by Hildegarde of Bingen. Native American dancers led participants in a traditional dance creating a circle of connectedness and unity of spirit in the group. The dance workshop gave participants an opportunity to create caring images. It was a group process to create one dance which carried the meaning of caring for each person. Coming together to create meaning in this form required an environment which was open and safe where participants could take a risk. How does one create a safe environment? Last year I had the good fortune to hear Judith Jamison speak at a lecture demonstration in modern dance technique at Radcliffe College. She shared her belief that the best dance performances happen when the dancer makes herself vulnerable to the audience. It is opening the heart which allows the audience to truly participate in the dance. As the workshop facilitator, I shared some examples of dances about nursing situations as well as stories of feeling vulnerable which helped create a trusting environment. Participants had varied previous dance experiences, from formal training to social dancing to dancing "in their hearts" to no dance experience. The participants worked with music and each other to create healing images. With a basic choreography of thematic movement and music to work with, they created a dance that was the group's own, stamped with their own personal signatures. The pleasure of doing this was evident in the number of times they danced the piece—over and over—and the joy and spontaneity experienced each time.

PATHWAY TO THE HEART

Dance as a means of expression is esthetic as well as a pathway to the heart. My teacher and friend, Martha Browne, director of the Guild Dancers in Lunenburg, Massachusetts, tells her adult dancers, many of whom did not have dance training as children that, "One must dance from the heart, with passion and care. It is more important than the depth of your plié in communicating with the audience." Participants shared feelings which got stirred up during the workshop. One woman shared that she always placed a high value on control and order in her life and she feared her body "might not do what I tell it to" but do something completely different. She was also trying to integrate her conception of what she thought her body should do and what it actually did. Another participant shared how watching a dance I choreographed about caring helped her to shape the words necessary to talk with a close friend about her life-threatening illness. The workshop group gave this woman a gift. We all lifted her carefully into the air, cradling her and rocking her to quiet song—an experience most of us only have memories of.

Appreciating the abilities and limitations of our bodies also created discussion of making the most of what each person has both professionally and personally.

RELEVANCE TO NURSING

How do we take this experience back to clinical practice? Our patients require that we be aware of their lived body experiences. Reading patient narratives I am often struck by accounts where physicians and nurses ignore this most important facet of a patient's experience with illness. By getting more closely in touch with our own bodies, our own vulnerabilities and strengths, and by taking risks with our bodies, we may have a heightened awareness of our patient's experience and honor it. We can come to appreciate each person's unique experience in their body. Arthur Frank (1991) in his book *At the Will of the Body* says, "Care begins when uniqueness is recognized" (p. 45). He believes this is the difference between treatment and caring. When his own body was incapacitated because of both an illness and its treatment, this long-distance runner reflected:

. . . listening to Bach's music gave me a sensation of movement. The origins of music are inseparable from dance and dance is one of the great metaphors of life itself. Until I was ill, I never heard so clearly the dance in the music, the music in the dance (p. 63).

Coming together to celebrate caring in dance was also a form of ritual expression. Perhaps such gatherings could occur as part of other clinical conferences or as part of clinical practice dialogues among colleagues.

CLOSING DANCE IMAGES

The last day of the conference I was asked to prepare a closing piece in which all conference members were invited to participate. This performance would complete the circle of dance. Members of the workshop group led others in moving in a circle to our dance music. As we prepared to dance in the grass, I noticed one person in a wheelchair which would not easily move in the thick lawn. I invited her to the center of the circle, to use her upper body to dance the caring images we had choreographed and with the music singing in her ears and with her eyes closed, she soared.

REFERENCES

Fraleigh, S. (1987). *Dance and the lived body.* Pittsburgh: University of Pittsburgh Press.

Frank, A. (1991). *At the will of the body.* Boston: Houghton-Mifflin.

Graham, M. (1991). *Blood memory.* New York: Macmillan.

11

The Personal Journal for Nurses: Writing for Discovery and Healing

Karen Vaught-Alexander

The sunlight glitters through the silt in the darkened water of the Kla-
math River. I wait under the protection of a tree root. I am a salmon.
One beam of light refracts over my stippled, dappled back. Weary from
my journey, I listen for a cleansing flood of cool mountain water, my
gills breathing laboriously but hopefully. I rest, almost touching, the
time-smoothed rocks of the stream bed.

This journalist, using metaphor analysis while listening to music, discovered a metaphor for herself. She was a salmon, threatened by silt
and warm waters, but she was still hopeful, a survivor against all odds,
weary but at peace and secure in her traditional culture, her home. Her
journaling allowed her to discover, to find meaning from her own
metaphor of herself as a salmon.

Writing is often described as a discovery process, a vision and revision process (Murray, 1978). We write about X and discover Y, and
from Y we may even discover Z. We find a long-lost childhood photograph of ourselves, Hershey chocolate-smeared, hugging our collie
dog. Rounding a corner in Portland, Oregon, we smell the crispy, pep-
pered, country-fried chicken of our midwestern youth. We hear B. B.
King on the radio, Lucille poignantly wailing as she did the night we
lost our first true love. Writing allows us to connect and explore such

verbal and nonverbal memories or reactions. We discover what we need to say, what we must say.

Writing can also allow us to problem solve (Connolly & Vilardi, 1989). From the moment we begin to write, we are taking action. As Emig (1983) suggests, we connect the hand, the eye, the mind through the act of writing. We talk on paper, releasing feelings and finding satisfaction or resolution, as the words and sentences reveal what we would not or could not articulate before. We figure out what we feel or perhaps what we need to do. We embrace the contraries: we doubt in order to believe, and we continue to believe until we find meaning—or meaning finds us (Elbow, 1986).

So writing allows us to make meaning out of the meaningless, to find hope in the hopeless. Writing chronicles our joys and our feelings in descriptive word pictures, detailed narrative slices of our worlds. Through writing, we create artifacts with which we can then interact. Nurses and nursing education, practice, and research often use journaling. This chapter, however, will discuss the personal journal as a different approach to journaling, with nurses using writing for personal exploration, healing, and growth.

AN OVERVIEW OF THE JOURNAL

The Academic or Ethnographic Journal

Academic or classroom journals have become a typical part of the writing-across-the-curriculum programs of the last three decades (Parker & Goodkin, 1987). These writing-to-learn journals emphasize the connecting of personal or prior knowledge to course theory or information (Vygotsky, 1962). Typical journals or logs for writing to learn include dialogue or response journals, observation logs, dialectic or double-entry journals, personal development journals, team journals, and "think books" (Fulwiler, 1987; Gere, 1985; Graybeal, 1987; Hallberg, 1987). Academic journals, shared usually with a professor and sometimes with peers as well, rarely are written exclusively for private use.

These course journals often emphasize the development of critical or reflective thought. Assignments are often designed to lead students from dualistic or received, to contextually-based or relativistic thinking, from silence to constructed knowledge (Belenky et al., 1986; Perry, 1970; Kurfiss, 1988). Typical of academic journals in other disciplines, nursing education uses peer reflective journals, dialogue journals, course clinical logs, student logs, learning logs, experiential diaries, and reflection journals (Cameron & Mitchell, 1993; Heinrich, 1992; Kelly, 1993; Kelly, 1992; Sedlak, 1992; Anderson, 1991; Keenen, 1988; Dunn & Crosby, 1988; Cooper, 1982; Jensen & Denton, 1991; Nelson, 1991) in order to encourage students to become personally involved in their own educational, cognitive, and professional discovery and growth.

From descriptive researchers like Lincoln and Guba (1985) and Yin (1984), we find the ethnographic value of the rich description of contexts, people, moments, and events. In field journals or observation logs, along with cassette- and videotapes, we record research stories, our own and those of others, so crucial to our understanding of underlying research patterns and themes. Through research journaling and its stories, we chronicle the anomalous, the personal, the contextual and intuitive, the richly and contradictorily human elements that more empirical research methods would omit. With field journals, activity logs, pain journals, accident logs, participant observation logs, sleep logs, or clinical logs, nurses and their patients can document subjective feelings or objective observations on daily activities like exercise, responses to chemotherapy, sleep patterns, or pain occurrences (Rogers & Aldrich, 1993; McGrath & Hillier, 1992; Solomons & Elardo, 1991; Gagliardi, 1989; Matocha, 1989; Getty & Stern, 1990; Coop, 1990).

The Personal Journal

Journals have a long and interesting history (Lowenstein, 1987). Some of the earliest journals, recorded during the first century A.D. in China and during the Classic Greek and Roman periods, were concerned with the life of the community or the polis. With its emphasis on the thoughts and feelings of the individual, the personal journal only appeared in Western civilization at the time of the Renaissance. As the Japanese pillow books of Heian court ladies in the tenth century and the war diaries of the American Revolution and Civil War show, the personal journal, while written for private use, often later became public, published for its historical or literary value.

Diaries or personal journals have practical purposes today. We adults may have kept travel diaries to record our reactions to food, monuments, landscapes, or people on our trips to Yellowstone or China. As adolescents, we kept diaries full of details about that memorable first date or kiss. In undergraduate or graduate programs, many of us mixed personal with academic responses in our response or learning logs (Fulwiler, 1987), making individual connections, to record and reflect about observations and discover personal insights about course material (Dewey, 1933).

We write personal journals to understand ourselves, "often in relation to other people, events, ideas, or religions" (Lowenstein, 1987, p. 91). We write journals in times of personal exploration or crisis, as we struggle to understand or to control that which seems inscrutable or uncontrollable. Journals let the inside out and the outside in (Kirby & Liner, 1988; Lukinsky, 1990).

The personal or autobiographical journal continues to have many uses. The personal journal has been central to the women's movement with its emphasis on bringing women out of silence by finding their voices and by telling their stories (Belenky et al., 1986; Lowenstein, 1987). Also many psychotherapists and counselors, as part of therapy and counseling, use personal journals to help patients discover their feelings and find closure for unresolved issues in their lives. Personal development journals, as suggested by Burnham (1987), can provide important reflective thinking and constructive change. Progoff (1975), through the use of his Intensive Journals, primarily in adult education and staff development workshops, seeks to promote changes in perspectives and then establish new perspectives and relationships for the journal writers.

The personal or autobiographical journal has much value for nursing. Narratives for detailing metaphors of caring (Vezeau, 1993), for exploring intuitions through pictures and words (Leners, 1993), and for describing and sharing the actualized caring moment through poetry (Euswas, 1993) begin to indicate the potential of writing personal journals for nursing practice. For example, gerontology, pediatric, AIDS, and oncology patients and their families use journal, letter, or poetry writing for reflective exploration and therapeutic release of feelings (Dodd, Dibble, & Thomas, 1993; Gaglialdi, 1989; Quinn, 1991; Lashley, 1989; Johnson & Kelly, 1990; Sourkes, 1991; Curley, 1982; Matocha, 1989; Getty & Stern, 1990). Certainly nurses, as well as their patients and the families of patients, can benefit from personal writing. The personal journal thus can preserve the narratives and stories, the feelings, experiences, and reflections, so richly woven into human care nursing, and can help nurses perceive writing as an important source of personal exploration, growth, and healing.

Getting Started With a Personal Journal

Henry David Thoreau, a noted transcendental diarist, declared his journal was "of myself, for myself" (quoted in Stillman, 1987, p. 79). The personal journal, first and foremost, belongs to the writer, reflecting his or her personality, composing style, and writing needs. Much of the following information I presented at a workshop, "The Healing Power of Journaling," conducted on May 17, 1993 at the Research Conference, Caring as Healing: Renewal Through Hope, May 16–18, 1993, at the University of Portland, Portland, Oregon. The personal journal excerpts included throughout this article came from that workshop.

A personal journal has many choices in format, as many as the creativity of the writer can imagine. If the journal is handwritten, different colors of pencils or ink, along with different kinds of pens or ways of writing, e.g., calligraphy, can be chosen for a permanently bound, spiral, or looseleaf notebook. If word-processing is used, font, clip art, and other design features can serve to personalize typed pages in a folder. Of course, a personal journal is not limited to narratives or stories but can include any writing genre like poetry or plays. Sketches, a pressed leaf or flower, photographs, paintings, videos, cassette tapes, compact disks—all may be included as the nonverbal integrates with the verbal to express and record the thoughts and feelings of the writer (Emig, 1983; Winterowd, 1979).

The color, the texture, and the design of the journal cover can express much about the mood or personality of the journalist. A black paper cover or a light blue burlap decorated with sketches of mountains and clouds set very different moods for writing. The texture and color of the paper add another personal touch. The tactile differences in smoothly or roughly textured paper, the aesthetic choice of cool gray or warm pink, even lined or unlined paper, all contribute to the writing tenor of the personal journal.

The time and place for journaling need to be comfortable and inviting for the inner self. Some journalists prefer to write on-demand, writing five times one day and then not again for two weeks. Others enjoy definite time schedules. Perhaps writing comes easiest in a favorite chair or with a cup of tea, either late at night before bedtime or early in the morning before dawn. Each journalist finds a special time and place for writing.

Some journalists write whenever, however, and on whatever they can—on the back of a grocery list as they drive on the freeway or on a napkin during lunch. When the need to write happens, feelings and ideas must be released, perhaps never to be read again. Some spontaneous entries serve to purge feelings and emotions, and then having served their cathartic function, are best destroyed. Other such entries may provide crucial retrospection in months or years to come and need to be put in a permanent folder with other journaling.

Trying Common Journal Writing Strategies

Sometime journalists may become bored or unproductive with one approach to journaling. The following common journal writing strategies may provide different vehicles for creating the metaphors and different frames for exploring the stories stored deep within. Personal journals allow writers to release emotions, feelings, and memories or to discover and preserve them. Freed from the worry of writing conventions like spelling, style, or syntax, we tap into our inner conversations, so saturated with verbal and nonverbal meaning (Vygotsky, 1962; Berthoff, 1981).

Freewriting or Focused Freewriting This idea-freeing technique called freewriting requires that the writer write without stopping, without lifting the pen from the page or without looking at the text on the computer screen. If no thoughts come, the writer is to write the statement: I can't think of anything to say, over and over and over until ideas begin to flow. Focused freewriting uses this same technique except the writer begins with a topic or focus in mind. Like brainstorming or free association in relation to that focus, focused freewriting frees the writer's hidden feelings and thoughts and lets them leap across the page.

Looping After freewriting or focused freewriting for a time period, the writer may pause and read what has been written. Then, circling or underlining the most promising or most productive parts of the passage, the writer loops back to focus on and continue to write about those nuggets of wisdom or flashes of insight captured in the freewriting process.

Dialogue Journaling A dialogue journal invites the writer to think of writing as a conversation or dialogue with oneself, a peer, professor, or chosen other reader. The spontaneity of conversation, along with the focus and motivation of a known audience, makes dialogue journals valuable records of those conversations that we hold in our minds and then lose after an hour, day, or week. Troyka (1993) mentions some invention strategies to help create these dialogues. Writers may need to list-jot or brainstorm ideas in no special order, or they may wish to use the questions of journalism—who, what, when, where, how, why—to explore an idea or situation. Mapping or clustering allows visual relationships to be explored without writing paragraphs or sentences.

Dialectic or Reflective Journaling   Berthoff (1987) among others encourages dialectic journaling in order to see beyond one perspective or viewpoint, to foster the ability to generate or appreciate different perspectives. The journal page is usually divided in half either horizontally or vertically to create visually the need for different perspectives. One column then can represent the perspectives of the now and the other those of a decade ago; one column can represent supporting evidence for a stand on an issue and the other column evidence for the opposite stance. Another strategy for stretching our ability to empathize with the perspectives of others is to write about a situation or conflict using a third person to describe the writer's feelings and first person pronouns (I, me, my) for the other(s) involved. Reflection by peers or by the writer about ideas and perspectives recorded in this journal is a key component. These journal entries are re-read and analyzed for personal criteria, overall growth, or ability to confront dualistic views and integrate contextually-based or relativistic perspectives (Perry, 1968).

An Unsent Letter

All of us compose letters in our minds that we never send. This strategy requires that the writer compose a letter to someone else. The following example shows the catharsis, the emotional release that such a letter can have:

Dear Mom,

I am a nurse now. Yes, me, the selfish, ungrateful brat that tried your very soul. I am a healer. At least, I am better at healing others than myself. I help others feel cared for and listened to. Ironic, huh? After all those years of never feeling cared for or listened to, I pride myself on giving that gift to others. I think that you would be proud of me. I have grown up so much since you died almost a decade ago. I was bitter and young. I never meant to let you go without telling you how much I loved you. I guess that's why I find it so easy, actually so necessary to give that love I forfeited to others. I keep looking in their eyes for your approval. I keep telling myself that you would be proud of me, that you too regret not saying that you loved me too.

Response Journaling   This journaling focuses on first feelings, reactions, and responses. Response prompts may be used, i.e., I feel _____ because, or Whenever I think about _____, I feel _____, in order to facilitate reactions and clarifications of feelings. A description of a critical incident in the writer's life or professional career (or series of such incidents) may help stimulate the discovery of hidden feelings and responses. A series of self-generated questions and answers (Q: and A:) may help writers discover or deal with questions and answers otherwise unexplored.

Verbal Portrait or Actual Sketch of a Person, Event, Feeling   To sketch with words or pictures a person, event, or feeling can do much to open up the hand, eye, brain connections mentioned by both Emig (1983) and Winterowd (1979). Different composing styles prefer the visual, the auditory, the kinesthetic. The creation of music or dance, oral composing with a tape recorder—all allow those ideas not ready to be written to be expressed.

Guided Imagery or Metaphor   One of the most powerful personal writing strategies is guided imagery or metaphor. Some writers use music, candles, colored lights or semi-darkness, along with statements like the following to help generate metaphors deep from within, i.e., I am a _____, or I see, feel, hear, taste, touch, or smell _____. Here is an example:

I am a leaf, bright green and in the fullness of my glory—but I have become unattached. I am floating down, down, down. I am so afraid that I will become part of that big pile of leaves. Meaningless, one of the crowd, raked and stuffed in a plastic bag. I am troubled. People tell me 'you are special, you do good work, you have a good reputation.' But I am burned out by having inadequate pay but a heavy work load; no power, no real authority but responsibility, lots of responsibility. I keep floating. The decision I must make scares me.

Discovering the Benefits of the Personal Journal for Nurses

Journals, especially academic and research journals, have provided nursing educators and researchers with rich and valuable educational and professional insights. The therapeutic benefits of logs and journaling for patients have also been well-documented. Certainly, the personal journal for the reflection and healing of nurses promises equally powerful benefits.

Indeed the personal journal may benefit the writer and the writer alone in her search for acceptance, healing, or closure. While writing for ourselves is a worthy goal, nurses in their personal journals may have stories to tell that will inspire, will resonant for, other nurses. Perhaps some of the examples in this discussion begin to illustrate the value of such collaboration and sharing. Publishing the poems, short stories, plays, or narratives that may evolve from personal journaling may provide the final stage of healing and growth—not only for the writers but for readers who then can share these heartfelt expressions of caring and self-discovery, "For it is in the dew of little things, the heart finds its morning and is refreshed" (Gibran, 1985, p. 58).

REFERENCES

Anderson, S. L. (1991). Preceptor teaching strategies: Behaviors that facilitate role transition in senior nursing students. *Journal of Nursing Staff Development, 7*(4), 171–175.

Belenky, M., Clinchy, B., Goldberger, N., & Tarule, J. (1986). *Women's ways of knowing: The development of self, voice, and mind.* New York: Basic Books.

Berthoff, A. E. (1981). *The making of meaning: Metaphors, models, and maxims for writing teachers.* Upper Montclair, NJ: Boyton/Cook.

Berthoff, A. E. (1987). Dialectical notebooks and the audit of meaning. In T. Fulwiler (Ed.), *The journal book* (pp. 11–18). Portsmouth, NH: Boyton/Cook.

Burnham, C. C. (1987). Reinvigorating a tradition: The personal development journal. In T. Fulwiler (Ed.), *The journal book* (pp. 148–156). Portsmouth, NH: Boyton/Cook.

Cameron, B. L., & Mitchell, A. M. (1993). Reflective peer journals: Developing authentic nurses. *Journal of Advanced Nursing, 18*(2), 290–297.

Connolly, P., & Vilardi, T. (1989). *Writing to learn mathematics and science.* New York: Teachers College Press.

Coop, L. A. (1990). Pain diaries, journals, and logs . . . writing pain journals. *Orthopaedic Nursing, 9*(2), 37–39.

Cooper, S. S. (1982). Methods of teaching—revisited experiential diaries and learning logs. *Journal of Continuing Education in Nursing, 13*(6), 32–34.

Curley, J. S. (1982). Leading poetry writing groups in a nurse home activities program. *Physical and Occupational Therapy in Geriatrics,* Vol. *1*(23–34).

Dewey, J. (1933). *How we think.* Chicago: Regnery.

Dodd, M. J., Dibble, S. L., & Thomas, M. L. (1993). Predictors of concerns and coping strategies of cancer chemotherapy outpatients. *Applied Nursing Research, 6*(1), 2–7.

Dunn, J. D., & Crosby, F. S. (1988). Teaching nursing diagnoses to school nurses: A curriculum plan. *Journal of Continuing Education in Nursing, 19*(5), 205–210.

Elbow, P. (1986). Embracing the contraries: Explorations in learning and teaching. New York: Oxford University Press.

Emig, J. (1983). *The web of meaning: Essays on writing, teaching, learning, and thinking* (D. Goswami & M. Butler, Eds.). Upper Montclair, NJ: Boyton/Cook.

Euswas, P. (1993). The actualized caring moment: A grounded theory of caring in nursing practice. In D. Gaut (Ed.), *A global agenda for caring* (pp. 309–326). New York: National League for Nursing Press.

Fulwiler, T. (Ed.). (1987). *The journal book.* Portsmouth, NH: Boyton/Cook.

Gagliardi, B. A. (1989). Three families' experience of living with a child diagnosed with Duchenne muscular dystrophy. Doctoral dissertation, New York University.

Gere, A. R. (1985). *Roots in the sawdust: Writing to learn across the disciplines.* Urbana, IL: National Council of Teachers of English.

Getty, G., & Stern, P. (1990). Gay men's perceptions and responses to AIDS. *Journal of Advanced Nursing, 15*(8), 895–905.

Gibran, K. (1985). *The Prophet.* New York: Alfred A. Knopf.

Graybeal, J. (1987). The team journal. In T. Fulwiler (Ed.), *The journal book* (pp. 306–311). Portsmouth, NH: Boyton/Cook.

Hallberg, F. (1987). Journal writing as person making. In T. Fulwiler (Ed.). *The journal book* (pp. 289–298). Portsmouth, NH: Boyton/Cook.

Heinrich, K. T. (1992). The intimate dialogue: Journal writing by students. *Nurse Educator, 17*(6), 17–21.

Jensen, G., & Denton, B. (1991). Teaching physical therapy students to reflect: A suggestion for clinical education. *Journal of Physical Therapy Education, 5*(1), 33–38.

Johnson, J. B., & Kelly, A. W. (1990). A multifaceted rehabilitation program for women with cancer. *Oncology Nursing Forum, 17*(5), 691–695.

Kelly, B. (1992). Professional ethics as perceived by American nursing undergraduates . . . senior baccalaureate nursing students. *Journal of Advanced Nursing, 17*(1), 10–15.

Kelly, B. (1993). The "real world" of hospital nursing practice as perceived by nursing undergraduates. *Journal of Professional Nursing, 9*(1), 27–33.

Keenen, E. A. (1988). A description of the influence of the learning environment on the cognitive development of registered nurse students in a baccalaureate nursing program. Doctoral dissertation, University of Maryland College Park.

Kirby, D., & Liner, T. (1988). Inside out: Developmental strategies for teaching writing (2d ed.). Portsmouth, NH: Boyton/Cook.

Kramer, D. (1990). Integrated skills reinforcement applied to nursing content in the senior year of a RN baccalaureate program. Doctoral dissertation, Columbia University Teachers College.

Kurfiss, J. G. (1988). Critical thinking: Theory, research, practice, and possibilities. ASHE-ERIC-Higher Education Report No. 2, Washington, DC: Association for the Study of Higher Education.

Lashley, M. E. (1989). *Being with the elderly in community health nursing: Exploring lived experience through reflective dialogue.* Unpublished doctoral dissertation, University of Maryland, College Park.

Leners, D. W. (1993). Nursing intuition: The deep connection. In D. Gaut (Ed.), *A global agenda for caring* (pp. 223–240). New York: National League for Nursing Press.

Lincoln, Y., & Guba, E. (1985). *Naturalistic inquiry.* Beverly Hills: Sage Publications.

Lowenstein, S. (1987). A brief history of journal keeping. In T. Fulwiler (Ed.). *The journal book* (pp. 87–97). Portsmouth, NH: Boyton/Cook.

Lukinsky, J. (1990). Reflective withdrawal through journal writing, J. Mezirow and associates (Ed.), *Fostering critical reflection in adulthood: A guide to transformative and emancipatory learning.* San Francisco: Jossey-Bass.

McAuley, E., & Jacobson, L. (1991). Self-efficacy and exercise participation in sedentary adult females. *American Journal of Health Promotion*, 5(3), 185–191.

McGrath, P. A., & Hillier, L. M. (1992). Phantom limb sensations in adolescents: A case study to illustrate the utility of sensation and pain logs in pediatric clinical practice. *Journal of Pain and Symptom Management*, 7(1), 46–53.

Matocha, L. K. (1989). The effects of AIDS on family member(s) responsible for care: A qualitative study. Doctoral dissertation, University of Delaware

Mezirow, J., and associates (Ed.). (1990). *Fostering critical reflection in adulthood: A guide to transformative and emancipatory learning.* San Francisco: Jossey-Bass.

Murray, D. (1978). Internal revision: A process of discovery. In C. Cooper and L. Odell. (Ed.) *Research on composing: Points of departure* (pp. 85–103). Urbana, IL: National Council of Teachers of English.

Nelson, D. A. (1991). Gerontologic learning and the development of practical knowledge in the nursing home setting. Doctoral dissertation, Kent State University.

Parker, R. P., & Goodkin, V. (1987). *The consequences of writing: Enhancing learning in the disciplines.* Upper Montclair, NJ: Boyton/Cook.

Perry, W. (1968). *Forms of intellectual development.* New York: Holt, Rinehart, & Winston.

Progoff, I. (1975). *At a journal workshop.* New York: Dialogue House.

Quinn, A. A. (1988). Integrating a changing me: A grounded theory of the process of menopause for perimenopausal women. Doctoral dissertation, University of Colorado Health Sciences Center.

Quinn, A. A. (1991). A theoretical model of the perimenopausal process. *Journal of Nurse Midwifery, 36*(1),25–29.

Rogers, A. E., & Aldrich, M. S. (1993). The effect of regularly scheduled naps on sleep attacks and excessive daytime sleepiness associated with narcolepsy. *Nursing Research, 42*(2), 111–117.

Sedlak, C. A. (1992). Use of clinical logs by beginning nursing students and faculty to identify learning needs. *Journal of Nursing Education, 31*(1), 24–28.

Solomons, H. C., & Elardo, R. (1991). Biting in day care centers: Incidence, prevention and intervention. *Journal of Pediatric Health Care, 5*(4), 191–196.

Sourkes, B. M. (1991). Truth to life: Art therapy with pediatric oncology, patients and their siblings. *Journal of Psychosocial Oncology, 9,* 81–96.

Staton, J. (1987). The power of responding in dialogue journals. In T. Fulwiler (Ed.), *The journal book* (pp. 47–63). Portsmouth, NH: Boyton/Cook.

Stillman, P. (1987). "Of myself, for myself." In T. Fulwiler (Ed.), *The journal book* (pp. 77–86). Portsmouth, NH: Boyton/Cook.

Troyka, L. Q. (1993). *A handbook for writers* (3rd ed.). New York: Prentice Hall.

Vezeau, T. M. (1993). Use of narrative in human caring inquiry. In D.

Gaut (Ed.), *A global agenda for caring* (pp. 211–221). New York: National League for Nursing Press.

Vygotsky, L. (1962). *Thought and language.* Cambridge, MA: MIT Press.

Winterowd, W. R. (1979). Brain, rhetoric, and style. In D. McQuade (Ed.), *Linguistics, stylistics, and the teaching of composition* (pp. 151–181). New York: Queens College, CUNY.

Yin, R. K. (1984). *Case study research: Design and methods.* (Applied Social Research Methods Series, Vol. 5). Beverly Hills: Sage.

Part V

Hope

12

Hope as Healing: Patient Voices

Linda Brown

I tell myself and I tell her that the bad times don't last forever. And that it always gets better. Because when she's really sick, we know and I think she knows too, even then, that when her meds are OK again we can get back to normal and we will do things again. And now I always keep in my mind during the bad times something to do, something that we will do when it's over. And I try to tell her about it too, so there is something to look forward to. We have to work, you know, at the times when she's really sick, to remember that it isn't always like this, because sometimes it seems like it will be, and to have an idea, a plan, for what we want to do when it is over.

Mother of a young woman with chronic mental illness

When I'm in the hospital, well, it's hard because whatever I want, whatever I think, it doesn't make any difference. They just want me to take my medicine and shut up. But when I'm out, I know that when I'm out, that it's different. When I'm out I know I can do things. Like I can get my own money and I can make my own plans. And I can decide what to do. Even when Ron, you know, my case manager, has ideas for me, he has to ask me. And knowing that, that I have some say, that's what keeps me going. And that is why I don't like to be in the hospital and I don't really like to live at (a group home) because it makes me feel

like, like whatever I do, it doesn't really matter. And that's when I just feel like giving up like I really am sick.
                    Thirty-five-year-old man with chronic mental illness

These are voices of individuals relating their experiences of living with illness and how they keep going in the face of this reality. They illustrate many dimensions of hope as it is experienced in the reality of illness. Heard within the context of a study of patient and family experiences with chronic mental illness, their voices reveal what they felt they needed and what they actually received from care providers. Participants were asked about the "burden" of illness in their lives and about the things they did or received from others that helped them with the burden. Hope was one of the fundamental things that helped individuals live with the illness. In this chapter we examine the meanings and structure of hope and identify critical components of the experience of hope. We explore the ways it is experienced by individuals as they live and heal in the presence of illness and suffering as we listen to people telling us their experiences. The relationship of hope and healing will also be discussed.

MEANINGS OF HOPE

Our theoretical understandings of hope have been influenced by the work of philosophers, behavioral scientists, and theologians. From philosophy, especially from the work of Marcel (1962, 1967), comes a view of hope as an important and, essentially mysterious, inner force for survival in the face of captivity, trial, or entrapment. Hope for Marcel was characterized by (a) an open sense of time that permitted the individual to transcend the present situation and recognize other possibilities, (b) a connectedness or bond between self and others in which hope could be both given and received, and (c) an active non-acceptance of defeat that was both patient and positive.

Hope has also been equated with experiencing meaning and value in life in the face of events of extreme hardship and threats to personal existence that are difficult to understand and explain (Frankl, 1959, 1990; Vaillot, 1970). Faith in the existence of a higher power that can be drawn upon to transcend the present situation and to give meaning to the experienced suffering has also been shown to be an important component of hope (Alfaro, 1970).

Lynch, a psychologist, described hope (1965) as an interior sense of possibility that develops in response to some difficulty in living. Hope involves the ability to imagine or "image" another perspective that permits the individual to move beyond the present difficulty and see a desired future as possible. Like Marcel, Lynch considered hope a personal experience that requires a response from an other to be fully realized. The "imaged" perspective needs to be shared and given reality in an act of collaboration or mutuality.

Hope has been described by other behavioral scientists as an expectation of goal attainment modified by the perceived probability of attaining it (Stotland, 1969), as an attitude or belief that moves the individual into the future (Tiger, 1979), as a positive motivation to move past immediate obstacles in a situation in which the outcome is uncertain (Taylor, 1989), and as a conviction that a good future is possible (Smith, 1983).

During the last decade, empirical knowledge of hope as an important variable in health care has grown as nurses and others have explicitly studied hope in individuals experiencing a range of health problems in various settings. Across health conditions and settings, hope has been shown to be an important factor in maintaining and regaining health (Hickey, 1986; Hinds, 1988; McGee, 1984; Raleigh, 1992), in coping with illness (Craig & Edwards, 1983; Rideout & Montemuro, 1986; Stoner, 1983), and in facing the end of life with peace and dignity (Herth, 1990; Scanlon, 1989).

In nursing, hope has been incorporated into the concept of care. Watson (1979) identified the instillation of faith-hope as one of the ten carative factors in nursing while others consider hope and the ways in which nurses enable others to hope as important processes of care (Benner, 1984; Brown, 1986).

From these meanings and views of hope, several common dimensions emerge that lead to a view of hope as a complex, multidimensional process characterized by:

- a situation that poses great threat or difficulty to the individual;

- an inner force for survival in face of threat;

- a future orientation that permits the individual to transcend the immediate situation;

- a positive but not certain expectation of attaining a desired goal in the future;

- relationship(s) with an important other(s).

Based on the multiple meanings and common dimensions of the experience of hope found in both the theoretical and empirical literature, and on work with patients in a variety of settings, I have come to describe hope in the caring practice of nursing as a multidimensional process through which an individual is able to transcend the suffering of a present situation and experience healing.

THE RELATIONSHIP OF HOPE AND HEALING

This view of hope as a process through which a suffering individual experiences healing requires consideration of the meanings of both suffering and healing. I am particularly indebted to Dr. Katie Eriksson for helping me clarify and deepen my understanding of suffering and it's place in the practice of caring (Eriksson, 1992). At the most basic level, suffering is the human response to situations of captivity, threat or great difficulty identified earlier as inherent to the experience of hope. Suffering is the anguish experienced when personal integrity (physical, psychological, social or spiritual) and being are threatened, when an individual perceives the possible disintegration of self as a whole, functioning unity (Cassell, 1991). It is in response to the suffering of another that the nurse becomes engaged with the other to provide the compassionate care essential to healing (Eriksson, K., personal communication, 1993).

Healing is the integration or reintegration of self in the presence of suffering. It is important to note that healing does not imply the absence of suffering. Rather it is the ability to experience self as an integrated, functioning unity in the presence of the threatening situation that has the power to evoke suffering. It is through hope in relationship with others that the individual moves from the anguish of suffering to healing. The processes of hope are a bridge by which the individual is able to transform suffering and experience healing. The relationships among suffering, hope, and healing are shown in Figure 12.1.

STRUCTURE OF HOPE

We will now examine what I have come to think of as the structure of hope. It is a structure in the sense of being made up of consistent

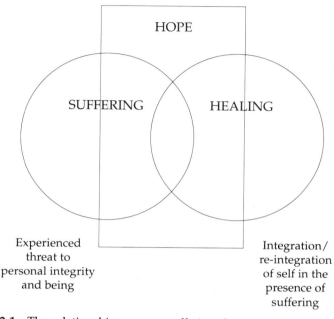

Figure 12.1 The relationships among suffering, hope, and healing.

elements that emerge as fundamental components in the experience of hope. While each person expresses the structure in unique and individual ways, all will utilize the underlying structure of hope as they transcend suffering. This will be seen as we more closely examine the experiences heard in the voices quoted earlier in this chapter.

The first structural element is a *time orientation* in which the individual anticipates a future that will be good or better than the present. It is essential that the person be able to see past the immediate situation of threat and suffering and realize the possibility for a different state of being at a different time. The future may be the next hour, the next day or any other time that has meaning for the individual and is perceived as possible and good. This structural element was expressed by the mother quoted earlier, when she says:

I tell myself and I tell her that the bad times don't last forever. And it will always get better because when she's really sick we know and I

think she knows too, even then, that when her meds are OK again we
can get back to normal and do things again.

The second structural element is a *personally meaningful goal* that is perceived as attainable in the future. While it is important that the goal be realistic in view of the situation, it is the perspective of the suffering individual that is most important in defining what is realistic. The goal may take the form of a concrete "project" that allows a person to "project" him- or herself into the future in very concrete ways as specific plans are made and actions are taken to realize a project that extends into the future. The element is illustrated as Lizabeth, a 38-year-old woman with schizophrenia, talks about the importance of projects or goals to her sense of being:

> *The things that I have to do are OK but the things I want to do, those*
> *are the really important things. Like right now one of my projects is*
> *with my sister. She's a teacher, you know, she teaches first grade, and*
> *I'm helping her make masks for the kids out of paper bags, you know,*
> *with eyes cut out and colors on the bags for their Halloween Party. And*
> *I know she needs help for Christmas too, and I know I can do that. And*
> *what I am doing is good for the kids and for my sister and for me.*

The third element is an *action orientation toward the goal* in which the individual mobilizes resolve and energy to do what is necessary to achieve the goal. We hear this element expressed by Ann, a 30-year-old woman with a long history of severe mental illness as she tells of the actions she took during a recent hospitalization to achieve her goal of leaving the hospital to return to her home and friends in the community:

> *And I knew, I just knew, that if I was going to be better again and get*
> *out of here, I would have to make myself start taking the medicine*
> *again. And I didn't really have to decide and do it on my own because I*
> *knew from before that sooner or later they would give it to me anyway.*
> *And I knew I needed it, but I just hate it, you know. But anyway, I*
> *decided that I would be the one to decide and I just got up my energy*
> *and I started taking the medicine on my own because I really wanted to*
> *get out of there.*

Uncertainty, the fourth, and last, structural element, is somewhat paradoxical in that all of the other elements are focused on positive expectations and perceptions while uncertainty explicitly acknowledges the possibility that the positive expectations and perceptions may not be realized. Uncertainty acknowledges the dynamic nature of hope as the individual strives to integrate the present and real threatening experience and the associated suffering with the wished for, anticipated, future in which suffering is alleviated. Uncertainty is an always present reminder of the multiple realities that surround every lived situation. Again we hear the voice of Lizabeth expressing uncertainty as she talks of her expectations and sense of the future. As Lizabeth talks we hear the combination of structural elements of hope that interact to contribute to her sense of integration and being. In this brief excerpt she identifies uncertainty, a sense of connection and affiliation, optimism that she is not always sick, and a sense of purpose in the projects that she is committed to carry out:

> *I know I can get sick again. My case manager keeps telling me that I can and I've been through it enough times to know. But I know that I'm not always sick and when I'm not there are projects and things that I want to do. And sometimes I don't remember them when I'm sick but they are always there somewhere and my sister always helps me remember them even when I'm sick.*

CRITICAL COMPONENTS OF HOPE

Within the structure of hope there are a number of critical components that contribute to the experience of hope and healing. These components can be considered the processes through which hope is realized. As such they provide guidance for specific nursing actions that can foster and promote hope. The first component is a *sense of meaning and purpose in life* that provides the individual a reason to live and to reach out into the future past the suffering of the present. The sense of meaning and purpose may be rooted in personal, interpersonal, or larger societal or spiritual concerns and commitments that serve to replenish, renew and affirm the threatened self. Later in the interview with the mother, she talks of the importance of seeing meaning and purpose in the experience of suffering and of ways she seeks this sense:

> *But it's really hard sometimes to understand why it keeps happening. Well, maybe it's not hard to understand because it is a disease, but it's*

really hard to, you know, accept or understand why it happened to Kay and to us. And that's when I have to talk with other parents and people who know about this. Because we're all in this together and I know it isn't just us and that we can work together to make things better for our kids and for other people who have this disease.

The second component is a *sense of connectedness, of mutuality and affiliation* in which the individual experiences being able to count on an important other(s) for affirmation and assistance. The sense of connectedness is fostered in relationships that are characterized by caring, sharing and trust in which there is a sense of belonging as a valued other. Especially for older individuals, a primary sense of connectedness and affiliation may be with God, or other spiritual force, or with a church group. The mother quoted above also illustrates the importance of connectedness, mutuality, and affiliation and how these components interact in the experience of hope and healing.

A *sense of optimism* is a third component of hope. Optimism encompasses a sense of possibilities and a search for cues that the possibilities are, indeed, real. Memories of past successes and past endeavors are important to a sense of optimism for these memories foster a sense of competence and success that can be aspired to again. Memories allow the individual to experience self in better situations and provide a sense of future possibilities that are grounded to past realities.

The fourth component of hope, *success with immediate goals in the situation*, is related to optimism. This component highlights the importance of the experience of achievement regardless of the seriousness of the present situation. While optimism can draw on memories of past successes and accomplishments, it is also important to experience self as competent in the present situation. Sam, a 28-year-old man with bipolar disorder, illustrates both a sense of optimism and the importance of success in the present situation as he tells of how he manages to keep going in the face of his illness:

I am starting a training program, a vocational rehab program next month. And I'm looking forward to it. I had to convince my case manager that I was ready again to do it. And I reminded him that I had been able to do it last year and that I kept the job they found for me until I got sick again. And he told me that Voc Rehab might not want to let me take another program but I told him I thought they would and that I could convince them that I was ready and so I went to the appointment and talked them into letting me into the program. I think my case manager was surprised but other people who know me, like people that I worked with before, they knew I could do it.

A fifth component of hope is a *sense of freedom* as in the ability to make decisions and choices about things that are personally important. The freedom to choose, even if within limited areas, fosters a sense of self as a competent and fully functioning individual who is able to maintain control over important aspects of existence. The importance of this component is clearly heard as Andy, a 35-year-old man tells of his experience with mental illness:

When I'm out (of the hospital) I know I can do things. Like I can get my own money and make my own plans. And I can decide what to do. . . . And knowing that, that I have some say, that's what keeps me going. And that is why I don't like to be in the hospital and I don't really like to live at _____ because it makes me feel like, like whatever I do, it doesn't really matter. And that's when I just feel like giving up, like I'm really sick.

A final component of hope is taking *mental and/or physical action*. Hope is not a passive experience but requires a state of readiness to act in response to the situation that threatens the integrity of being. Action does not have to be strenuous or physical and may be directed toward the mental work of reviewing memories to experience past successes or identifying meaning and purpose in one's life. The important component of taking action is investing energy in transcending the present situation and reaching ahead. We hear this component of hope in the voice of a 27-year-old woman with a long history of schizophrenia as she tells of a recent hospital experience:

And I knew, I just knew, that if I was going to be better again, I would have to make myself start taking the medicine again. And I didn't really have to decide and do it on my own because I knew from before that sooner or later they would give it to me anyway. And I knew I needed it, but I just hate it, you know. But anyway, I decided that I would be the one to decide and I just got up my energy and I started taking the medication on my own because I really wanted to get out of there.

The voices we have heard tell of the experience of illness and suffering and of the ways individuals experience hope and healing. They clearly illustrate the structure and critical components of the experience of hope. The fundamental role that hope, in its many manifestations, plays in the ability of the person to transcend suffering and to heal have been vividly portrayed. We, as nurses, have the privilege, opportunity, and responsibility to assist those for whom we care in these transformations.

REFERENCES

Alfaro, J. (1970). Christian hope and the hopes of mankind. In C. Duquac (Ed.). *Dimensions of Spirituality*. New York: Herder and Herder.

Benner, P. (1984). *From novice to expert: Excellence and power in clinical nursing practice*. Menlo Park: Addison-Wesley.

Brown, L. (1986). The experience of care: Patient perspectives. *Topics in Clinical Nursing, 8,* 56–62.

Cassell, E. J. (1991). *The nature of suffering*. New York: Oxford University Press.

Craig, H. M., & Edwards, J. E. (1983). Adaption in chronic illness: An eclectic model for nurses. *Journal of Advanced Nursing, 8,* 397–404.

Eriksson, K. (1992). The alleviation of suffering—the idea of caring. *Scandinavian Journal of Caring Science, 6,* 119–123.

Frankl, V. (1959). *Man's search for meaning: An introduction to logotherapy*. New York: Simon and Schuster.

Frankl, V. (1990). Facing the transitoriness of human existence. *Generations, Fall,* 7–10.

Herth, K. (1990). Fostering hope in the terminally ill. *Journal of Advanced Nursing, 15,* 1250–1259.

Hickey, S. (1986). Enabling hope. *Cancer Nursing, 9,* 133–137.

Hinds, S. S. (1988). Adolescent hopefulness in illness and health. *Advances in Nursing Science, 10,* 79–88.

Lynch, W. F. (1965). *Images of hope*. Baltimore: Helicon Press.

Marcel, G. (1962). *Homo Viator: Introduction to a metaphysics of hope*. New York: Harper & Row.

Marcel, G. (1967). Desire and hope. In N. Lawrence and D. O'Conner (Eds.) *Readings in Existential Phenomenology*. Englewood Cliffs, NJ: Prentice Hall.

McGee, R. F. (1984). Hope: A factor influencing crisis resolution. *Advances in Nursing Science, 6,* 34–44.

Raleigh, E. D. (1992). Sources of hope in chronic illness. *Oncology Nursing Forum, 19,* 443–448.

Rideout, E., & Montemuro, M. (1986). Hope, morale and adaptation in patients with chronic heart failure. *Journal of Advanced Nursing, II,* 429–438.

Scanlon, C. (1989). Creating a vision of hope: The challenge of palliative care, *Oncology Nursing Forum, 16,* pp. 491–496.

Smith, M. B. (1983). Hope and despair; Keys to the sociopsychodynamics of youth. *American Journal of Orthopsychiatry, 53,* 388–399.

Stoner, M. (1983). Hope and cancer patients. (Doctoral dissertation, University of Colorado, 1982). *Dissertation Abstracts International, 44,* 115B.

Stotland, E. (1969). *The psychology of hope*. San Francisco: Jossey-Bass.

Taylor, S. E. (1989). *Positive illusions: Creative self-deception and the healthy mind*. New York: Basic Books.

Tiger, L. (1979). *Optimism: The biology of hope*. New York: Simon and Schuster.

Vaillot, N. C. (1970). Hope, the restoration of being. *American Journal of Nursing, 70,* 268–273.

Watson, J. (1979) *The philosophy and science of caring*. Boston: Little Brown.

13

A Journey With Breast Cancer: Telling My Story

A. Lynne Wagner

I was running scared, angry and confused inside, calm and calculating outside. Diagnosed with breast cancer, I was hungry for every piece of information there was on the subject. The objectivity shielded me for a while, but the time had come to make a decision and I was forced to look inside. I saw only confusion; I found no answers for me. Then a different type of search began, not through medical journals, in library stacks, or by listening to others' stories. The initial frantic search and lists dissolved into a more meditative, flowing expression of observations, needs, and reflection recorded in a journal.

As my journey with breast cancer unfolded, I wrote sporadically of illness and fear, choices and confusion, despair and pain, new found strengths and resources, and the healing celebration of life—not for posterity—but for momentary comfort. My journal was a release of emotion and a description of senses to an untelling audience. The blank pages gave me permission to discuss anything and everything without required feedback. In my safe rambling of thought, decisions sorted themselves out, high-peaked emotions leveled. As my journal grew, I never became retrospective. New days led to new feelings and my journey propelled me forward rapidly to new decisions and coping skills. Through my writings, which flowed with an inexplicable ease and art, I touched my core of humanness, focused my perspective of living, and transcended academic realism and daily demands.

A year after my journey had stabilized, idle curiosity sparked a re-view of my journal. I was amazed at the volume, at the fever of emo-tion, at the honesty, at the portrayed intimacy of my spirit, at the cre-ativity. I did not remember much of the writing for it had been my unconscious voice, but I recognized that I had utilized a special expres-sive talent that had been healing for me. As I relived my journey again through my words, I was exhausted, but better appreciated from where I had traveled and how I had survived. My story was powerful and hopeful in the midst of challenge. What struck me was this story was no longer just mine. It belongs to many other women and their families and friends. I had been given a gift that needed to be shared. Thus my story passed from a personal account of hidden thoughts to a public sharing of human despair and hope.

I did not know how my story would be received or if 1 had enough courage to become vulnerable in telling it. Once I decided to take the risk, creative thoughts abounded on how best to present the material. Nature has always spurred my imaginative curiosity, and photographic attempts to capture its magic have been a longtime hobby. I was sur-prised that much of my poetry and prose centered my struggles and mortality in the seasons of nature. I envisioned complementing the verbal with visual stimulus, and developed a presentation of my writ-ing with slides to portray the full meaning of my journey.

After three days of validating the importance of patients' qualitative accounts in understanding and fostering caring and hope, my first au-dience at the International Caring Conference in Portland, Oregon was primed to hear my story. I had been given safe and fertile ground to move forward. Hours before my presentation, I scrapped my original introduction for a more personal comment: "Over the last three days, we have shared. We have gathered together, learned together. We have been thoughtful and playful. We have prayed, cried, laughed. We have danced and encircled our spirits. We have questioned and con-firmed our beliefs. So many of you have given me gifts. I now give you a gift. I give you my story. Once I release it, it is yours and it will change."

I proceeded to bare a fraction of my soul as my verse and prose spoke of diagnosis and despair, of frantic busyness and caged feelings, of nakedness and paralysis, of a growing toward wholeness with new understanding of self. My winter season blossomed into the spring of hope as I sought help from a Greater Power and awakened to the col-ors of my world. I described how I vacillated between the enmeshment of pain and the healing salve of nature. Personal relationships, body image, and sexuality healed through acceptance, humor, friendship, and a new perspective of a hopeful present. The words and images did their magic. Although I entered a protective twilight zone as I was absorbed in the reliving of my journey, I was aware of my audience in a global sense during the presentation. I felt the energy flow between us, the connectedness pull us together as we swayed from despair of illness and change to the hope of the seasons. We entered a synergetic state and when the spell was broken, we were both exhausted and exhilarated by the power of the common experience.

In so telling my story, I have changed and people who listened changed. Like any story, it carries a message of time and space, and as the message moves through new audiences, new listeners, the words will stay the same, the meaning will change for each person. I now understand that storytelling is a vehicle to encourage discussion, foster a sharing of experience, and validate feelings. It is a two-way communion. Both the listener and the storyteller gain new perspective of the worth of honest reflection and penetration of feelings. A good story is like hugging each person in the audience, for it individually touches the person's intimate sense of self and leaves a warm afterglow of connectedness. I must thank the listeners of my story, for they gave me the gift of response that adds to my understanding and energy to heal. I was inspired to write the following poem after the conference.

Strength Through Sharing

> *A simple and heartfelt story brings the beauty out of change,*
> *And points to the inner growth we can all accomplish,*
> *When challenged to look anew at ourselves.*
> *With growing understanding of how great life is,*
> *We are powerful in controlling—if not our destiny,*
> *Then at least the quality of our path.*
> *Lead on in the adventure of self-direction.*
> *With conviction that life offers challenges we can absorb.*

I continue to write of hope, for my healing is a daily adventure. I cannot change the past, it is and will remain so to be remembered. The present is an unfolding, changeable state of being, a product of the past, but able to be molded, challenged. It is giving and hopeful. It lives. The future is yet to be defined, but will be influenced by past and present. Its gossamer-like shape haunts those who search too hard. The future is unreal, untouchable, and gives hope only from the present view. It promises nothing and its strength comes from the hopeful dreams of the present. Hope is perspective of yourself within the universe, when body, mind, and spirit share a fluid connectedness that melds past memories into present activity with a flexible view of the future without bounds of time and space.

Health care providers who offer hope are beacons for patients floundering in the sea of diagnosis, choices, and despair. Another person's hope can bolster a flagging soul until the patient is safely in harbor where his or her own senses have gained perspective again with new awareness of life's perils. Caring is the ability to give that hope through bedside care, a smile, listening, help in attaining small goals, a touch, a forgiving presence. My healing came from many sources, but it was the people around me who allowed me to look deep within myself to find inner strength and to discover nature's colorful power which dissipated my despair. My journey with breast cancer continues to carry me to both familiar and unknown places of many colors. I will absorb it all, be energized by the gifts that were always there, but are now experienced with greater partnership. Nature comforts me with gentle reminders of the cyclical seasons that complement my mortality as expressed in a poem I wrote during my recovery.

The Seasons of Nature's Mortality

Grow tree, grow
I am watching, I am praying.
Grow tree, grow.
I am watering, I am caring.

Winter will bend you, shape you,
As you stand dormant weighted by heavy snow,
A sentinel of potential.
Spring will nourish you, energize you,
As you reach out in new directions,
Bursting forth, branching outward,
Upward, always toward the golden light.
Summer will clothe you, fan you,
As your green finery sparkles with dew,
Your strength a resting place for visitors,

Your foundations spreading invisibly underground.
Fall will decorate you, adorn you,
As your coolness turns to vivid colors,
A passing glory to end in rest.

Grow tree, grow.
I am changing, I am rooting.
Grow tree, grow.
I am learning, I am living.

Sharing my story has captured the essence of my healing, for my writings helped me confront my feelings, and my listeners helped validate those feelings as normal progression toward recovery. The audience also gained perspective in their own unexpressed feelings. It is through such open, honest communication between caring people that hope blossoms and living gains value.

14

Hoping for the Best:
Live-In Parents' Experiences

Philip Darbyshire

*Only now after six days in the hospital am I beginning to feel at ease.
It's like living in a goldfish bowl. After the accident my confidence is
shattered and simple tasks like changing nappies (diapers), feeding and
giving drinks are a nightmare. At first I felt as if I was continually
being watched by nursing staff. I feel so helpless not being able to help
him get better and [having] only my love and company to give.*

*I feel totally devastated by the accident and I know I'm surviving on
coffee and nerves. The Mothers' Unit [shared accommodation block] is
adequate but the thought of going up to bed at night and usually finding
a different mother in the next bed is off-putting. Don't get me wrong, I
don't know how I could even begin to cope if I couldn't stay here, knowing even at night, a phone call from the ward and within two minutes I
can be beside him, settling him.*

Extract from a mother's diary

There can be few more traumatic events for parents than their child's
illness or injury and consequent hospitalization. For over 30 years now,
especially (in the United Kingdom) since the publication of the Platt
Report into the welfare of children in hospital (Ministry of Health,

*I gratefully acknowledge the support of a Scottish Home & Health Department Nursing
Research Training Fellowship which enabled me to undertake the study upon which this
paper is based.

1959), attempts have been made to humanize the experience of hospitalization for children and their families.

A central tenet of this move toward family-centered care and increasing parental participation has been the encouragement of parents to live-in with their child during their hospitalization. In the UK the latest government advisory document on children in hospital is clear on this point:

> *A cardinal principle of hospital services for children is complete ease of access to the child by his parents, and other members of the family (as well as a mother or father 'a parent' could be a grandparent, aunt, uncle, sibling, nanny or close friend of the family). This is not a luxury.*

> Welfare of Children and Young People in Hospital.
> (Department of Health, 1991)

However, when it was first seriously proposed in the early 1960s, this approach was not particularly popular with some pediatric nurses. For example, one wrote of parents in *Nursing Times* as late as 1970 that:

> *Some are a support to the child and a help to the nurse. Some, fussy and neurotic, manage to be neither. Some again are unbelievably stupid—or perhaps it is too easy to forget that they just do not know things that any nurse takes for granted.*

> Anstice (1970)

As a pediatric nurse-teacher in the 1980s I was aware that the move toward parental living-in was being urged more as a slogan and being seen more as a panacea. I was concerned that parental living-in was being viewed as essentially unproblematic.

The rather simplistic reasoning seemed to be that parents living-in equals 'good,' therefore the more parents living-in and the longer that they live-in equals 'even better.' As children's nurses we seemed to be advocating and promoting an approach without having tried to truly understand the nature of this experience of living-in from either the parents' or the pediatric nurses' perspective.

STUDYING PARENTS' AND NURSES' EXPERIENCES

This was the opening for my study. The broad purposes of the study were threefold:

1. To better understand the lived experiences of parents who lived-in with their hospitalized child.

2. To better understand the experiences and practices of pediatric nurses as these related to resident parents.

3. To explore the nature of the relationships which existed and developed between parents and nurses.

For this study I drew on a wide tradition of interpretive phenomenology which was essentially hermeneutic and grew more so as the study and interpretation progressed (Darbyshire, 1992).

Fieldwork and data collection took place in a large Scottish pediatric hospital. Two wards were chosen; a general medical ward where the length of parents' stays was comparatively short, perhaps a week or two, and a burns and plastic surgery unit where parents could be living-in for up to three months.

Thirty parents were interviewed, either individually, as a couple, or in small focus group interviews. Twenty-seven qualified nurses were also interviewed either individually or in small focus groups (see Table 14.1).

The interview transcripts and fieldnotes were interpreted with a focus on participants' understandings, explanatory accounts, perceptions, and practices. Major themes were identified and while I sought to remain close to participants' everyday understandings, I also tried to bring further horizons of possible meaning (Gadamer, 1975) to bear on their accounts, where meanings were not taken to be private possessions but were viewed rather as common, relational, and constitutive of the person.

This brief description of methods is necessarily something of a gloss. The reality of interpretive research was captured much more faithfully by the Scottish curriculum theorist, Lawrence Stenhouse (1975) when he observed in relation to curriculum that:

> *The distance between plan and practice is not unlike that between Haig's headquarters and the mud of Flanders.*

Table 14.1 Living-in Interviews

Parents Interviewed, $n = 30$

	MOTHERS	FATHERS
Interviewed Individually	9	1
Interviewed With Partner	2	2
Interviewed in Four Focus Groups	15	1

Nurses Interviewed, $n = 27$

Interviewed Individually	12
Interviewed in Four Focus Groups	15

This study's findings suggest that previous attempts to understand live-in parents in primarily functional and instrumental terms of roles and responsibilities have given us a very limited insight into the meaning of their lived experience. Drawing on the work of Heidegger (1962) and Benner (1989), I have followed an ontological turn which sought to uncover more of the nature of Being-in-the-world as a parent, and particularly, of being a resident parent with your hospitalized child. Many of the parents' experiences were extremely difficult for them to articulate and they often echoed Van Manen's (1990) observation that parenting, ". . . is something primordial which defies literal language."

PARENTS' EXPERIENCES

The particular findings presented in this paper relate specifically to how resident parents' relationships with each other could foster hope, strength and healing, and how nurses' particular caring practices could support parents in this endeavor. My previous experience as a pediatric nurse had made me aware that some nurses treated the relationships between live-in parents with some suspicion. I suspected that "Unofficial parents groups," as I termed them, were often perceived to be a source of uninformed gossip or that they were dangerous in that parents would swap information about children's treatments, or more seriously, that they were a conspiracy of criticism against the nurses. The parents' accounts in this study however, suggested that their relationships were every bit as complex as those between parents and nurses.

Parents as Being "All in the Same Boat"

Like all researchers, I began the study with assumptions. One of my initial assumptions was that parents might consider that they had a common bond or purpose, by virtue of the fact that they were all live-in parents of a sick child, that they might see themselves as being "All in the same boat." However, the parents' accounts showed that this was too simplistic an assumption. Two mothers in a Focus Group interview discussed this shared bond:

> Mother # 2: *The girl I'm sharing a room with now, I don't see her all day and I've only slept with her two nights (laughs) . . . and I feel I've got to know her quite well and I could say that I really like her. I feel that even in this short time I know her as well as, well, somebody in my street that I only say 'Good Morning' to.*

> Mother # 4: *And you're kind of bonded anyway, because everybody's child's ill.*

> Mother # 2: *Well, that's right.*

> Mother # 4: *. . . so you've got that common thing between everyone.*

But the qualifying "kind of" is significant, for parents often felt isolated and alienated from each other by the uniqueness or severity of their child's condition. As one mother of a very seriously ill baby explained:

> *There's nobody comes and says, 'I've been through that,' my daughter was exactly the same, you know. They'll say 'I had a niece who had an*

accident and she was very bad but she's fine now.' But to be very bad and exactly the same is completely different.

However, there were many other factors which determined the nature of live-in parents' relationships. For many of the parents, the nature of their child's illness was a major factor in constituting their relationships with each other. I have described the parents' experiences in this respect as being "alone together." While parents may have felt a sense of connectedness and communality with other parents, they could also feel isolated and alienated by the uniqueness or by the severity of *their* child's condition. One mother described this vividly:

> *The mothers of the children with leukemia, they stick together because they're coming across the same problems. But Jamie's so peculiar, Jamie's problems are all of his own, nobody's like him. I can't really talk to the other mums about it because they're in here with their own problems and if they're not in here with a really bad problem, you . . . You don't really want to talk to somebody that's in with a kid that's got tonsillitis, although that can be serious, but you know . . . when your baby's life's in real danger . . .*

Jamie's mother articulated this dilemma well. His unique medical biography had isolated her even from the other parents' informal support group. She was in a "Catch 22" where she could not speak to mothers of seriously ill children for "they had their own worries," which her own experience had taught her were considerable.

Nor could she speak with mothers of comparatively less ill children for their experiences could have no real resonance with hers. In this situation, where individual differences were stressed by both parents and nurses, no one's child was quite the same as yours and not to be identical was to be significantly different.

Mutually Supporting and Helping

Parents described a range of ways in which they supported and helped each other, from listening to each other's concerns and anxieties to physically helping with the care of each other's child. But the most frequently described forms of supportive contact were talking and listening. Parents described how they *"just* listened" or *"just* talked" to each other. As in nurses' descriptions of their caring practices, the "justs," in Hochschild's (1983) memorable phrase, are used to linguistically smuggle caring out of the discourse.

Ironically, parents sensed that this sharing of their stories of their child's illness or treatment was considered to be something of an illegitimate, but nonetheless widespread activity. As one mother who lived in the Mothers' Unit [a small shared accommodation block within the hospital] noted:

> *There's a notice up in the Mothers' Unit [which says], 'Please Do Not Discuss Your Child's Illness With Other Parents As This Could Lead To Distress,' but it does go on—I mean, that's all that goes on all the time is talking about what's wrong with yours and theirs.*

What was the manager or administrator thinking of who devised such a sign? The mothers ignored it because it ignored them and their concerns. Their child's illness or injury was so overwhelmingly *omnipresent* in this situation, and such an inalienable part of their being as parents that it was inconceivable that the parents could spend a day without thinking and talking about their child. For me, the parents' accounts of their sharing of experiences and concerns allowed them to do what Benner and Wrubel (1989) described as "setting up the possibility of giving help and receiving help."

As with their relationships outside the hospital, there were varying degrees of closeness among parents. As one mother explained:

> *I suppose it's just the same as anywhere else, there are people that you will be able to talk to and get on with and there will be people that you will not. It's not that you are all in the same boat really, because you can still be in the same boat with someone and still not have anything in common with them and still not be able to talk to them.*

Some parents were able to establish relationships which moved beyond superficial politeness to a level where more meaningful and painful feelings could be shared. One significant factor here was that parents described how they needed to "get out"—or "get away from it all." Some of the parents' most valued conversations took place in a bar near to the hospital. Unfortunately space does not permit a fuller exploration here of the phenomenological notion of lived space in relation to the parents' and nurses' experiences and practices. One of the interesting questions raised by the study participants' accounts was

"Whose place was the pediatric ward?" Was it the parents' because they "lived" there but didn't "work" there, or was it the nurses' because they worked there but didn't "live" there?

Parents described the importance of maintaining hope if they were to "be there" in both the physical and existential sense, for their child and for the rest of the family. In addition to sharing concerns, parents would make a point of encouraging and trying to boost the morale of their fellow residents.

For example, one father, whose child had received massive scalds and was in the Burn Unit's intensive care area, stopped one day in the ward corridor to speak to two parents who were waiting outside the treatment room while their newly admitted child was being treated for comparatively minor scalds to his feet. This father then went into the treatment room to see the child and asked the nurses if the other parents could come in. He came out to tell the waiting parents that their son was fine, that he wasn't crying and that his scalds were really comparatively insignificant in comparison with his own son's injuries. Now to professionals this might seem incredibly insensitive and inappropriate, essentially to say that *your* worries and *your* child's injuries are minor—in comparison to *his*. But in his interview, this father made the telling point that any talk of "appropriate" levels of distress is itself inappropriate, because, as he said, "when it's *your* child, it's different." Interestingly here, in my interview with the two parents who were sitting in the corridor, they related this incident as one of the things which had been most helpful to them; the chance to speak to someone who had been through a similar experience as themselves.

Their accounts suggested that the relationships which existed among parents were of greater importance than nurses had previously assumed. Far from being involved in insensitive gossip, cliquishness or conspiracy, parents, through their quiet presencing were bearing witness to each other's distress and were creating more of a community of caring between themselves than they were able to articulate.

In saying this, however, the parents' accounts also showed that it would be wrong to romanticize this relationship or to see it as being unproblematic. Resident parents, like the rest of us, both liked and disliked other people. They made what we could call, qualitative distinctions and practiced a finely modulated comportment in their interactions. A very delicate social balancing operated between the expression of caring concern for another parent's well-being and insensitive prying. In their accounts, several parents brought out the difficulties involved in what I have called "parenting in public"—in being the parent of a sick child in a public arena where once private concerns, feelings and childcare practices could be pressed into becoming common property.

If parents were to maintain a sense of hope and if they were to move in from the moral margins of parenthood where some had been exiled, it helped enormously if they developed relationships with other parents who had, "gone through what they had gone through." Here, a collective identity based upon the child's unique illness or injury seemed especially important to parents. This gave a clearer focus to their sharing than did the more general bond which existed between all parents of a sick child in the hospital. While the latter was invoked to suggest more general changes which would be of universal benefit, such as improved living facilities, the disease-specific sharing seemed to provide something of a more uniquely personal value.

Fostering Hope Through Nurse Caring

I turn now to the nurses in this study and examine the ways in which their caring practices helped to foster and nurture a sense of hope and optimism among the resident parents. Firstly, I should say that it was so much more easy for nurses to dash and crush hopes than it was to strengthen them. The briefest comment, the slightest glance, was often enough to send parents' hopes plummeting. For example, one mother of a pre-teen girl who was semi-comatose following a head injury told of how she would keep a watchful vigil beside her daughter's bed, scanning her for the slightest sign of arousal or awakening. (Please don't suggest to me that parents couldn't quickly learn to do any routine observations!) If she moved slightly or seemed to respond at all to her, the mother would rush to tell the nurses, only to be told that these were not signs of recovery but, simply "neurological quirks" or "just reflexes." The nurses themselves agreed that this was a commonplace approach, for above all, they feared doing what several nurses described as "giving the parents false hope."

However, parents did also describe nurses' caring practices which fostered inclusion and involvement rather than exclusion and alienation, which valued and empowered rather than which leapt in and took over, and which supported and encouraged rather than demoralized. It was no surprise to learn that the parents were acutely aware of the abilities and different approaches of each nurse on the ward.

Parents did indeed "hope for the best" nurse but more than that, they would actively seek out those nurses whom they perceived to be "the best," i.e., the most caring.

They valued nurses who took time, found time, and spent time with their child. For example, when I asked a mother to tell me about anything that a nurse had done which she felt had really stood out for her or had really helped her daughter she told the story of "Sally" and her daughter's pillow. Sally, a final year student nurse, had been walking down the ward toward the door when she had seen that the child's head looked uncomfortable. She detoured across to the bed, gently rearranged the pillow, spoke briefly to the child and then went out of the ward on her original errand. How, we might ask, could such a trivial and insignificant action have become this mother's "paradigm" or exemplar of what was good nursing care for her daughter? The answer of course is that this nurse's caring practice was anything but trivial and was laden with significance. Through Sally's involved, caring stance, she had *noticed* that this child looked uncomfortable where another nurse might simply have passed by oblivious. Sally had *understood* the nature of discomfort and comfort and knew that these were elemental and fundamental nursing concerns. Sally had also *acted*, and through her caring practices of making comfortable and speaking with had affirmed for this mother that her daughter was still a person, despite the fact that she was comatose.* This "taking time," confirmed for parents that they and their child were not merely names on a kardex or care plan or bodies beside a bed.

Nurses whose approaches were warm and friendly were actively sought out by parents for these nurses helped parents feel less alienated and helped them reaffirm their sense of personhood.

One father, whose child was in intensive care, told of how he appreciated nurses who shared his sense of fighting optimism. He explained that:

> *I was just crying at the cot (crib) there and holding his hand and praying and saying to him 'fight it' and the nurse that was there, she comforted me and said, 'just keep hoping and it'll be alright, he's going to be alright.'*

---

*I owe this idea of "noticing, understanding and acting" to Martha MacLeod. For a sustained discussion of this idea in relation to expertise see MacLeod, 1990.

A mother similarly revealed how parents could gain strength from the nurses who were so supportive toward her and who had really "got behind" her baby in his fight. She observed that:

There are certain nurses who have cared for him quite often and I feel really care for him, not obviously as much as I do but who are really behind him . . . basically they keep your spirits up, they've kept mine up.

Nurses, Parents and Hope-full Relationship

Finally, I want to describe how the nature of the nurse-parent relationship could develop and become the involved, caring, connected, way of being with others where hope could be best fostered. A mother explained how nurse caring enabled her relationship with nurses to work out in practice:

Mother: *The relationship changed from them doing a job and me just being there. Basically, it wasn't really a relationship. They were just the nurse and I was the patient's mother . . . and they were always friendly but they were just doing their job. They were just being friendly to you because you were in distress, whereas now I feel they are more friends . . . you know they all do care so much, it's grand, it really is . . . because it is a relationship now.*

When I asked her what else she would have liked from nurses, she continued:

PD: *What would you have wanted from the nurses that wasn't given?*

Mother: *Not really anything. . . . I can't think of something . . . I honestly can't, because they've just given everything, they really have. It's made it possible for me to live through all this. . . . certainly I never feel at any time that they've forgotten about me, because although they're looking after Anna, I still feel that they care about me as well . . . I don't feel that I'm just there and nobody cares about me . . . I feel I'm part of the whole set up.*

Not all nurses were however, able to make parents feel "part of the whole set-up." Some nurses felt that parents' presence diminished their importance and their role in caring for the child. But other nurses lived out in their caring practices, a vision of participation which Gadamer (1984) articulated so well when he noted that:

> *Participation is a strange word. Its dialectic consists of the fact that participation is not taking parts, but in a way taking in the whole. Everybody who participates in something does not take something away, so that others cannot have it. The opposite is true; by sharing, by our participating in the things in which we are participating, we enrich them; they do not become smaller, but larger.*

CONCLUSION

In conclusion, this study suggests the need to reconceptualize live-in parents. We need to move beyond an instrumental notion of parents and of parenting as being a series of discrete child care activities. We need instead to consider being a parent as a unique way of being in the world with children.

We need the humility to listen to parents before we plan services for them. We need to learn from them before we presume to teach them. I believe that nurses need to develop a greater understanding of how live-in parents experience being in the hospital with their child, for only from a basis of such shared understandings can a system of genuinely shared care evolve.

REFERENCES

Anstice, E. (1970). "Nurse, where's my mummy"?, *Nursing Times*, 66(48), 1513–1518.

Benner, P., & Wrubel, J. (1989). *The primacy of caring: Stress and coping in health and illness.* Menlo Park: Addison-Wesley.

Darbyshire, P. (1992). *Parenting in public: A study of the experiences of parents who live-in with their hospitalized child, and of their relationships with pediatric nurses.* PhD Thesis, University of Edinburgh.

Department of Health. (1991). *Welfare of children and young people in hospital.* London: HMSO.

Gadamer, H-G. (1975). *Truth and method.* London: Sheed and Ward.

Gadamer, H-G. (1984). The hermeneutics of suspicion. In *Hermeneutics: Questions and prospects,* Edited by G. Shapiro and A. Sica. Amherst: University of Massachusetts Press.

Heidegger, M. (1962). *Being and time.* (J. Macquarrie & E. Robinson trans.) NI: SCM Press Ltd.

Hochschild, A. R. (1983). *The managed heart: The commercialization of human feeling.* Berkeley: University of California Press.

MacLeod, M. L. P. (1990). *Experience in everyday nursing practice: A Study of 'experienced' ward sisters.* PhD Thesis, University of Edinburgh.

Ministry of Health. (1959). *The welfare of children in hospital (The Platt Report).* London: HMSO.

Stenhouse, L. (1975). *An introduction to curriculum research and development.* London: Heinemann.

Van Manen, M. (1990). *Researching lived experience: Human science for an action sensitive pedagogy.* Ontario: Althouse Press.

Part VI

Invited Papers

15

A Naturalistic Inquiry of Post-Operative Pain After Therapeutic Touch

Rosze Barrington

Recovery time from surgical procedures such as open heart surgery is hastened when post-operative pain is well-controlled. No single method of pain management is right for every patient. To maximize comfort, nursing caring modalities potentiate, augment, or replace pharmacological intervention. Nurses use Kreiger's (1979) Therapeutic Touch (TT) as one caring modality to facilitate pain reduction. This study is a qualitative evaluation of outcomes to the nursing intervention of TT. The purpose of this study was to examine the patient's lived experience of TT during post-operative pain phenomena.

Therapeutic Touch

Therapeutic Touch involves the nurse's intent to help and to heal as she or he attempts to unblock the flow of life energy in order to promote healing. TT has been taught in both undergraduate and graduate schools of nursing throughout the world (Krieger, 1990). TT is a unique caring modality of the nurse's therapeutic use of self.

I wish to thank the following for rendering support, guidance, and consultation to this study: University of Portland School of Nursing, Center for Nursing Research; Delores Gaut, PhD, RN; Rod Galyen, MN, NP, RN; Nancy Powers, DN, NP, RN; Rita Herlong, MS, NP, RN; Sylvia McSkimming, PhD, RN.

Nurse scientists have engaged in researching the process of TT and its effects, and speculated on the mechanism of action. The basic assumption one accepts in order to understand the practice of TT is that humans act in totality as open systems in constant and mutual interaction with environment. Humans and environment are energy fields, each maintaining their own integrity in a universe of open systems (Rogers, 1990; Krieger, 1981).

TT derives from an ancient religious practice of "laying on of hands." Formalized for use by nurses without a religious context, Krieger (1979) outlines four phases of TT: (a) *Centering*, through which the nurse enters a meditative state; (b) *Assessment*, for the purpose of identifying imbalances within the patient field by placing hands two-to-six inches over the patient's body in a head-to-toe fashion; (c) *Smoothing*, in which nurse's hands move in a sweeping motion head-to toe over the patient field to remove congestion; and (d) *Modulation*, through aligning nurse and patient energy with intent to mobilize the patient's intrinsic healing pattern. Assessment phase is then repeated.

LITERATURE REVIEW

Quantitative Evaluation of TT Effects

Research and theory development are ongoing surrounding the effects and mechanism of action of TT. Four primary effects of TT have been suggested: Decreased anxiety (Heidt, 1981; Quinn, 1984, 1989; Randolph, 1984), induced physiologic relaxation (Krieger, Peper, & Ancoli, 1979; Krieger, 1979), decreased post-operative pain (Meehan, 1990), decreased pain due to tension (Keller & Bzdek, 1986), facilitation of the healing process (Wirth, 1990; Grad, Cadoret, & Paul, 1961; Krieger, 1973; Quinn & Strelkauskas, 1993), and facilitating growth process in plants (Grad, 1965). Most studies have been primarily experimental in design.

Qualitative Study of TT

Three qualitative studies sought to define the lived experience of TT through interviewing both TT practitioners and/or their ongoing clients. It is significant to note that the recipients of TT who participated in this study were familiar with the concept and practice of TT. Samarel

(1992) reports that study respondents expressed a fulfilling experience which facilitated personal growth from engaging in TT. Data suggest a shift from physiological sensations to emotional and/or spiritual awareness. Lionberger (1985) focused on the phenomenon of nurses' interpretation of their practice of TT. Heidt (1991), through grounded theory, studied reports of highly experienced TT practitioners who described the concept of opening to the flow of a universal life energy. This study refined the original four phases developed by Dr. Krieger as data identified components of the TT experience to include: quieting, affirming, intending, attuning, planning, unblocking, engaging, and enlivening.

Speculations of TT Mechanism on Pain Reduction

The exact mechanism behind why TT works to reduce pain is unknown. Boguslawski (1990) speculates that the pain is blocked through the reduction of anxiety, decreased edema which relieves pressure placed on the nerve endings, or any increased activation of the body's own analgesics—the endorphins. Some practitioners envision TT as a communication tool used to accentuate the nurse-patient therapeutic relationship (Heidt, 1990). Many nurses who perform TT believe that: (a) There exists a universal, healing energy that can be accessed through intent of the practitioner and (b) That the universal energy is then transmitted through the interaction of human energy fields (Krieger, 1979; Heidt, 1990; Jurgens, Meehan, & Wilson, 1987).

Controversy over methodology and evaluation of TT effects has characterized the TT research to date. Studies on pain management have attempted to evaluate what is defined as a human subjective phenomenon. Pain is a unitary, whole person phenomenon involving cognitive and physiologic components which are interpreted through the perception of the person in pain. Human pain is a lived experience. The person in pain determines the nature, location, and meaning of the pain experience. It is uniquely personal. There is minimal qualitative data reporting the effects of TT on the human phenomenon of pain. The naturalistic inquiry method of phenomenology would seem appropriate to studying pain perception phenomena.

Until this study, there was no study of surgical patients which described qualitatively the patient's perception of pain experiences pre- and post-operatively after receiving TT. No previous qualitative study reported had selected participants who were unaware of the potential effects or theoretical basis of the practice of TT.

Theoretical Rationale

Caring is often expressed through modes of touch. Touch has been used as a therapeutic gesture since ancient times. From a caring nursing model, touch is seen as intentional communication of empathy, support, and nurturance. The nurse, involved in therapeutic use of self, uses touch as effective and intentional communication to enact healing. In TT, nurses use compassionate intent to potentiate the patient's capacity to mobilize self-healing.

A primary theoretical base which guided this study is Rogerian Nursing Science of Unitary Human Beings (Rogers, 1970). A central theme is the Rogers' Principle of Integrality which envisions that humans are energy fields, with characteristics of integrality, motion, and patterning in constant and mutual process with their environment. Energy signifies the dynamic nature of the field (Rogers, 1970).

In TT, one focuses attention to the hands in order to sense the energy field of another. Humans as energy fields co-exist within a cosmos of environmental energy fields. Interaction between fields occurs in totality. When fields interconnect, a new field is created encompassing both fields through mutual process. Rogers (1992) suggests that patterns are the detectable manifestation of the mutual process. Patterns manifest pandimensionally in the form of a person's experience, perceptions, and expressions (Cowling, 1990).

Disease, illness, and pain are pattern manifestations which may signify disruption in the organization of the human field (Rogers, 1970). The disruption may be a result of energy loss, energy accumulation, or energy blockage. In health, one has the pattern of abundant and flowing energy.

Theoretical Assumptions

The assumptions underlying this study were as follows:

1. People are irreducible unitary beings who are open vibrating energy fields extending beyond the skin and interacting totally and pandimensionally with environmental energy fields through energy patterning.

2. Health is a relative index of field patterning, evolving from a continuous mutual interaction of human energy fields with environmental fields.

3. Nurses engage in intentional therapeutic use of self to mobilize a client's intrinsic healing pattern.

4. Pain is a subjective, multifaceted unitary field phenomena which warrants a holistic treatment approach.

PURPOSE

The purpose of this study was to study the nurse caring modality of therapeutic use of self through Therapeutic Touch. The study examines the patient's lived experience of TT during a person's post-operative pain phenomena.

METHOD

Design

The study utilizes naturalistic inquiry in a Level I, qualitative descriptive design. The phenomenological method followed is that developed by Beekman of the Utrecht School, which aims to uncover the foundations of certain phenomena by analysis of situations (Lynch-Sauer, 1985). This project followed the themes of Reinharz's (1983) five steps of phenomenological experience transformation into knowledge. These steps are: (1) Experience is transformed into language which then (2) transforms what we see and hear into understanding, then (3) transforms understanding into clarifying concept categories, then (4) transforms concept categories into a written document, then (5) the audience transforms the document into an understanding of the human experience described.

Informant Sample

The target population was persons experiencing post-operative pain. The purposive sample, *n* of six, ages 39–77 years old, five males and one female, expressed a wide range of socio-economic and educational levels. Informants were selected from stable hospitalized patients scheduled for coronary artery bypass surgery within 24 hours of my initial contact. Potential participants were approached the evening prior to surgery to elicit their participation and secure informed consent. Participants were provided with a written description of how TT is performed without explanation of energy field theory or expectations to outcomes. None had previous experience with TT.

Excluded from participation were those people who: Were unable to communicate in spoken English; had mental or cognitive impairment; and/or exhibited neurosensory deficits. Any informants who would have suffered complications requiring re-transfer to intensive care unit or surgery were to be eliminated from the study. One participant dropped midway through the study voluntarily.

Operational Definitions

Therapeutic Touch   TT, defined through the Krieger Protocol (1979), was performed in the following manner with each participant:

1. The researcher removed distractions by closing the door to the private patient room.

2. The informants, dressed in hospital gowns, were positioned either supine or sitting. The informant was asked to take deep breaths and think calm thoughts. Eyes remained closed or open.

3. The researcher entered a meditative state. She then moved her hands slowly two-to-six inches from the informant's body surface in a head-to-toe direction, making mental note of any sensations felt.

4. *Smoothing* and *Modulation* were then performed.

5. With hands held two-to-six inches from the informant's body surface, the researcher placed hands over any area where imbalances were detected. Intentional healing energy, caring, and love were directed to the informant.

6. Reassessment then occurred. When continued imbalances were perceived, the researcher repeated Steps 4 and 5.

The Pain Experience   Pain is defined by the McCaffery (1972) definition. "Pain is whatever the experiencing person says it is and exists whenever he says it does" (p. 8).

Perception   The informant's perception of pain was defined as the informant's verbal description of quality, duration, severity and intensity of pain. The informant's correlation of provoking and relieving factors were included as perception of the pain experience. Any non-verbal cues (grimacing, wincing, frowning, posture guarding, shallow breathing) that the researcher determined to possibly signify pain, were validated by open-ended questioning, such as "What are you experiencing now?"

Post-Operative Experience　　The experience was described as days two through five, post-coronary artery bypass surgery and occurred in a hospital intermediate care unit.

Medications　　Medications were considered as extraneous variables and defined as any pharmaceutical analgesics or tranquilizers administered. These were equivocated.

Instruments

Instruments used were:

1. Therapeutic Touch, Krieger (1979) Protocol.

2. Five semi-structured interviews per informant.

3. McCaffery-Beebe (1989) Vertical Visual Analog Scale (VVAS).

4. Reinharz (1983) Five-Step Phenomenological Process.

5. Krieger Subjective Experience of Therapeutic Touch Survey (SETTS) Tool (Ferguson, 1986).

6. Bracketing Tool of a Researcher Log.

Procedure

The researcher, an experienced practitioner of TT, used the Krieger SETTS Tool in order to assess her TT performance competency criteria. A high score was recorded indicating an experienced TT practitioner.

The setting chosen was a large metropolitan hospital, prominent for the provision of comprehensive care of people with cardiovascular disease. The study was conducted in the private patient room on an intermediate care unit in the summer of 1992.

Potential informants were approached the evening prior to surgery. Informed consent was attained. The initial pre-surgical semistructured interview was held and tape recorded in the informant's hospital room.

The purpose of the pre-operative interview was to establish pattern identification of one's perception, expression, and experience of pain and "best feelings they had ever experienced."

Two post-operative TT sessions occurred. One was 48–56 hours after surgery and the second, 24 hours later. An audiotaped interview documented the informant's perceptions of the pre-TT pain experience including quantification through the VVAS. TT was then performed, after which a second interview was conducted to ascertain a description of the pain levels and experiences felt, thought, or envisioned during the TT. This procedure was repeated the next evening using the same format.

Within one hour after the close of each TT/interview session, the researcher bracketed using the Researcher Log entry of personal experiences and reflections which occurred during the TT session and interview. The Log, used to expose and release preconceived meanings of the researcher, also aided in documenting a transformation of the lived experience of the researcher. TT, as a field phenomena, has the potential to transform and repattern the energy field of the researcher (Reeder, 1993; Quinn and Strelkauskas, 1993) through mutual process.

Analysis of Data

The taped interviews were transcribed by the researcher. The transcriptions were analyzed in a method where themes of experiences were extracted. Exact words were used. The themes of all informants were compared. The analysis transformed the informant's perceptions of the pain and the TT experience into categories. The data were then reduced to concepts into a descriptive matrix to combine parallel data from the multiple interviews. The computer analysis was performed through ethnographic principles and the use of Spradley's (1979) universal semantic relationships as a guide. An independent nurse researcher reviewed all transcripts for the purpose of confirming theme forms that emerged as categories. The same analysis format was used to examine the Researcher Log.

FINDINGS

Analyses of findings were guided by Cowling's (1990) template for pattern-based practice. Use of the template assisted in the identification of patterns manifested as experience, perception, and expression. Pre-operative pattern identification revealed that all had significant past history of pain experiences. It is significant to note that none of the subjects reported colors, visions, or other sensations during past pain or pain treatment experiences.

In 66 percent of the cases, the "best feeling" described pre-operatively was grossly similar to what the informants reported to have felt during TT. This phenomena has not previously been reported in the literature.

Post-TT interview analysis revealed a pandimensional manifestation of the pain experience during and after TT sessions. After the TT session which lasted three-to-eight minutes, informants' patterns were: (a) *Experiences* relating to comfort, sensations, visions, and energy flow; (b) *Expressions* relating to a changed affect noted by the researcher; and (c) *Perception* relating to insights received during or after TT.

Pandimensional experiences are outlined in Figure 15.1. In 100 per-

EXPERIENCES	$n=6$	
Comfort	No.	%
Pain reduced or eliminated	6	100
Relaxation reported	5	83
Breathing better—"more air"	3	50
Physical and Visual		
No sensations	1	16
Did not respond to question	1	16
Soothing	2	33
Pain, discomfort being drawn away	4	66
Peace	1	16
Colors—vivid scenery	3	50
PERCEPTIONS		
Insights	4	66
Felt and "energy"	4	66
Temperature changes	4	66
Aware of nurse-patient intuitive connection	3	50
EXPRESSIONS		
Affect Change	6	100
Febrile episodes, (possible immunological response) Temp. >38.4° C after first Therapeutic Touch Session.	3	50

Figure 15.1 Pandimensional Experience.

cent of the cases, pain was eliminated or significantly reduced. Relaxation was reported in 83 percent of the informants. Fifty percent of the informants reported that they had more air and could breathe better. Sensations, reported by 66 percent of the informants, were soothing feelings, peace, and/or a sensation that pain and discomfort were being drawn away from their bodies. Vivid colors or scenery were seen by 50 percent of the informants.

Experiences   Examples of experiences follow: One informant, who had his eyes closed during the session nearly described the four phases of TT per Krieger protocol: ". . . it feels like a part was drawing energy or soreness out or something. Part of it felt like warmth, like I was holding my granddaughter. . . part of it felt like, at night, when I go to sleep and my back is aching and I try and force myself to relax . . . warm . . . soothing."

A second informant did not report visions or sensations initially, but did begin seeing colors after the first session. Researcher Log reveals that the researcher had visualized the newly formed coronary artery bypass delivering flowing life-giving blood during the TT session. The informant's second session revealed that during the evening after TT, he had begun to experience visions each time he closed his eyes:

> I see the color red. I see things all bright red. I have never seen red before . . . It is the brightest pinkest red . . . I am seeing swirls, I am seeing movement.

The second TT session began. The researcher reported looking outside the window to see a blue-gray cloud cover. After the TT the informant reported:

> I started seeing red when I first closed my eyes. And, then I never saw it again. It changed to a mild, light blue-gray, a comfortable gray. . . . I have flowing feelings, that things were changing position in me. It's like a magnetism.

Perceptions   The perceptions involved an awareness beyond experience. Sixty-six percent of the informants reported having insights which "came to them" either during the session or the evening after the first TT session. One stated, "I kind of got the idea that there are just more happier things to look forward to." Sixty-six percent of the informants reported that they felt "energy" or temperature changes.

Fifty percent indicated that they were aware of a nurse-patient intuitive connection. The researcher noted feeling burning, heat, tingling, cramping sensations in her hands during assessment and modulation, which is commonly reported by TT practitioners. During one encounter, the researcher felt an overwhelming feeling of sorrow and a sadness which was powerful and fleeting in nature. The informant then stated in the post-TT interview, "I know you felt it, I know you felt it. You must have felt that pain. I know, didn't you?" Another informant stated, "You felt the vibes coming off me." This phenomena may be a replication of what Quinn and Strelkauskas (1993) reported as a connectedness between nurse and client during TT suggesting that nurse and client resonate in a pattern of shared consciousness.

Expressions The expressions of the pain experience after TT showed a marked change in affect in 100 percent of the informants. All cases exhibited a decreased rate of breathing and talking in lowered vocal pitch and intensity. Their eyes, glazed and watery, exhibited a dreamlike state. They all exhibited delayed answer-response time in questioning.

In 50 percent of the cases, informants experienced an oral body temperature reading of $>38.4°$ C. during the evening after the first TT session, lasting approximately four hours. Medical workup, independent of this study, did not reveal a significantly causative pathology. The fevers spontaneously resolved without sequelae.

All but one of the participants rated the TT intervention to be a good thing. One participant was dropped after the first TT session. He became irritated and hostile after the TT and stated that he thought that the study was "kooky." He was, however, the only person to express an understanding of the concept behind TT, "If what you are trying to say is that there is some kind of energy that takes place between you and the patient, uh, I question that." No participant was told of the concept of energy field patterning which underlies TT.

DISCUSSION AND SUMMARY

The study offers several important findings. Primarily the data offer substantial evidence that TT reduces or eliminates post-operative pain, produces perceived relaxation, soothing, calming, and an overall feeling of well-being.

Two incidental findings involve immunity and intentionality. First, data suggest a possible increased immune response in 50 percent of the patients who exhibited transient febrile episodes. This finding may serve to build on early studies that exhibited accelerated wound healing in mice (Grad, et al., 1961) and increased hemoglobin levels (Krieger, 1973). Quinn and Strelkauskas (1993) are currently engaged in studying the immunological effects of TT, noting increased helper T_4 cells and decreased suppressor T_8 cells in people who participated in TT.

Secondly, the reports of participants substantiate the existence of mutual process pattern manifestations between energy fields. Participants in the study reported that intent to care on the part of the TT practitioner is received by the recipient of TT as pattern manifestations in the form of visions, feelings, and insights. The Researcher Log reported experiencing sensations, colors, and visions that parallelled those of the informants.

Limitations

There were three possible limitations to the design of the study. One was the use of the researcher as the TT practitioner, possibly affording bias to the informants' reports. A second limitation was that of the previous TT experience of the researcher offering potential bias to the analysis of the transcriptions. Bracketing and Researcher Log were used to offset this bias. A check for representativeness was made through utilizing an independent researcher to read the transcripts and review the descriptive matrix. Ideally, further studies investigating the concept of intentionality would be better performed by two researchers: one performing TT and a second as interviewer while the Researcher Log is written. A third limitation was the possible confounding effect of medications. The nature and time of administration of medications were evaluated. Because the pain was relieved within three-to-eight minutes of TT initiation, and medications had been administered one to ten hours prior to the TT session, it was determined that there was no significant confounding effect of medication in this study.

Implications for Nursing

The study provides a basis for expanding the alternatives to pain management. Positive outcomes in reducing the patient's pain in a short amount of time may entice more nurses to learn this technique, and health care institutions to support its use by nurses.

The study lends support to Rogers' Science of Unitary Human Beings. Data provide a basis to support Rogers' principle of integrality in the description of pandimensional experience and mutual process.

The concept of "Intention to Care," one criteria of Caring Nursing Science outlined by Gaut (1986) is a basis for caring action within the practice of TT. The findings of this study suggest positive outcome of caring intention.

Future Research Suggested

As we continue to investigate the phenomena of lived experiences, it may be wise to investigate the concept of "Intention" as it affects the outcome of mutual process between nurses and their clients. Further studies, perhaps, involving triangulation of quantitative and qualitative methodology, would be appropriate to investigate immunological effect of TT that may have been evident in the febrile episodes documented.

SUMMARY

Intention to help or to heal, perhaps, is a primary criteria for mobilizing a nurse's therapeutic use of self. TT enhances the mutual process relationship of nurse and patient, allows for the nurse's conscious intent to care, and results in a positive client outcome.

REFERENCES

Boguslawski, M. (1990). Unitary human field practice modalities, pp. 83–92. In Barrett, E. A. (Ed.), *Visions of Rogers' science-based nursing.* New York: National League for Nursing Press.

Cowling, W. R. (1990). A Template for unitary pattern-based nursing practice, pp. 45–65. In Barrett, E. A. (Ed.), *Visions of Rogers' science-based nursing.* New York: National League for Nursing Press.

Ferguson, C. K. (1986). *Subjective Experience of Therapeutic Touch Survey (SETTS) psychometric examination of the instrument.* Doctoral Dissertation. Austin: University of Texas.

Gaut, D. (1986). Evaluating caring competencies in nursing. *Topics in Clinical Nursing, 8,* 77–83.

Grad, B. (1965). Some biological effects of the laying-on of hands: Review of experiments with animals and plants. *Journal of the American Society of Psychical Research, 59,* 95–127.

Grad, B., Cadoret, R. J., & Paul, G. I. (1961). An unorthodox method of wound healing in mice. *International Journal of Parapsychology, 5,* 5–24.

Heidt, P. R. (1981). Effect of Therapeutic Touch on anxiety levels of hospitalized patients. *Nursing Research, 30*(91), 32–37.

Heidt, P. R. (1990). Openness: A qualitative analysis of nurses' and patients' experiences of Therapeutic Touch. *Image: Journal of Nursing Scholarship, 22*(3), 180–186.

Heidt, P. R. (1991). Helping patients to rest: Clinical studies in Therapeutic Touch. *Holistic Nursing Practice, 5*(4), 57–66.

Jurgens, A., Meehan, T. C., & Wilson, H. L. (1987). Therapeutic Touch as a nursing intervention. *Holistic Nursing Practice, 2*(1), 1–14.

Keller, E., & Bzdek, V. M. (1986). Effects of Therapeutic Touch on tension headache pain. *Nursing Research, 35*(2), 101–106.

Krieger, D. (1973). The relationship of touch, with the intent to help or to heal, to subjects' in-vivo hemoglobin values: A study in personalized interaction. In *Proceedings of the Ninth American Nurses Association Research Conference.* New York: American Nurses Association.

Krieger, D. (1979). *The Therapeutic Touch: How to use your hands to help or to heal.* New York: Prentice Hall Press.

Krieger, D. (1981). *Health nursing practices, the renaissance nurse.* Philadelphia: J. B. Lippincott Company.

Krieger, D. (1990). *Imprint.* NSNA.

Krieger, D., Peper, E., & Ancoli, S. (1979). Therapeutic Touch: Searching for evidence of physiological change. *American Journal of Nursing,* (79), 660–662.

Lionberger, H. J. (1985). An interpretive study of nurses' practice of TT. Doctoral dissertation. University of California at San Francisco. *Dissertation Abstracts International, 46*(8), 2624B.

Lynch-Sauer, J. (1985). Using phenomenological research method to study nursing phenomena. In Leininger, M. M. (Ed.), *Qualitative research methods in nursing.* Orlando: Grune & Stratton, Inc.

McCaffery, M. (1972). *Nursing Management of the patient with pain.* Philadelphia: J. B. Lippincott Co.

McCaffery, M., & Beebe, A. (1989). *Pain: Clinical manual for nursing practice.* St. Louis: C. V. Mosby Co.

Meehan, T. C. (1990). The science of unitary human beings and theory-based practice: Therapeutic Touch, 67–82. In Barrett, E. A. (Ed.), *Visions of Rogers' science-based nursing.* New York: National League for Nursing Press.

Quinn, J. F. (1984). Therapeutic Touch as energy exchange. Testing the theory. *Advances in Nursing Science, 6(2),* 42–49.

Quinn, J. F. (1989). Therapeutic Touch as energy exchange: Replication and extension. *Nursing Science Quarterly, 2(2),* 79–87.

Quinn, J. F., & Strelkauskas, A. J. (1993). Psychoimmunologic effects of Therapeutic Touch on practitioners and recently bereaved recipients: A pilot study. *Advances in Nursing Science, 15(4),* 13–26.

Randolph, G. L. (1984). Therapeutic and physical touch: Physiologic response to stressful stimuli. *Nursing Research, 33(1),* 33–36.

Reeder, F. (1993). Personal Communication, Portland, OR.

Reinharz, S. (1983). Phenomenology as a dynamic process. *Phenomenology and Pedagogy, 1,* 77–79.

Rogers, M. E. (1970). *An introduction to the theoretical basis of nursing.* Philadelphia: F. A. Davis Company.

Rogers, M. E. (1990). Nursing: Science of unitary, irreducible, human beings: Update 1990, 5–12. In Barrett, E. A. (Ed.) *Visions of Rogers' science-based nursing.* New York: National League for Nursing Press.

Rogers, M. E. (1992). Personal Communication. New York, NY.

Samarel, N. (1992). The experience of receiving Therapeutic Touch. *Journal of Advanced Nursing, 17(6),* 651–657.

Spradley, J. P. (1979). *The ethnographic interview.* New York: Holt, Rinehart & Winston.

Wirth, D. (1990). The effects of non-contact Therapeutic Touch on healing rate of full thickness dermal wounds. *Subtle Energies, 1(1),* 1–20.

16

Harmony: The Path to Health

Carol L. S. Simonson

HARMONY: A NATIVE AMERICAN PERSPECTIVE

As nurses, we care for others as they strive to maintain, regain, establish, or promote their own or significant others' health. What do we mean when we use the term "health"? We need to consider this meaning because it serves as a guide for our nursing interactions with these others. Without a clear understanding of the goal toward which we are striving, how can we care appropriately for them? In this paper, I am proposing that we look more closely at the term "harmony" as descriptive of the path toward and the destination for anyone seeking "health."

The Navajos use the word *hozho* to describe "the intellectual concept of order, the emotional state of happiness, the moral notion of good, the biological condition of health and well being, and the aesthetic dimensions of balance, harmony and beauty" (Witherspoon, 1977, p. 154). According to Witherspoon, *hozho* is a concept central to Navajo culture; it is descriptive of "a unity of experience, and the goal of Navajo life" (p. 154); it encapsulates the ontology of the Navajo.

The faculty of the University of New Mexico-Gallup Campus Nursing Program (UNM/Gallup) which I studied in 1990 had adapted this Navajo term for use in their philosophy and conceptual framework as descriptive of a major concept guiding their program. They, however, substituted the word "harmony" for *hozho* to make it more understandable to English-speakers. As I studied and worked with this faculty, I asked how they were using the term harmony and began to consider its potential for guiding nursing actions as a descriptor of health. While giving credit to the Navajos and Witherspoon, the UNM/Gallup "Philosophy" explains:

> *Harmony is a term used to describe the human experience of maximum potential of wellness in the mental, physical, and spiritual dimensions. . . . A harmonious state exists when the individual and his relation to society, family, spiritual and natural worlds is [sic] in accord. The individual is not only internally consistent but also in a positive relationship with his external environment. The individual strives consistently to meet the demands of his internal and external words. When his behavior results in meeting his needs harmony is produced, when a deviation occurs disharmony results.* (University of New Mexico-Gallup Campus Nursing Program, 1989, pp. 4–5.)

I am proposing that harmony, as explained in the UNM/Gallup "Philosophy," is not only descriptive of a potential for wellness, it appropriately describes health. I further propose there are other aspects to the concept of harmony, or *hozho*, which suit it for use by nurses as a synonym for health. I believe this concept of harmony is useful in directing our caring as nurses because of its holism and inclusiveness. In this paper, I will explore the concept of harmony as defined in the preceding excerpt. Additionally, I will explain other uses of the term that can enhance and expand our understanding of the concept as descriptive of health.

HARMONY RELATED TO NURSING

Our description begins with a reference to "the human experience." Here the emphasis is clearly placed upon the human, the person, as the focus. It is the experience of that human which must be considered, the phenomenon of that person's existence which is important. In nursing we deal with a client's responses to problems or potential problems in health-related matters, according to the American Nurses Association (1973). This means we focus upon the experience of that client, the world as that individual perceives and understands it. The nurse's perception and experience of the world are not what are of prime importance. What is important is the manner in which the client is experiencing the world. That experience is embodied within the client and cannot be reduced to a scientific, quantifiable interpretation imposed from the outside. As nurses, we work with the client and together define priorities, plan interventions, and evaluate the results of our interactions.

Next is the reference to "maximum potential." Again, we are dealing with the potential for this client, not some abstract potential for people in general. What is this client capable of, and what are the resources available to this client, nurses, and other health care workers assisting this individual? What does this client envision as possible and can we expand that vision through education or bringing to bear resources which might enhance this client's potential? The maximum potential may be restoration of full physical capabilities following an injury. It may be a healing of interpersonal conflicts with significant others. It may be learning to accept assistance with activities of daily living during or following a debilitating illness. It may be assisting the client with a peaceful death. Whatever the potential is, given the client and the health-threatening situation, we assist clients to achieve what is maximally possible for them in their situation.

Harmony involves "the mental, physical, and spiritual dimensions" of a person's life. This is an inclusive view. Every dimension of one's life is intertwined with every other dimension. It is not possible to separate out the physical, for example, and not to expect a physical change to impact the other dimensions. When we care for a person experiencing pain, as nurses we recognize its psychological aspects (McCaffery & Beebe, 1989). In speaking of the broader condition of suffering, Cassell has stated, "Just as the sufferer is unique and individual, suffering is unavoidably social. . . . It is not the severity of the pain or insult that is crucial to suffering, but rather what is believed it represents or will become" (1992, p. 6). As nurses we take into account all dimensions of a client's life as necessarily interrelated and acknowledge that what impacts one dimension impacts all dimensions. This is also part of maintaining a holistic view of persons.

A faculty member in the UNM/Gallup program gave the following example:

> When I discuss [harmony] with the students, . . . I usually . . . start
> out with all the needs being met—oxygen and safety and all those
> needs—but even if you have all those needs met, that doesn't mean

you're in a state of wellness. We have to consider the relationship is-sues. Things like how you are with your family, how you are with the world, how you are with the natural and the supernatural. . . . And then I try and discuss what it means to be fairly physically healthy but to feel like you've lost touch with your roots or any sense of the spirit. Or what it feels like to be physically healthy but have had a terrible argument with your mother—that sense of disharmony being that sense of being cut off. (Simonson, 1991, p. 59)

Because we as nurses view persons holistically, we know we must in-teract with the client, taking into account all dimensions of their life.

The above quote speaks also to the statement "the individual and his relation to society, family, spiritual and natural worlds." In a 1970 article, Luckmann spoke of the many small life worlds we each inhabit. In one sense Luckmann argued that people live in and move between many different worlds or contexts as they go through their lives, worlds which may or may not be connected. But in another sense Luckmann pointed out that through the life of the individual those worlds are connected and the connections are constructed by that indi-vidual's existence. Harmony reveals the congruent relationship be-tween all those small life worlds. In harmony, those worlds are in accord.

The fifth part of the statement speaks of the individual being "inter-nally consistent." One way to think of this is to think of homeostasis. *Taber's Cyclopedic Medical Dictionary* (1993) defined homeostasis as a "state of equilibrium of the internal environment of the body that is maintained by dynamic processes of feedback and regulation . . . a dynamic equilibrium" (p. 909). As nurses we work with our medical colleagues carrying out dependent and collaborative functions, many of which are aimed at assisting the individual to retain or regain ho-meostasis. It may be a little troubling if one thinks that harmony can only be achieved when a state of homeostasis exists. What, then, of the dying client or the client with a long-term or chronic illness? Go back to that portion of the statement which speaks of "maximum potential." Taking the statement as a whole, harmony, or health, is reaching the nearest state possible to homeostasis for that client at that time. One is not held up to an impossible goal but the dynamic status of the internal aspects of the individual is recognized, and maximum potential, not perfection, is the goal.

"A positive relationship with his external environment" is the next consideration. "Positive" implies that something is helpful, cooperative, useful, effective. To be in a positive relationship means to be in a relationship that is working, that contributes to well-being. One's actions can promote effective use of one's self within all the small life worlds one inhabits. In harmony, one is able to act in a way which contributes to the achievement of one's maximum potential. If there are threats to the client's physical well-being, the client utilizes resources to deal with those threats which lessen or eliminate their impact. If there are threats to the client's emotional or spiritual well-being, the client is able to cope with those threats in order to maintain an effective way of life.

The final portion of the preceding explanation meshes with the previous two, "strives consistently to meet the demands of his internal and external worlds." This statement reflects the dynamic state in which an individual lives. In striving to maintain homeostasis, one's body is constantly monitoring feedback and regulating itself, attempting to maintain itself "within normal limits" as we commonly phrase it. The same is true of our responses to the external world. Paying attention to feedback as one interacts with all one encounters in one's surroundings is essential to the enactment of appropriate responses to meet the demands of that external environment. It is important to keep in mind, also, that it is the individual who attaches meaning to what is occurring and it is that meaning which directs the response (Benner, 1985). The quote from Cassell, earlier, about the meaning of suffering also speaks of this. And whether we are referring to internal regulatory mechanisms or innate or learned responses to external stimuli, the individual exists in a dynamic state of adjustment. As another faculty member from UNM/Gallup explained about harmony:

> *I think, to the credit of the Native American population, that they have had that [harmony] as part of their cultural heritage all along. . . . To me it is the realization that all frameworks of your life must be in alignment, almost like homeostasis in your system. And if they are not, if something is out of alignment, it's going to impact on the homeostasis of the physiological system. I think that 'harmony' is a term that [nurses] should have had a long time ago.* (Simonson, 1991, p. 56)

HARMONY RELATED TO MUSIC

At this point I shall move on to a different aspect of the concept of harmony which may enhance your understanding of how it serves as descriptor for both the path toward and the destination of health. Almost immediately when you ask anyone what harmony means to them, they refer to music. With this in mind, I asked three musicians, two of whom use music in their work, to tell me what harmony meant to them and if they felt there was any relationship between harmony and health. Their responses were illuminating and provided a perspective which expanded my own understanding of harmony.

First, they all stated, in one way or another, that the term harmony conveys a sense of balance in that notes are combined in such a way that pleasing chords or sounds are produced. One person stated that harmony is "where parts have relationship and where the whole is greater than the sum of the parts—a gestalt situation" (J. Ballard, personal communication, January 8, 1993). There was no attempt to define harmony in terms of a particular tonal scale, for instance, or to tie the definition to a particular type of music, just that the notes went together in a pleasing way. The musicians spoke of a sense of tranquility, peace, and well-being which comes when one listens to harmonious music. They spoke of harmony as producing wholeness and indicating that things were in balance. They used the terms "dissonance" and "discord" to indicate disharmony or the opposite of harmony. When asked to respond to any relationship they perceived between harmony and health, one volunteered that, "Health results when one's physical, mental, and spiritual sides (or body, mind, spirit) function in harmony with each other" (L. Foshee, personal communication, January 2, 1993). Another commented, "Health is wholeness, is a state of harmony" (J. Ballard, personal communication, January 8, 1993).

The preceding statements can be analyzed as was the previous description of harmony. (It must be stated that none of the musicians had read or heard the UNM/Gallup statement about harmony.) A sense of balance, for instance, is descriptive of the "harmonious state [which] exists when the individual and his relation to society, family, spiritual and natural worlds is [sic] in accord" (University of New Mexico-Gallup Campus Nursing Program, 1989, p. 4). The reference to harmonious music producing tranquility, peace, and well-being in the listener also speaks to this. The musician's statement that the whole is greater than the sum of the parts equates to the holism with which nurses view their clients. The description of health as resulting from all aspects of one's life functioning in harmony mirrors the UNM/Gallup statement that harmony results when behavior meets one's needs and deviation produces disharmony.

HARMONY AS DESCRIPTIVE OF HEALTH

As stated earlier, I am proposing that harmony very appropriately describes health and is a term which we, as nurses, can use to guide our interactions with clients. You have heard, I am sure, the example that in English we have only the one word for "snow" while Eskimos have many words to describe many different kinds of "snow." We are limited by our language when trying to express the full meaning of any concept. This paper is an example of just how limited we are by our language as I have attempted to explain using harmony to mean health and its attainment. Nurses can use harmony as a benchmark from which to work with clients to assist them in achieving their maximum potential. With this perspective of health, nurses of necessity must consider the entire context of a client's life, seeking out the meanings that client has attached to what is occurring in both their internal and external worlds in addition to all the objective data available about the client. This term harmony, adapted from the Navajo concept *hozho*, describes a perspective of health which is holistic and inclusive. Harmony, quite appropriately, can be referred to as the path toward and the destination of health.

REFERENCES

American Nurses Association, Congress for Nursing Practice. (1973). *Standards: Nursing practice.* Kansas City, MO: Author.

Benner, P. (1985). Quality of life: A phenomenological perspective on explanation, prediction, and understanding in nursing science. *Advances in Nursing Science, 8*(1), 1–14.

Cassell, E. J. (1992). The nature of suffering: Physical, psychological, social, and spiritual aspects. In P. L. Starck & J. P. McGovern (Eds.), *The hidden dimension of illness: Human suffering* (1–10). New York: National League for Nursing Press.

Luckmann, B. (1970). The small life-worlds of modern man. *Social Research, 37*(4), 580–596.

McCaffery, M., & Beebe, A. (1989). *Pain: Clinical manual for nursing practice.* St. Louis: C. V. Mosby.

Simonson, C. L. S. (1991). A lived experience of caring in an educational environment. *Dissertation Abstracts International-B, 52*(02), 751.

Thomas, C. L. (Ed.). (1993). *Taber's cyclopedic medical dictionary.* Philadelphia: F. A. Davis.

University of New Mexico-Gallup Campus Nursing Program. (1989). *Nursing program philosophy.* Gallup, NM: Author.

Witherspoon, G. (1977). *Language and art in the Navajo universe.* Ann Arbor: The University of Michigan.

17

Dream Sharing:
A Narrative Approach to Self-Care

Mary-Therese B. Dombeck

Narrative knowledge has been described as the impulse to story life events into order and meaning (Sandelowski, 1991). Narratives assume many forms and are usually encoded in the language of particular communities. For these reasons it is essential that nurses develop epistemological consciousness; that is, the awareness of whose voices are heard, and what knowledge is revealed or concealed in particular narratives (Dickson, 1990; Hays, 1989). Story can be a method of organizing and communicating nursing knowledge when it is grounded in nursing experience (Boykin & Schoenhofer, 1991). In this paper, I propose that dream-telling facilitates personal storytelling at many different levels. An experienced dream is a way of being with oneself. A told dream is a way of telling about oneself and of being with another. In a gathering of nurses dream-telling has potential for communicating personal and communal stories and of retelling nursing mythology. By "nursing mythology" I mean traditional, historical tales and paradigmatic events told by nursing communities. Myths can be and usually are regarded as the repository of symbolic truth and paradigmatic knowledge for the communities that tell them. Nursing history, nursing theories comprise nursing mythology. But so do informal narratives told by and for nurses. Myths are multivocal (Ricoeur, 1981). This literally means "many voices." Metaphorically it means that knowledge, experience, and history are communicated in multiple paradigms and are understood at many levels. When hearing myth, one is forced to move beyond old patterns of knowledge and fixed perspectives. As connections are made between old knowledge and new perspectives, the capacity to see new dimensions of oneself is enhanced, and old patterns gain flexibility. The joining together of different aspects of oneself is profoundly satisfying: It is an experience of integration. In a dream sharing group personal and communal experience and knowledge can be not only revealed and understood, but also integrated and transformed. Thus, the process can become a ritual of re-creation and self-care for the participants.

In this paper I describe the rationale, structure, process and analysis of an experiential dream sharing group of seven nurses: six graduate students and one faculty member. The dream sharing experience demonstrated that personal knowledge and nursing knowledge were communicated in fundamental ways. Carper's (1978) classification of patterns of knowledge was used to analyze the participant's responses to the dream sharing experience. It was useful in demonstrating the complexity and diversity of the nursing knowledge embedded in the dream sharing experience. I also propose that the *connexional* and *dynamic* aspects of dream sharing, that is, the connections and movement between different meanings and levels of understanding, made the experience transformative.

BACKGROUND AND RATIONALE

Dreaming is one of the ways that persons experience, reflect on and process knowledge about their bodies, their contexts, and their life events. Dreams are symbolic stories we tell ourselves and others by making pictures out of our words. Therefore, dreams are linguistically and culturally constituted. Dream-telling is a social experience that represents and creates personal and social mythology. Much can be learned about societies and particular communities by studying the way they narrate and interpret dreams. Personal and social characteristics, including social stereotypes common in a particular society appear in dream material of persons in that particular society (Ullman, 1988a; Hillman, 1988). Historically dream-telling has been an important activity in Western societies, but since the modern scientific era* dream-

---

*The era of modern philosophy is conventionally considered to begin with Descartes in the seventeenth century. Descartes was profoundly doubtful of his dreams. Scharfstein

telling became regarded either as a trivial activity, or as a restricted one reserved for encounters with experts in psychotherapy. However, the practice has retained its popular and human appeal and has continued to be important in artistic endeavors. Recently, there has been a resurgence in the interest in dreams in the scientific and art communities, including nursing (Dombeck, 1991; Thompson, 1991).

Sharing dreams in the context of a group is valuable not only in psychotherapeutic but also in self-help modalities (Ullman, 1988b; Taylor, 1992). The ritual aspects of the group process are enhanced by the mythological aspects of the dream. Dombeck discovered that group mythology and group development issues appeared in dreams that group members chose to share in a group (1988) and that dream telling and dream interpretation were contextually connected to issues of personhood, gender, social status and hierarchy (1991). Therefore, dreams can be considered a source not only of personal information but also of information about social contexts and situations. For all these reasons a dream sharing group of nurses was considered a valuable source of personal knowledge as well as nursing knowledge. As the dream experience and the nursing experience are shared among trusted colleagues, there is a potential for improved understanding of the communal context, for feeling bonded to others, for giving and receiving support, and of experiencing playfulness and humor. It allows nurses to experience knowledge as a valuable resource in self-care and healing.

The Structure and Process of the Group

It is important for all participants in a group to feel safe and free within a structure that allows them to achieve their purposes. In a dream sharing group this is emphatically the case. Dream material is very sensitive and personal; therefore the dreams and each member must be treated with care by all concerned if the group is to be a healing experience. Ullman (1988b) and Taylor (1992) described group methodologies that address safety issues and discovery issues in dream sharing

---

(1969), after describing several dreams of Descartes in the context of his life, tells us about Descartes, "I struggle with his dreams which failed his test of indubitable truth: It is his dreaming that lives, or, rather his dreaming concealed behind his mask of reason, or perhaps, his dreaming mingled insensibly with his open-eyed reason. He stands at the point where the difference cannot easily be made out" (p. 316).

groups. Although Wheeler and Chinn (1989) did not specifically describe dream sharing gatherings, their feminist process could be adapted to the sharing of any topic to which the members are committed. The emphasis on awareness, empowerment, and evolvement would make a dream sharing group, using their process, a healing experience.

The Theme-Centered Interaction Model was used as a basis for the dream sharing group. This model has not been customarily used as a modality for therapy groups. It was first developed as a format for clinicians to gain self-awareness and receive support. It is based on existential philosophy and aims at balancing the cognitive, the subjective/affective and the interactional aspects of the group (Dombeck, 1983, 1986). The assumptions are that as these aspects are allowed to emerge freely, and in balanced proportions, participants become spontaneous, respectful, attentive, and sensitive toward the topic and toward each other. The dream (one's own or someone else's) is honored as a topic worthy of attention and thought. It is expected that participants will not separate their affect from their thought, nor will they restrict their subjective reactions. The structural aspects of the group, such as group leadership, justice issues, the freedom to disagree, and to be different from other members in the group, are all allowed to emerge and are not suppressed.

The operating principles of the Theme-Centered Interaction Model were adapted to this group and were stated explicitly as follows:

1. Dreams are creative unique communications that can be enjoyed if I and the rest of the group choose to do so. Dreams are special and unique communications from each participant to oneself and to the rest of the group. A dream is honored as a gift from the dream reporter.

2. Participants are helped to appreciate, understand and learn about dreams by their discussions, expressions, and feelings about dreams.

3. The dream reporter is the final authority on her/his own dream. The dream reporter is free to share as much or as little about her/his dream and personal life—no more—no less.

4. Themes are explored by playing word games, and by remembering personal, social and communal associations. A

theme that has been explored in one way can be explored at a different time or with a different participant. Themes are never finalized or "wrapped up" because dream symbols have many meanings.

5. Participants are not therapists, analysts, or interpreters of each other's dreams. They are rather participant explorers of a dream or the theme from a dream, brought to the group by a dream reporter.

6. Dream exploration is not a problem-solving activity. However, through the exploration of dreams, new perspectives can be gained, old concepts modified, and changes could occur if the participants choose to make these changes.

7. All participants will have an opportunity to share dreams if they choose to do so; however, there is no pressure to share dreams if one does not choose to do so.

8. It is important that the group atmosphere be acknowledged and stated. A supportive communal milieu is essential for participants to explore their dreams.

9. If the group atmosphere is tense or conflicted, addressing the interactional issues must take precedence over accumulating more dreams.

10. The facilitator's main function is to balance the cognitive, subjective/affective and interactional aspects of the group. The facilitator's responsibilities can be rotated if the group chooses to do so.

Summary Description of Group

A group of students who knew that my personal, practice, and research endeavors involved dreams asked if I could facilitate a dream sharing group for them. I agreed, and suggested an optimal number of eight participants. Eight members were recruited from a large graduate student body by placing announcements on student bulletin boards. The group was understood to be an extracurricular self-care experience. Membership was voluntary. The participants' understanding was that the group would meet two hours weekly for ten meetings. They expected to learn about dreams and dream exploration and to have an opportunity to share their dreams. This would be done for relaxation and fun in the context of a very rigorous graduate study program.

It was notable to me that, at that time, I was not the instructor for any of the participants in formal classes. This would have put us in dual relationships. If that had happened, the participant would not have been turned away but the relationships would have received special attention by the whole group.

First Meeting Eight participants attended the first meeting. All were women. Most of them knew each other's names and faces but did not know other personal facts about each other. Some were classmates but even they were excited by the possibility of getting to know each other better. The themes which emerged were "sharing dreams," "confidentiality," and "dream recall." This happened as the Theme-Centered Interactional Method of conducting groups was proposed. No one mentioned any difficulty with dream recall and apparently no one was worried about the lack of confidentiality. They eagerly focused on the theme of "sharing dreams" and were very clear with me that they did not want a course on dreams. Although they wanted to learn about dreams, they wanted to do it by sharing dreams for fun and as a means of self-awareness. As they continued to talk about sharing dreams, anxiety mounted about the process itself. One member explicitly mentioned the possibility that listening to others might not be a comfortable thing to do. Most members agreed with her. Then a member volunteered to share a dream (see table 17.1). The symbols were striking: a big fish like Moby Dick, a woman with a scarred face, a little boy chained to the fish, and a mother taking the back seat in a car. There was great interest in the dream and fascination with the symbols. A member told the dreamer, "I could have dreamed this dream myself." Participants agreed with the dreamer's understanding that the dream portrayed the vulnerability of weak and little people to "big fish." There may have been an identification by the group members with the anxiety that strong members would overwhelm weak ones in the group. One participant said that powerful persons in institutions usually overwhelm weaker ones. The other participants emphatically agreed.

Second Meeting Six members came. Two members had contacted me to inform me that they would be dropping out, one of them for reasons of difficulty in scheduling and one because the goals of the group did

Table 17.1   Dreams   (Nine of the twenty dreams)

1. There was a big fish like Moby Dick. There was a woman whose face was scarred in every possible place. There are barnacles all over the big fish. There is a little boy chained to the big fish. The mother takes a back seat. (First Meeting)

2. I had a dream of being naked to the waist and my boyfriend trying to cover me. I guess it must mean I'm conscious of baring my chest to the group. (Second Meeting)

3. A nurse is cradling the partially decapitated head of a man and telling it to stay on. (Third Meeting)

4. I am inserting green soft contact lenses aboard an ocean liner on the Persian Gulf. (Third Meeting)

5. I was in my nurse's uniform and cape running to help in a fire. There was an orange glow in the distance. I was side-tracked in drugstore by woman with orange hair. (Sixth Meeting)

6. I went into a burning house. On the first floor there was an old woman living in ignorance and poverty. On the second floor lived an intellectual, a sort of academic. On the third floor there was an old man who saw things. The whole upstairs is upside down and slanted and had an orange glow. (Seventh Meeting)

7. I'm on stage. Hostages—we are supposed to recite the pledge of allegiance. I cannot do it. I cry. (Eighth Meeting)

8. I am in a kitchen. The woodwork needs painting specially the drainboard and sink. An upstairs room has a hole in the floor. You can see into the kitchen. (Ninth Meeting)

9. I am in a group of 10–12 women. Someone is giving a talk about dreams. F is in the audience. I tell the class about optical chiasm. F tells me to sit down. Nurses already know about that. (Tenth Meeting)

not match her own. The six members who came expressed anxiety about the survival of the group and renewed their own commitment to return. These statements were made in terms of commitment to oneself, and a decision that attending the group was a personal priority. I introduced the theme of "exploring dream language." This exploration included the suggestions that it was helpful to play word games, find puns, make images out of dream words, and make words out of dream pictures. The suggestions were accepted and used as the dream reporter interpreted a dream where she was naked to the waist as a reluctance to "bare her chest" or disclose personal things in the group. However, this preliminary interpretation by the dreamer, though it was accepted by the group, was passed over quickly. Group members indicated that their major concern was the loss of a member and the possibility that other members would drop out and that the group would have to dissolve. This general feeling was reinforced when the second dream reporter announced that she had entitled her dream "Let her come back." This title was met with amusement and a mild lessening of tension as they recognized that their general concern was reflected in the title of her dream.

Third Meeting Five members were present. One member was absent because of illness. Although word games continued, the members spent much time discussing the "loss of the group members" and the "stability of the group." There were two dreams reported: the first one was about a nurse cradling the partially decapitated head of a person and telling it to stay on. Someone recognized this as a fear of fragmentation. There were no ideas about why "the head" was coming off. But there was much conversation about difficult practice sites. Members told stories of their practice. One nurse said, "Sometimes I get so busy and tired I feel as though I'm cut in two." Others connected her statement to the dream.

The second dream was about inserting green, soft contact lenses aboard an ocean liner in the Persian Gulf. The dreamer understood this to reflect her own excitement about seeing things in a new way through the dream sharing group. She considered the group analogous to an exotic journey. She communicated her excitement to other members, who then became excited themselves. The atmosphere became playful.

Fourth and Fifth Meetings On the fourth meeting I was away because of an urgent family situation. The members met without me. On the fifth meeting all the members were present. Although I introduced the theme of "amplification of symbols," the members listened with interest but spent much of the time and much of their energy discussing "illness" and "loyalty to the group." There was much concern expressed for my personal issues and again mention of lost group members.

The dream reported introduced some novel themes: buying a defective game, prosecuting the salesman, and getting money back. There was general satisfaction that the dreamer got the full value of her game at the end of the dream. The dreamer and members did not initially make connections between the dream and the group emotion. The dream may have expressed concern that the group survive even if I was away. Their decision to take action and realize the value of the group for themselves by meeting without me was subsequently understood in a new light.

Sixth Meeting All members were present. Much of the time during this meeting was spent discussing the previous meeting. They described the previous meeting as "trance-like" and quiet. One of the members told of an ill relative. They discussed the themes of illness and grief, remembering losses in their own lives and in their current patients with sadness. They comforted each other by making supportive comments. I introduced the theme of "archetypes" and "complementarity" from the Jungian approach to dreams. The members were intrigued with the themes of complementarity and opposition in dream symbols. The dreamer reported a very frightening dream with symbols of fire, burning, orange hair, and orange glow. The group discussed complementarity of symbols that conveyed images of heat and cold. This meeting culminated in a decision to move to a cooler room because of the heat. Then they discussed their own action in light of the dream.

Seventh Meeting All members were present. They were overwhelmed, exhausted, and angry with school issues and with their courses. They all seemed agitated when they came in. I suggested that it was possible to do content analysis of dreams. This was met with a generally lukewarm response and lack of enthusiasm. One member announced that she had had a nightmare about a flood in her house. This sparked much interest and even before she told her dream members were exploring the symbol "house." The dream portrayed a flooded basement, a tidal wave, tugging a boat, and hope for survival. There was animated discussion of being overwhelmed by school work and of survival in school. The members were enthusiastic, cohesive and supportive in their exploration of the dream. It was clear that all were using the dream to express how overwhelming their lives were, but also expressing hope for survival. In this session they talked about the "house" as a religious symbol in all the faiths represented in the group. Members said the dream was beautiful.

Eighth Meeting This meeting occurred after school spring break two weeks later. It was clear that they felt much better and were able to express that. The dream reporter agreed to do a dialogue with one of the symbols in her dream to illustrate the Gestalt method. The dream was about "being on stage" and presented the dreamer's difficult feelings about her parents. The dreamer chose to dialogue with the image of her father in the dream. It was a moving experience for all. The theme of lightening of baggage since the last meeting became related to the expression of disappointment in parents, parent figures, and teachers. The dreamer received support, admiration, and applause for the depth of her sharing.

Ninth Meeting All members were present. Although I introduced the subject of the approaching termination of the group, members chose not to focus on it but chose to talk about the previous week's meeting instead. The dream presented was about the dreamer's aunt who was driving erratically. In the dream the dreamer was somewhat uncomfortable but did not feel that there was danger. The dream was interpreted by the whole group as reflective of their discomfort with the process of the Gestalt method dialogue of the previous meeting, and therefore the dream was acknowledged to be a *group dream*. A group dream is the dream of one member of the group that appears to be representative of the current group situation (Dombeck, 1988, p. 97). The similarity of feelings in their expressions of discomfort made them feel cohesive and safer.

Tenth and Last Meeting All members were present and talked at length about the group, each other, themselves and the ending of the group. Three members presented dreams. The feelings were of sadness and abandonment because of the ending of the group. One of the dreams was about the dreamer taking a leadership role and teaching a class and being chided by a faculty member. The dreamer acknowledged that although she felt competent in many ways it was frightening to take leadership because of the fear of criticism of superiors and teachers. The ending of the group symbolized the ending of school and of being out in the "real world," functioning in a new role.

This short summary does not convey the range of symbols, images, feelings, statements of commitment to healing, to caring, to themselves and to nursing that were expressed and articulated. The summary, however, conveys the flow of events, ideas, and experiences as they occurred over the ten-week period. The group experience became a story in which they all participated, and a community to which they all belonged.

Analysis of Selected Dreams and Participants' Responses to Them

Although each dream reported was significant and important to participants, only selected dreams and the responses of group members can be analyzed for the purposes of this article. Examining the dreams from the perspective of different patterns of knowledge is useful in demonstrating the breadth and depth of the dream sharing experience, the diversity and complexity of nursing knowledge, and nursing resources which can be accessed by such an experience.

Empirical Pattern of Knowledge in Dream Group Analysis

The most prevalent method of analyzing dreams is the content analysis of dreams. Through this method dreams are collected and classified according to themes. The symbols in the dreams are coded, counted, differentiated into items such as: cast of characters, emotions, activities, animals, man-made materials and natural materials. The theory is that people's dreams are representative of the situations in their lives, and, therefore, much can be learned about a person or a group simply by observing, counting and analyzing the content of their dreams (Hall & Van de Castle, 1966).

When nurses dream and tell their dreams to one another, one would expect that many of the dreams would depict nursing activities, interactions, common feelings and even common values. In the process of this group twenty dreams were presented. The characters in the dreams were most often women, the activities depicted were of a helping and caring nature. Most of the dreams showed a high level of frustration. There were also several statements of survival and success. Out of the twenty dreams three dreams depicted the actual presence of a nurse. However, several other dreams depicted nursing activities such as caring, rescuing others, comforting someone, and teaching.

The predominant themes, however, dealt with images of authority, status, power and powerlessness. In talking about the dreams the most intense interactions were generated by symbols which depicted the member's situation of being a student: namely, a classroom, a difficult game, an academic man, a faculty member. Other images were being small and powerless, being helplessly attached to a whole, being in a strange place with a frightening glow, being overwhelmed, drowning, being disappointed in parents and parental figures, being hostages and made to recite the pledge of allegiance, being driven in a car erratically by someone in an older generation, being reprimanded and put in one's place. There were also positive images of exploring new and exotic territory, being heroic, surviving danger, having the capacity to teach others.

Only two of the dreams were considered to be nightmares. The dream reporters expressed being frustrated in many of the dreams, but the dreams were not considered "bad" dreams. It was the dialogue that followed the dreams that revealed the resources and the knowledge embedded in their situations. The participants told stories of their difficult clinical situations in support of the dream of the dreamer who was holding the head of the man. They also comforted the participants who told of ill relatives and dying patients. Their understanding of each other as caring persons, and as rescuing persons, became a point of cohesion as their dreaming lives showed as much similarity with each other as did their waking lives. Even their frustrations as students became an opportunity for cohesion and the building of a repertoire of student "war stories." If one were to create a composite story from the content and collective experience, one could say that the story would be about the trials by fire endured by students, and about the comforting aspects of being a community of people with similar experiences.

The dream reporters were emphatically descriptive of sensory details in their dreams. There was, however, one notable experience involving a sensory event which became more memorable than the rest to the participants.

On the sixth meeting the following dream was shared:

I went into a burning house. On the first floor there was an old woman living in ignorance and poverty. On the second floor lived an intellectual, a sort of academic. On the third floor there was an old man who saw things. The whole upstairs is upside down and slanted and has an orange glow.

There were many associations to the dream, including the suggestions that the house represented the poverty of students, the class system in society or in the hospital. The symbols were puzzling—especially the color orange. The dreamer admitted she did not like the color orange—

being Irish she preferred green. Did the color orange symbolize the color of the enemy? At this point one of the members mentioned that the color orange was a hot color. The whole dream conveyed heat. One of the group members commented on the heat in the room. All the participants concurred and it was spontaneously resolved that we should move to a cooler room. This was done with no apparent realization about the similarity of the sensation of heat in the dream and the sensation of heat in the room. When I asked playfully "What's the matter? You couldn't take the heat?" they were awestruck by their collective experience and their own ritualistic action (Van Der Hart, 1983). They felt empowered to try to move symbolically to a new psychic place.

Recognizing the Esthetic Pattern of Knowing in the Dreams

The experience just described was also recognized by the members as an experience of the esthetic dimension of dreams. They told the dreamer her dream was "colorful" and "beautiful" as they experienced its dimensions at different levels. The experience was remembered and discussed again on the seventh meeting when the members became aware of how the symbol of "house" was sacred in all the faiths represented in the group. The dream had become a medium for esthetic expression.

Carper identified empathy as the marker of the esthetic pattern of knowing. Meleis suggested that this focus on empathy confuses the issue (Meleis, 1991, p. 438). Although empathy is, at times, involved in the esthetic experience, it is because that experience is also marked by unity particularity and rhythmicity. These markers of the esthetic experience often inspire empathy.

Dewey thought that, "in art, integration of experience always occurs" (Dewey, 1934 [reprint 1958], p. 259). Not only does art involve experience, it constitutes it (p. 214). The unique way in which an artist expresses his or her art ensures that an expression of art cannot be expressed in exactly the same way twice. The viewer or appreciator of the art is also drawn into the experience and integrates it. A dream is a unique creation that is seldom duplicated, or ever repeated in exactly the same way. A dream connects sleeping life with waking life. The experience of telling dreams draws the listeners into the dream in such a way that the dream and the dreamer are engaged, as in other works of art. "The purpose that determines what is esthetically essential is precisely the formation of *an experience*" (Dewey, 1958, p. 294).

Contemplating the Personal Dimensions of Dreams

It is not hard to see the dream as a personal experience. But in Western society dreams are not usually recognized as a source of personal knowledge. Dreams are often trivialized or pathologized. Many regard them as meaningless or abnormal (Dombeck, 1991). However, dreams can reveal bodily conditions and needs, psychological states, spiritual longings and personal mythology (Feinstein & Krippner, 1988).

An example will illustrate:

> *I am in the kitchen. The* woodwork *needs painting, especially the* drainboard *and* sink. *An upstairs room has a hole in the floor. You can see into the kitchen.*

The dreamer described clearly the hole in the floor. She said she felt tired in the dream; in her waking life she was drained with the end of semester classwork. The conversation was about why nurses always work so hard, and about surviving the school ordeal. The students spent much time talking about schoolwork with anxious animation. Since there was no possibility of seriously decreasing their workload they decided to help each other survive. As they contemplated the dream further, some members began to regard the dream with humor as they played with the words telling the dreamer, "Of course! If you are *drained, bored* and *sink*ing, you *would* not *work!*" There was general hilarity about this play on words. The dreamer made a decision to take a night off in order to fix her personal and psychological "drainboard and sink." The dream meant much to the dreamer. The other members also were forced to consider the fact that nurses tend to neglect themselves and not to play enough. This was important personal knowledge that they shared, realizing it was also part of the nursing ethos.

Other personal understandings were learned in the group, some not mentioned due to confidentiality considerations. Dreams presented themselves to the dreamer with a kind of stark honesty that was less accessible in waking life. The dreamers learned new things about themselves. Ricoeur advocated a hermeneutic of suspicion, as well as a hermeneutic of faith (Ricoeur, 1981, p. 34) in order to deal with one's own false consciousness. He meant that persons need to factor into their interpretations of their dreams the human tendency to deceive oneself. Dreams often show the symbolic "warts" that dreamers prefer to cover up or conceal.

Although it was difficult to learn about previously unknown and potentially unflattering things about oneself, it was also a healing experience. The reasons for this were discussed in the group. Many of the dreams that were shared were difficult and frustrating, yet the group experience was extremely positive. It feels good to be known by trusted colleagues and friends. It also brings together (integrates) within oneself new knowledge and old knowledge, past and present, positive things and negative things. The feelings induced by restriction and fragmentation are acknowledged. The different and compartmentalized parts of oneself begin to flow together. One also discovers that others are also experiencing similar things, and a sense of bonding develops.

Bringing to Light the Ethical Subtleties of the Dream

The dreams shared in this group provided a rich source of the ethical aspects of knowledge. Carper stated that "the ethical pattern of knowing in nursing requires an understanding of different philosophical positions regarding what is good, what ought to be desired, what is right of different ethical frameworks devised for dealing with the complexities of moral judgements" (Carper, 1978, p. 21).

Barthes, in his philosophical literary criticism, suggested that the critic look at "what goes without saying"; that is, what is so embedded in one's social consciousness that it appears to be taken for granted (Barthes, 1957, p. 11). In a similar vein Ullman (1988a) proposed that social prejudices appear in dreams because they are embedded in our language, images, and value systems. Benner suggested that nursing practice narratives provide the basis for skilled ethical comportment on which procedural ethics and the posing of ethical dilemmas depend (Benner, 1991).

The following three dreams demonstrate this:

1. *I am in a group of 10–12 women. Someone is giving a talk about dreams. F (a faculty member) is in the audience. I tell the class about optical chiasm. F tells me to "Sit down, nurses already know about that."*

2. *I'm on stage. Hostages—we are supposed to recite the pledge of allegiance. I cannot do it. I cry.*

3. *There was a big fish like Moby Dick. There was a woman whose face was scarred in every possible place. There are barnacles all over the*

big fish. There is a little child chained to the big fish. The mother takes a back seat.

In the first dream the assumption is that knowledge is to be transmitted by lecturing, that an expert always knows best, that students can be silenced even if they tell what nurses "already know." The dreamer said that, in the dream, she felt reprimanded and shamed. She also said that her nursing education experience had been one in which she had not been free to express her "dreams" for her nursing career. The other students, after comparing undergraduate experiences, concurred that that experience is common to most nurses in nursing education experiences in many schools.

The second dream finds the dreamer feeling like a hostage having to agree and pledge allegiance. I asked if the dream-telling group was becoming oppressive. None of the students felt this way about the group. Although they had been in different undergraduate schools, they had all experienced the power of the systems of education to take strong measures to make them conform. There were discussions about the limiting of curiosity and about the regulation of knowledge in nursing.

The dream of the big fish was the most evocative. The dreamer related the dream to personal facts in her life, but the following comments were made by other members, indicating that this was a group dream: "I could have dreamed your dream" and "This is a place where we can all be scarred and look at all the big fishes out to eat the little fishes." The members of the group had a chance to acknowledge the inequities and abuses of nursing and hospital institutions and to discuss the power of institutions of learning (Foucault, 1972; Roberts, 1987). That was a first step to working toward one's own survival.

The most significant thing for me was that students were able to speak openly and honestly in the presence of a member of the faculty. This was possible in the supportive atmosphere of the group, and it led to the enrichment of all of us.

Carper's classification of patterns of knowledge in nursing (1978) is helpful in broadening our understanding of the dream-telling experience. These patterns are not mutually exclusive nor are they static. I propose that it is the connexional and dynamic aspects of dreams that make the dream-telling experience transformative. Dreams, like myths, are multivocal; they speak in many voices and use multiple nuances of meaning. Therefore, for tellers and hearers of dream narratives it is profoundly satisfying when a dream can be perceived to have multiple levels of meaning. This was acknowledged to be true of most dreams that were shared in the group. The dream of entering the burning house was a good example, demonstrating the connexional aspects of dreams. At a personal level the dreamer was reminded of family relationships and the reality of the risk-taking and satisfying parts of her work. However, the group members were also reminded of hierarchical realities and inequities in their work settings and in the society at large. The convergence of these meanings, the particularity of the dream, including its color and symmetry induced some group members to experience the dream esthetically and to tell the dreamer that the dream was beautiful.

Finally, the empirical and sensory aspects of the dream caused the group members to connect the heat in the room with the heat in the dream. The multiple meanings of the dream moved them to symbolic action (Van Der Hart, 1983) and to the understanding of the symbolic significance of movement, change, and transformation in their lives. This dream narrative in the context of the group is an example for the transformative power of the dream. The nurses reiterated this transformative power in word and demeanor.

Summary

This paper describes the rationale, structure, process and analysis of an experiential dream sharing group of seven nurses. Carper's classification of patterns of knowledge was useful in guiding the analyses. Dreams were meaningful when they were considered in the light of each of the four patterns of knowledge. However, in addition to that, it was the connections between paradigms which were most moving and most satisfying, because it had a liberating effect on tendencies to be fixed on static old patterns. When one acquires the capacity to connect old knowledge with new perspectives, the self is restored, the new dimensions of the self begin to emerge. The self is re-created. In dream telling one's voice is discovered, empowered, and transformed in the telling.

REFERENCES

Barthes, R. (1957, reprinted 1972). *Mythologies*. New York: The Noonday Press.

Benner, P. (1991). The role of experience, narrative, and community in skilled ethical comportment. *Advances in Nursing Science, 14*(2), 1–21.

Boykin, A., & Schoenhofer, S. O. (1991). Story as link between nursing practice, ontology, epistemology. *Image: Journal of Nursing Scholarship, 23*, 245–249.

Carper, B. A. (1978). Fundamental patterns of knowing in nursing. *Advances in Nursing Science, 1*(1), 13–23.

Dewey, J. (1934, reprinted 1958). *Art as experience.* New York: G. P. Putnam & Sons.

Dickson, G. L. (1990). The metalanguage of menopause research. *Image: Journal of Nursing Scholarship, 22*, 168–173.

Dombeck, M-T. (1983). The theme-centered model in professional education. *Small Group Behavior, 14*, 275–300.

Dombeck, M-T. (1986). Faculty peer review in a group setting. *Nursing Outlook, 34*, 188–192.

Dombeck, M-T. (1988). Group mythology and group development in dream sharing groups. *Psychiatric Journal of the University of Ottawa, 13*, 97–106.

Dombeck, M-T. (1991). *Dreams and Professional Personhood.* New York: Albany State University of New York Press.

Feinstein, D., & Krippner, S. (1988). *Personal mythology: The psychology of your evolving self.* Los Angeles: Jeremy P. Tarcher.

Foucault, M. (1972). *The Archaeology of Knowledge.* New York: Harper & Row.

Hall, D., & Van de Castle, R. (1966). *The content analysis of dreams.* New York: Appleton-Century-Crofts.

Hays, J. C. (1989). Voices in the record. *Image: Journal of Nursing Scholarship, 21*(4), 200–204.

Hillman, D. J. (1988). Dream work and field work: Linking cultural anthropology and the current dream work movement. In M. Ullman & C. Limmer (Eds.), *The Variety of Dream Experiences*, 117–141. New York: Continuum.

Meleis, A. (1991). *Theoretical Nursing: Development and Progress.* Philadelphia: J. B. Lippincott Co.

Ricoeur, P. (1981). *Hermeneutics and the human sciences.* London: Cambridge University Press.

Roberts, S. J. (1983). Oppressed group behavior: Implications for nursing. *Advances in Nursing Science, 5*(7), 21–30.

Sandelowski, M. (1991). Telling stories: Narrative approaches in qualitative research. *Image: Journal of Nursing Scholarship, 23,* 161–166.

Scharfstein, A-A. (1969). Descartes' dreams, *Philosophical Forum, 1*(3), 293–316.

Taylor, J. (1992). *Where people fly and water runs uphill: Using dreams to tap the wisdom of the unconscious.* New York: Warner.

Thompson, J. L. (1991). Exploring gender and culture with Khmer refugee women: Reflections on participatory feminist research. *Advances in Nursing Science, 13*(3), 30–48.

Ullman, J. (1988a). Dreams and society. In M. Ullman & C. Limmer (Eds.), *The Variety of Dream Experience,* pp. 279–294. New York: Continuum.

Ullman, M. (1988b). The experiential dream group. In M. Ullman & C. Limmer (Eds.), *The Variety of Dream Experience,* pp. 1–26. New York: Continuum.

Van Der Hart, O. (1983). *Rituals in psychotherapy: Transition and continuity.* New York: Irvington.

Wheeler, C. E., & Chinn, P. L. (1989). *Peace and Power: A handbook of feminist process.* New York: National League for Nursing Press.

18

Healing Rituals Experienced by Persons Living with AIDS

Janet M. Lakomy

The presence of the Human Immunodeficiency Virus (HIV) and Acquired Immune Deficiency Syndrome (AIDS) have become fatal diagnoses for an increasing number of persons. The AIDS epidemic continues to spread rapidly and the victims are stigmatized by society. At the present time there is no cure for this disease and the afflicted persons are labeled with a terminal, devastating diagnosis which prompts them to reevaluate their lives. Consequently, the quality versus the quantity of their lives predominates their definition of life and well-being. Since AIDS is most prevalent in the male sector, the male pronoun will be used throughout this chapter.

The need for quality and compassionate care for persons who are HIV-positive is paramount in society. Persons with HIV-related infections are desperately seeking care for their disease. Ninety-four percent of the needs and services required by persons with HIV related infection is nursing care. The Institute of Medicine (1986) recommended a community-based model rather than hospital or medical clinics for the delivery of care for persons with related HIV infections. In spite of this recommendation, adequate health care services and sufficient facilities remain limited and many times unavailable to these persons. Thus, a major gap exists in our health care delivery system to meet the needs of persons living with HIV related infections.

The concept of caring has gained greater awareness and emphasis in nursing and nursing research. Caring has been posited as the essence of nursing (Leininger, 1981, 1984; Noddings, 1984; Watson, 1979, 1985). One of nursing's major goals is to gain a richer understanding about the client, how to facilitate his caring needs, and how to enhance his well-being. Understanding the meaning of human caring from the perspective of the client provides the health care professional with a rationale for the delivery of care. When caring is experienced by both the nurse and a person who is HIV positive, the nurse gleans a richer understanding about the client, his caring needs, and how to enhance his well-being. Thus, through the caring experience, the nurse is provided with the rationale for the care delivered.

When persons feel they are experiencing a depth of relatedness referred to as an "I-Thou" relationship (Buber, 1965), feelings of well-being are believed to ensue which can affect bodily processes. Frank (1975), for example, stated that positive mental states and faith can greatly influence health. Watson (1985) held that when clients experience caring, they have the capacity for self healing. During the caring interaction, the client perceives that he is being recognized by the nurse as a unique, thinking, and feeling human being. Also, during this interaction, the nurse is a participant in the client's world and appreciates and responds to the client on an "I-Thou" level (Riemen, 1986). Therefore, nurses play a major role in helping the client to gain inner strength, power, and self healing through the caring transaction(s) (Watson, 1985).

Smerke (1988) conducted a hermeneutical study to discover the meanings of human caring from nine disciplines: anthropology, ethics, fine arts, humanities, nursing, philosophy, psychoneuroimmunology, socio-behavioral sciences, and theology. Healing modalities emerged as one of the seven major meanings of human caring and this meaning was shared by all nine disciplines. Healing represented touching, enabling actions, centering, experiencing technical competence, using imagery/visualization, using humor/laughter, experiencing the outcome of healing, activating the self healer, listening to music, and engaging in holistic/transcendental modalities (Smerke, 1988). These representations of healing display a variety of potential healing practices for persons who have experienced a caring interaction.

Pilisuk and Parks (1986) stated that healing enhances, promotes, and preserves the person. Through healing there is cosmic harmony and renewal within the person. Buber (1965) stated that existential healing is at the root of the person's being and takes place through meetings. Caring transactions promote congruence between the perceptions and experiences of the person and promote self as real versus ideal self. Harmony within a body-mind-spirit gestalt is created. Through the caring transaction inner power and strength are released. This helps the person gain a sense of inner harmony, and thus the self-healing processes are potentiated and the meaning in the experience is found (Watson, 1985). When nurses are caring with persons who are HIV-positive in a humane and compassionate manner, there is the potential of impacting the quality of their lives. Human caring transactions with persons living with AIDS will promote their personhood and self healing processes and they will experience and practice a variety of healing rituals.

RESEARCH QUESTIONS

Healing is an important concept to nursing and especially when caring with persons with AIDS. Research studies need to be conducted that discover the meaning of healing rituals and processes engaged in by persons living with AIDS. Thus, the research question for this study was: What are the healing rituals experienced by persons living with HIV-related infections?

Methodology

Phenomenology was used for this study. Oiler (1986) stated that the aim of phenomenology is to describe the experience lived by the people. The investigator gains access to the human experience through the person's perceptions and experiences. Hence, the phenomenological description is one of the most effective methods of communicating the insights of human experience. In descriptive phenomenology, the investigator uses direct investigation, analysis, and description of the phenomenon under study while bracketing any preconceived beliefs and presuppositions. In a descriptive and exploratory study, the investigator is searching for factors to paint a picture of the phenomenon. Diers (1979) documented the factor-searching study as, "the method is to begin with as open a view as possible of the situation . . ." (p. 107). Ray (1985) documented that through deliberate and structured reflection on the experience, an awareness of the wholeness or gestalt of the human experience emerges.

The phenomenological method as explained by Speigelberg was followed in this study. The process of phenomenology includes: bracketing oneself from one's own knowledge base, beliefs, and values on the healing rituals experienced. During the first reflection, each participant's descriptions were read for a sense of the whole. Themes were formulated and coded onto the computer as they emerged that directly pertained to the healing rituals. From these themes, meanings were formulated during the second reflection. The formulations illuminated and discovered the meanings and experiences hidden in the various contexts and horizons of healing rituals which were present in the original descriptions. Finally, the universal experience of healing rituals emerged during the third reflection (Speigelberg, 1971, 1981).

Setting

A community-based nursing-directed center was the setting of the investigation. The Center provides physical care, psychoemotional support, self-care education, and coordination of services to clients and their families throughout all phases of HIV infection. Key features of the Center include the coordination of services and delivery of quality, compassionate, and comprehensive nursing care in a nontraditional setting.

Sample

The target population was composed of those clients enrolled in the Center with a diagnosis of HIV positive or AIDS. Ten male clients were selected on the basis of their medical diagnosis and their ability to verbally communicate in English their experiences of healing rituals. Four clients were diagnosed as HIV positive and six clients were diagnosed with AIDS. Participants ranged in age from 28 to 55 years. Nonstructured tape recorded interviews provided the investigator with in-depth data for analysis of the experience of the healing rituals.

Human Subjects Protection

After approval of this study was obtained from the Institutional Review Board, the investigator obtained verbal and written permission of the clients to participate in the study. Both verbal and written consent was obtained from each participant for the interview to be tape recorded. Participants were interviewed in a private office at the Center. Participants were told that responses to the interviews would be kept confidential. Demographic data regarding age, marital status, education, occupation, length of time since HIV-positive diagnosis, and current medical condition were recorded on tape just prior to the taped interview.

Data Generation

The participants were interviewed using nonstructured tape recorded interviews regarding their meaning of the healing rituals and processes they experienced. Some sample questions asked were: "Tell me what healing means to you?" "Tell me what healing rituals mean to you?" "What healing activities or rituals do you engage in?" "Have these rituals changed since your diagnosis of HIV-positive?" Interviews lasted between 45 minutes to one-and-one-half hours. Each interview was transcribed onto computer disks and subjected to phenomenological analysis. Following transcription, the tapes were destroyed. Finally, no names were used in the interviews so that confidentiality of the participants was maintained. The Ethnograph software program was used to assist with data manipulation tasks (Seidel, 1988).

The following steps were used to analyze the data (Speigelberg, 1971, 1981):

1. The investigator bracketed herself from her own knowledge base, beliefs, and values on the meanings and experiences of healing rituals.

2. During the first reflection, the investigator read such participant's descriptions of the meanings and experiences of healing rituals for a sense of the whole. Themes were formulated and coded onto the computer as they emerged from the participant's descriptions, phrases, or statements that directly pertained to the investigated phenomenon.

3. During the second reflection, the investigator reflected on the healing ritual themes that emerged during the first reflection. The themes were then organized into clusters of themes that reflected the participants' descriptions of their experienced healing rituals.

4. During the third reflection, the universal experience of healing rituals for all of the participants was described. This representative description of the healing rituals was a statement of the essential or fundamental structure of healing rituals for the participants.

To assess the trustworthiness of the data, the investigator requested that the participants assess the relevancy of the emergent themes and the universal experience of their healing rituals. After the participants read these, they affirmed that their healing ritual experiences had been fully captured through the themes and the universal experience.

FINDINGS AND DISCUSSION

The findings from this study included descriptions of healing rituals practiced by persons living with the HIV virus. Healing rituals were defined by the participants as activities or events that they engaged or participated in for the promotion of self or group healing. The participants always mentioned the Center in their descriptions of healing. For some of the clients, the Center represented their first encounter with caring and healing.

During the first reflection, some of the descriptions of the healing rituals experienced by persons who are HIV-positive included: maintaining a positive attitude in life, seeking environments and places that were positive, having supportive friends and family, following their health care regimens, socializing with others, engaging in health-promoting therapies, experiencing the genuine presence of others, experiencing positive affection by others, reliving memories of the death of others who had lived with AIDS, enabling the power within to heal, and experiencing the caring process.

During the second reflection, six formulated experiences of healing rituals for persons who are HIV-positive emerged (see Table 18.1). The first healing ritual engaged in by the participants was a positive philosophical outlook on life. One participant stated: "I've learned and realized that people are a lot sicker than I am and their attitude is so

Table 18.1   Six Formulated Experiences of Healing Rituals

Positive philosophical outlook on life
Involvement with caring, spiritual environments and places
Experience of the caring process
Activation of the self healer within the person
Engagement in a variety of healing therapies
Reliving the memories of the dying process from persons who had lived with
   AIDS

positive, it's just like a miracle and I can say to myself I can do this too." Another participant shared the following: "More positive thinking actually makes you feel better. It does in my life." Finally, another participant stated:

> It's just positive thinking. A thought to me is the strongest thing in the universe. I have seen people who have had negative thinking that have died because they won't open up. They refuse to believe or even want to go on with other energy to stay alive longer because negative energy can kill you just as fast as anything else.

A second healing ritual shared by the participants was being involved with caring, spiritual environments and places. One participant shared the following experience:

> There is something about this Center that once you get here, even if you're on a down, there is something in the building, in the caring, the feeling here that lifts your spirit and makes you smile. Makes you feel good. You want to take a piece of it home with you. We're like a big family here.

Another participant related the following: "You need a space where you can go and sit and think about what's happened. Kind of care about that for a moment." Finally, a third participant stated: "I read the Bible. I pray more now, it really means something to me when I pray now. This time it's meaningful."

The experience of the caring process was a third healing ritual shared by the participants. One participant shared the following experience: "You could feel that she cares about the people around her. And there's just a real kind of loving, warm feeling that kind of goes up through your body and you really, I can't pass by her and not smile."

A fourth healing ritual experienced by the participants was the activation of the self healer within the person. One participant related the following: "Before being diagnosed HIV-positive, I didn't realize that the power was in me." Another participant stated: "Anyone who is having any health care problem must participate in his/her health care and must take responsibility. People who do take responsibility for their own health get better and people who don't get worse."

The participants described their engagement in a variety of healing therapies. Some of the therapies utilized included: therapeutic touch, meditation, lit candles, crystals, playing soft music, support group meetings, humor, buddy systems, massages, listening to tapes, and picnics. In addition, several participants described their experiences of following their health care regimens as an example of a healing therapy. Finally, many of the participants actively engaged in a variety of self care activities. Some of the self care activities included: improving diet, practicing safe sex, writing a blue novel, exercising, getting plenty of rest, and pacing oneself.

The last healing ritual discussed by the participants was their reliving the memories of the dying process from persons who had lived with AIDS. One participant related the following experience:

> *I go and visit AIDS patients in the hospital. I go in to see life and to see if I can't create another day for someone else. I want to go in and the very first day I went in, it was very difficult. I went home and I was an emotional wreck seeing these bones and flesh laying there gasping for breath, not being able to eat, being paralyzed, because I saw myself laying there and then I looked at myself and I thought, well boy if you are just not wasting your time, you know you are wasting your time looking at yourself. You need to look at them and just go on about it and gain knowledge from it so you can keep yourself from getting into that position if (you can) at all possible.*

Another participant talked about his reflections: "Memory is still there of the person, the things you used to do together, places you might have gone, just little things might trigger off something you've done together. It's still a very caring and loving feeling that you get. It's an on-going process all your life."

During the third reflection, the universal experience of healing rituals for all of the participants emerged. For persons living with AIDS, healing rituals occur when actively caring with self and with others (see Table 18.2). Upon being diagnosed with the HIV virus, these persons actively engage in healing rituals. One participant described this experience:

> *When I was diagnosed with the HIV virus, I realized that my time might be limited. That brought a whole new dimension into my life about looking at myself, and looking at my friends, and looking at my world, and about caring about people, and about loving people.*

Table 18.2   Universal Experience of Healing Rituals

ACTIVELY

Caring process

Activation of the self healer within the person

Reliving the memories of the dying process from persons who had lived with AIDS

Involvement with caring, spiritual environments and places

Nontraditional and traditional healing therapies

Gaining a positive philosophical outlook on life

WITH SELF AND WITH OTHERS.

Participants are constantly seeking modalities that provide positive experiences for their lives and well-being. In addition, they actively search for traditional and nontraditional therapies that enhance their well-being. Finally, one participant summed it up by this experience: "I'm not ready to die yet and as long as I have people who care about me, I don't think I will, or it will be very hard for me to die if I know that somebody depends upon me." Healing rituals as a form of human caring can be construed as self care interventions for persons living with AIDS. When working and caring with persons with HIV-related infections, nurses need to facilitate opportunities for the person to gain a positive attitude toward living; a caring and healing environment; the energy to release the power within the person to begin healing; the availability of nontraditional and traditional healing therapies; and a space and time for sharing memories. Then nurses will have provided and delivered the highest quality of care possible for these persons. Through actively caring with self and with others, persons living with AIDS have the capacity for enhanced self worth, self growth, and self healing.

REFERENCES

Buber, M. (1965). *The knowledge of man: A philosophy of the interhuman.* New York: Harper & Row.

Davis, A. (1978). The phenomenological approach in nursing research. In N. Chaska (Ed.), *The nursing profession: Views through the mist* (pp. 186–197). New York: McGraw-Hill.

Diers, D. (1979). *Research in nursing*. Philadelphia: J. B. Lippincott.

Frank, J. (1975). The faith that heals. *The Johns Hopkins Medical Journal, 137*(3), 127–131.

Leininger, M. (1981). *Caring: An essential human need. Proceedings of three national caring conferences*. Thorofare, NJ: Charles B. Slack.

Leininger, M. (1984). *Care: The essence of nursing and health*. Thorofare, NJ: Charles B. Slack.

Noddings, M. (1984). *Caring: A feminine approach to ethics and moral education*. Berkeley: University of California Press.

Oiler, C. (1986). Phenomenology: The method. In P. Munhall & C. Oiler (Eds.), *Nursing research: A qualitative perspective* (pp. 69–84). Norwalk: Appleton-Century-Crofts.

Pilisuk, M., & Parks, S. H. (1986). *The healing web: Social networks and human survival*. Hanover: University Press of New England.

Ray, M. (1985). A philosophical method to study nursing phenomena. In M. Leininger (Ed.), *Qualitative research methods in nursing* (pp. 81–92). New York: Grune & Stratton, Inc.

Riemen, D. (1986). The essential structure of a caring interaction: Doing phenomenology. In P. Munhall & C. Oiler (Eds.), *Nursing research: A qualitative perspective* (pp. 85–108). Norwalk: Appleton-Century-Crofts.

Seidel, J. (1988). *The Ethnograph: Version 3.0* (Computer program). Littleton, CO: Qualis Research Associates.

Smerke, J. (1988). The discovery and creation of the meanings of human caring through the development of a guide to the caring literature. *Dissertation Abstracts International* (University Microfilms No. 8828059).

Speigelberg, H. (1971). *The phenomenological movement* (2nd ed.). The Hague: Martinus-Nijhoff.

Speigelberg, H. (1981). *The context of the phenomenological movement.* The Hague: Martinus-Nijhoff.

The Institute of Medicine. (1986). *Confronting AIDS: Update 1988.* Washington, DC: National Academy of Sciences.

Watson, J. (1979). *Nursing: The philosophy and science of caring.* Boston: Little, Brown.

Watson, J. (1985). *Nursing: Human science and human care. A theory of nursing.* Norwalk: Appleton-Century-Crofts.

19

Caring as Perceived During
the Birth Experience

Maureen G. Propst
Laura K. Schenk
Sherry Clairain

The phenomenon of giving birth is one of life's most sacred moments. The nursing profession in caring for the woman and family has the unique privilege of sharing witness to this miracle of creation. The caring that is provided and experienced can be ". . . used to describe those rare, precious moments of unique encounter when the participants recognize their common base of humanity" (Roach, 1992, p. 18). Sister M. Simone Roach (1992) identifies care as the fundamental phenomenon of human existence. To care and to be human are tantamount. During birth, in the unequivocal event of experiencing what it is to be human, caring cannot be separated or categorized as something nice to have. It is paramount for nurses to look at "caring as the most common, authentic criterion of humanness" (p. 2) for woman and to embody caring in the nursing role of assisting in the "being" experience of birth.

Nurse scholars (Benner & Wrubel, 1989; Leininger, 1981; Ray, 1981; Joach, 1992; Watson, 1988) have depicted caring as the essence and moral imperative of the nursing profession. Through caring nurses are given the privilege of sharing in the sacredness of the birth and life

The researchers acknowledge the Yvonne Bertolet Research Center, The University of Mississippi School of Nursing for assisting in funding this study. We extend our sincere gratitude to Deborah K. Bockmon, PhD, RN, who served as consultant.

experience. Therefore, it is critical for perinatal nurses to explore the woman's perspective of what caring is in the childbearing process.

The goal of this research was to allow the woman to tell her story of birth—focusing on caring. The central research question posed was: How did the woman perceive she was cared for during labor and delivery? A woman's life phenomena can only be gleaned from an external perspective. The vantage point comes when the woman shares her lived experience. Through the phenomenological perspective the nurse is allowed to become immersed into the woman's noumena.

CARING DURING THE BIRTH EXPERIENCE

Through a recent search in several data bases, caring is addressed in a multitude of topics but not during the intrapartum period and/or using a phenomenological design from the client's lived perspective (Beaton, 1990; Beck, 1992; Crowe & von Baeyer, 1989; Green, Coupland, & Kitzinger, 1990; Sequin, Therrien, Champagne, & Larouche, 1989; Tulman & Fawcett, 1991; Weaver, 1990). Several researchers have focused on the second stage and used videotaping to explore clients' perceptions (McKay, Barrows, & Roberts, 1990). The roles of the nurse and the client during birth have been explored utilizing quantitative methodologies (Beaton, 1990). The phenomenological perspectives of caring have been researched but not in the intrapartum period (Beck, 1992). A phenomenological perspective is needed in the current research literature. The knowledge base for the nursing profession will be expanded by "listening" to the women tell their stories.

PHENOMENOLOGICAL APPROACH

The phenomenological approach is considered to be most appropriate in nursing research because of the nature of human beings and the nature of nursing (Munhall & Oiler, 1986; Morse, 1989; Parse, 1987). Nine low-risk primigravida, who had vaginal deliveries, were asked to tell the story of their birth experiences within the first 48 hours postpartum. The focus of the participants' stories was their thoughts and feelings on the caring they experienced. Using Colaizzi's (1978) seven-step method the stories were audiotaped, transcribed, then analyzed.

The three investigators:

1. Read all interviews to obtain a feel for them.

2. Identified important statements and deleted duplications to recognize significant statements.

3. Drafted interpretations by spelling out the relevance of each significant statement into formulated meanings.

4. Organized the aggregate formulated meanings into clusters or themes. Validated the themes by going back to the original interviews for verification and omission.

5. Integrated the clusters of themes into an exhaustive description of the phenomena under study.

6. Formulated the exhaustive description into a fundamental essential structure.

7. Returned to the participants and asked if the descriptions formulated validated the original experience (Figure 19.1).

The three researchers came together and set up a sacred space—at work but away from their offices and after hours—to immerse themselves in the data. Work sessions varied from four-to-eight hours. Each member of the research team separately read the entire transcript completely the first time with initial fear that little was to be found. With elation the team discovered that after the first read the transcripts held exciting and valuable information. Transcripts were re-read an additional two-to-three times to assure completeness. Consensus was reached with minimum effort or controversy. Formulated meanings came to be grouped through a table top technique of shuffling and rearranging the typed slips of paper until the meanings naturally clustered. The team marvelled at the experience of the results emerging from the data—a non-analytical analysis, a right brain experience. The team experienced a high level of compatibility and camaraderie. An effort was maintained at *all* avenues of the research process to have group consensus and personal affirmation of the endeavor.

FORMULATED MEANINGS AND THEMES

Five themes were revealed through data analysis of the women's significant statements: techniques of the professional, constant presence,

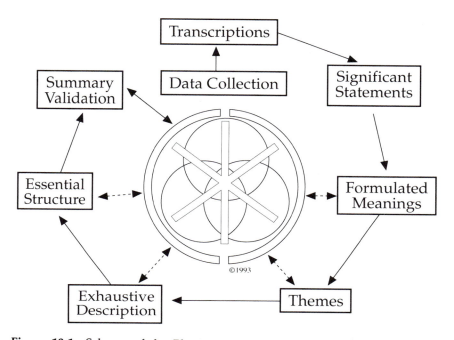

Figure 19.1 Schema of the Phenomenological Approach. Model: Birth (six-point star); Woman, Family, and Nurse (three interlocking circles); mirror-imaged "C" (Phenomena of Caring). Copyright © 1993 by M. Propst, L. Schenk, and S. Clairain.

need to be in company, going beyond the limit, and the nurse's positive manner/being. Select significant statements and formulated meanings and the five themes are presented in Table 19.1.

EXHAUSTIVE DESCRIPTION

From the integration of the clusters of themes, an exhaustive description emerged:

For the woman the process of birth has no other measure like it in life—nothing else in life compares to it. Perceptions of caring enhance this unique experience.

Caring was experienced through the enactment of the nursing role in responding to the woman's needs. Physical needs, such as pain relief, were dealt with in a timely manner. Serving as teacher and coach,

Table 19.1 Themes that Emerged from Clustered Formulated Meanings with Select Examples of Significant Statements

Themes	Formulated Meaning(s)	Significant Statement(s)
1. Techniques of the professional	1. Physical needs, such as pain relief or oxygen administration, were met.	1. "She really helped me through the epidural . . . it was a big help"
2. Constant presence	2. The constant helping presence of the nurse extended beyond just "being there" and encompassed the totality of the experience.	2. "She stayed the whole time."
3. Need to be in company	3. Nurse facilitated maternal-newborn attachment by placing baby in mother's arms.	3. "They gave her [baby] to me as soon as she came out, so I got to see her then. Then they weighed her . . . and then they gave her back to me. . ."
4. Going beyond the limit	4. Nurse exceeded the patient's expectations.	4. "She left one time for about three minutes, to go eat a sandwich but then she came right back."
5. Nurse's positive manner/being	5. Nurse's positive manner, both to the patient and the family, was seen as significant and helpful.	5. "Always asking very politely when to leave the room and went to get them [the family] as soon as they were through: never forgot about them."

the nurse gave options to the woman that facilitated the labor process. Encouragement was received through the nurse's communication of the woman's progress.

Caring was experienced through the presence of the nurse. The experience was enhanced because of the nurse's constant attendance. The nurse and the woman experienced a communion of persons that became an I-Thou relationship. Members of the health care team practiced continual assessment and information sharing. Encouragement of the woman's active participation was enabled by the nurse's constant presence.

The need to be in company during the birth experience included teamwork between and among the nurse, woman, and family. To facilitate teamwork role expectations were shared. Caring was conveyed through the nurse's cognition and acceptance of family needs. As a result, the nurse incorporated the family within the care. This was both valuable and helpful to the woman. Through the nurse's presence and touch, the woman experienced a sense of well being. After delivery, the mother's need to be in company with the baby was facilitated through the nurse placing the baby in the woman's arms.

The woman's perception of caring was enhanced as the nurse went beyond the limit of the woman's expectation of care. The nurse offered to stay beyond her assigned shift, doing more than duty required. The woman both valued the nurse's role and felt valued because the nurse requested to care for her.

Nurse's affect and personality communicated warmth and positive regard both to the woman and the family. The woman's potential for success was positively affirmed by the nurse. The nurse's positive manner was seen as significant and helpful.

ESSENTIAL STRUCTURE

The following essential structure was the fundamental result of this research:

Perceptions of caring enhance the unique experience of birth for the woman. The nurse's presence, attending, and caring is a desired and valued way of being. This communion with the woman's labor and birth becomes an I-Thou—intimate and personal—experience.

The need to be in company during birth includes the woman, the family, and the nurse. A need for togetherness is facilitated through their immersion into the phenomena of birth. The invitation to share is extended mutually. The threads of caring are reflected in the intricate fabric of labor and birth, as the nurse goes beyond minimum expectations of assignment and role.

Through an experience of caring, the woman values the nurse's way of being and the nursing role, thus enabling an appreciation of the woman's own value. Caring is emulated through the enactment of the nursing role, the nurse being with the woman.

DISCUSSION AND IMPLICATIONS

Evidence in other research studies provided support for the validity of the five themes: techniques of the professional, constant presence, need to be in company, going beyond the limit, and nurse's positive manner/being.

Techniques of the Professional

The techniques of the professional embrace the basic core of the art and science of nursing. The provision of the techniques and the time in which they are provided are critical. Nurses are employed to be there to meet physical needs, such as pain relief or oxygen administration, and timeliness contributes to the value the person will place on the nursing care received. Assistance with the gratification of human needs is one of Watson's carative factors (Watson, 1979).

A crucial factor in satisfaction is competence in the profession demonstrated through listening to and recognizing concerns and responding to questions and needs (Field, 1987; Larson, 1984; Shields, 1978). Larson (1984) reported similar findings in that patients identified the technique "monitor" and the action "following-through" as the most significant in the care they received. Von Essen and Sjödén (1991) found patients ranked competent technical skills highest of nurse caring behaviors. Gaut (1983) and Watson (1979) substantiate the need for awareness, knowledge, and the intention to act emphasizing that acts be based on knowledge which provides the value in the caring provided.

Mayeroff (1990) writes that in caring, the person experiences the other as having potentialities and the need to grow, and that there is also the need of the other for the person to care in order to grow. This is vividly portrayed through the nurse/client caring occasion. The power of caring the nurse has with the client is a sacred trust, it is the embodiment of the American Nurses Association code for nurses (*Code for Nurses with Interpretive Statements*, 1980). This trust becomes our devotion to the other, our affirmation of the other's being (Mayeroff, 1990).

Constant Presence

Sister Roach (1992) eloquently writes of caring and presence: "The human is a relationship with others, a power of experiencing the presence of another, of sharing intimacy. To be a person is to possess spiritual unity, sharing intimacy, inwardness and openness" (p. 22). The focus on individuals has supplanted the human community or group (p. 105). From the classic work of Buber (1937) to the current research of Eriksson (1992), the communion of persons persistently finds support as the basis for humanity. Gilje (1992) presents an analysis of the concept of presence that supports the work of Forrest (1989) who identified ". . . a preference for 'being with' rather than 'doing to' a patient." Thus the theme of constant presence is validated as a part of the essential structure of caring for this work.

Need to Be in Company

Caring is being with the other as well as being for the other (Mayeroff, 1990). Two beings exist on a level of equality. When the other person has this feeling of "being with," they do not feel alone but feel understood. Understanding comes from the nurse "being with," by knowing what it is like to be the client. There is an expressed need to avoid isolation, a need to feel the companionship or community with the family or meaningful others. The family needs to be incorporated into the birth experience and not to seem "in the way." Allowing others to "be with" the woman contributed to the feelings of both kindness and value (Cartwright, 1987).

Going Beyond the Limit

Personal value and esteem are accentuated when the person experiences caring beyond expectations. The nurse does not treat the person as an assignment with the boundaries of shift time or length. The nurse is involved in her work and makes it a personal experience for the person. The work is more than a duty or assignment (Field, 1987). Noncaring is identified in the absence of "going beyond the limit" (Hancock & Krohn, 1992).

Nurse's Positive Manner/Being

The way in which the nurse chooses to be, her attitude, manner, tone of voice, inflection, nonverbal expressions, give validity to her sincerity and genuiness. Women persistently affirm the decisive skill of communication: encouraging the parents, telling the woman she had done well, listening to and respecting the mother's opinion (Field, 1987). Acting as an advocate and receiving unique care based on their needs demonstrated respect (Field, 1987) and promoted the woman's self-worth.

The research results yield valuable information to nurses (both in practice and in education) and other health care providers to guide their actions and add to their repertoire in caring for these women and their families.

Practice

Defining the caring behaviors valued by the woman in the birth experience yields validation for the nursing profession and the delivery of care. Considering the woman's perspective impacts how the nurse will approach her care. The phenomenological methodology provides the window to view woman's lived experience—a way of knowing the woman from her perspective—her noumena. Sharing from the woman's point of view will allow the nurse to be existentially present or "in-company."

Practice implications become a marketing strategy for clients who are likely to choose the hospital for future care (Duffy, 1992; & Valentine, 1991). The positive, warm regard for care received will serve as vital to public relations.

Research

Implications for future research evolved through the conduction of this inquiry. Will this essential structure of caring be the same at times other than the immediate postpartum period? Will women who have had more than one experience of childbirth relate different needs of caring? A replication of this work could be explored with other populations. Inquiry into both caring and non-caring experiences merits consideration.

Education

Research and practice both advances and contributes to education. Phenomenological inquiry will yield the essential structure that will direct educators to impart caring sensitivities to the undergraduate nursing students. The formalized meanings clustered into themes that serve as a logical framework to present areas of caring needs. A holistic paradigm is imparted when the woman's perception of caring is used to assist students learning to nurse the childbearing family. To be "in-company" the student will need to know personal biases, as well as the woman's, to appreciate each person's value of caring behaviors. Through enactment of current research, the student's practice will be authentic for the woman and her family. Existential ways of thinking and the modeling of valued behaviors are requisite for the being of caring to exist.

The "what" to teach and the "how" to change curricula receive direction from research and practice. Valid programs that yield a marketable professional nurse are evidenced with the incorporation of research findings derived from the practice core—the lived experience.

REFERENCES

American Nurses Association (1980). *Nursing: A social policy statement*. Kansas City, MO: Author.

Beaton, J. I. (1990). Dimensions of nurse and patient roles in labor. *Health Care for Women International, 11,* 393–408.

Beck, C. T. (1992). The lived experience of postpartum depression: A phenomenological study. *Nursing Research, 41,* 166–170.

Benner, P., & Wrubel, J. (1989). *The primacy of caring: Stress and coping in health and illness*. Menlo Park: Addison-Wesley.

Buber, M. (1965). *The knowledge of man* (M. Friedman & R. G. Smith, Trans). New York: Harper & Row.

Buber, M. (1945). *I and thou* (3rd ed., English edition). Edinburgh, England: R & R Clark. (Original work published 1937.)

Cartwright, A. (1987). Who are maternity services kind to? What is kindness? *Midwife: Health visitor and community nurse, 23,* 21–24.

Colaizzi, P. F. (1978). Psychological research as the phenomenologist views it. In R. S. Valle & M. King (Eds.), *Existential-phenomenological alternatives for psychology* (pp. 48–71). New York: Oxford University Press.

Crowe, K., & von Baeyer, C. (1989). Predictors of a positive childbirth experience. *Birth, 17,* 15–24.

Duffy, J. R. (1992). The impact of nurse caring on patient outcomes. In D. A. Gaut, (Ed.), *The presence of caring in nursing* (pp. 113–136). New York: National League for Nursing Press.

Eriksson, K. (1992). Nursing: The caring practice "being there." In D. A. Gaut (Ed.), *The presence of caring in nursing* (pp. 201–210). New York: National League for Nursing Press.

Field, P. A. (1987). Maternity nurses: How parents see us. *International Journal of Nursing Studies, 24,* 191–199.

Forrest, D. (1989). The experience of caring. *Journal of Advanced Nursing, 14,* 815–823.

Gaut, D. A. (1983). Development of a theoretically adequate description of caring. *Western Journal of Nursing Research, 5*(4), 312–324.

Gilje, F. (1992). Being there: An analysis of the concept of presence. In D. A. Gaut (Ed.), *The presence of caring in nursing* (pp. 53–68). New York: National League for Nursing Press.

Green, J. M., Coupland, V. A., & Kitzinger, J. V. (1990). Expectations, experiences, and psychological outcomes of childbirth: A prospective study of 825 women. *Birth, 17,* 15–24.

Hancock, K., & Krohn, B. (1992). Caring is a gift of the heart. *Journal of Neuroscience Nursing, 24,* 110–112.

Larson, P. J. (1984). Important nurse caring behaviors perceived by patients with cancer. *Oncology Nursing Forum, 11,* 46–50.

Leininger, M. M. (1981). *Caring: An essential human need*. Thorofare, NJ: Charles B. Slack.

Mayeroff, M. (1990). *On caring*. New York: HarperCollins. (Original work published 1971.)

McKay, S., Barrows, T., & Roberts, J. (1990). Women's views of second-stage labor as assessed by interviews and videotapes. *Birth, 17*, 192–198.

Morse, J. M. (1989). Qualitative nursing research: A contemporary dialogue. Gaithersburg, MD: Aspen Publications.

Munhall, P. L., & Oiler, C. J. (1986). Philosophical foundations of qualitative research. In P. L. Munhall & C. J. Oiler (Eds.), *Nursing research: A qualitative perspective* (pp. 47–63). Norwalk: Appleton-Century-Crofts.

Parse, R. R. (1987). *Nursing science: Major paradigms, theories, and critiques*. Philadelphia: W. B. Saunders.

Ray, M. A. (1981). A philosophical analysis of caring within nursing, in M. M. Leininger (Ed.), Caring: An essential human need, pp. 25–36. New Jersey: Charles B. Slack.

Roach, M. S. (1992). *The human act of caring*. Ottawa, Ontario: Canadian Hospital Association Press.

Seguin, L., Therrien, R., Champagne, F., & Larouche, D. (1989). The components of women's satisfaction with maternity care. *Birth, 16*, 109–113.

Shields, D. (1978). Nursing care in labour and patient satisfaction: A descriptive study. *Journal of Advanced Nursing, 3*, 535–550.

Tulman, L., & Fawcett, J. (1991). Recovery from childbirth: Looking back six months after delivery. *Health Care for Women International, 12*, 341–350.

Watson, J. (1979). *Nursing: The philosophy and science of caring*. Boston: Little, Brown.

Watson, J. (1988). *Nursing: Human science and human care—A theory of nursing*. Norwalk: Appleton-Century-Crofts.

Weaver, D. F. (1990). Nurses' views on the meaning of touch in obstetrical nursing practice. *Journal of Obstetric, Gynecologic, & Neonatal Nursing, 19,* 157–161.

Valentine, K. L. (1991). Comprehensive assessment of caring and its relationship to outcome measures. *Journal of Nursing Quality Assurance, 5,* 59–68.

Von Essen, L., & Sjödén, P. (1991). The importance of nurse caring behaviors as perceived by Swedish hospital patients and nursing staff. *International Journal of Nursing Studies, 28,* 267–281.

20

Caring and Learning: A Mosaic

Kathryn Stewart Hegedus

A mosaic is an exquisite piece of art with hues, textures, and dimension that portrays feelings, diverse perspectives and proverbial messages. Nursing practice, with all of its artistic dimension and intricacies of expression, has the patchwork of a mosaic. This is evident in the daily work of nurses as they deliver care in the community while visiting clients in their homes. The purpose of this article is two-fold: (1) to describe the instrument and process that was used to evaluate students' clinical work during their community health practicum and, (2) to discuss the caring components of learning.

It is the personal belief of the writer that the way faculty care about students is the way in which they will care for their patients. Therefore, part of the socialization into the discipline of nursing and the modeling of the meaning of "caring" is through the interpersonal aspects of teaching. It is an added dimension that spans time even though the teaching may be subtle and the learning retrospective.

In this instance, in the community setting described here, the faculty was privileged to witness caring about and among students, staff, and families. Individually and collectively they strove forth though they came from diverse backgrounds and operated from, at times, sad moments in their personal lives. For example, one student drove to the home of her patient with tears streaming down her face because the student's sister had been hospitalized during the previous weekend after a near fatal auto accident.

BACKGROUND

The community setting is especially challenging for students who are new to this area of practice. The skillful match between student and preceptor (senior staff nurse in the agency) is crucial to a smooth student entry and continued learning.

One of the many challenges is the evaluation of the students' clinical performances. The approach chosen was one that allowed for the input from all who participated thus valuing their contributions and work. The experience was in a Visiting Nurse Agency which covers a relatively small geographical area but services a diverse population with varied health needs ranging from the debilitated elderly in affluent neighborhoods, to the child with AIDS in an inner city area. In this situation, I (the faculty) saw the strength, beauty, and fragility of staff, students, and clients as they coped with risky and complex environments.

As the faculty representative, I developed and presented the plan for evaluating the students' work. The approach that was agreed upon by the preceptors, students, and faculty consisted of the following: (1) a self evaluation from the student, (2) an evaluation from the preceptor and, (3) an evaluation from the faculty. The clients were not asked for their perception of care, nor did we use peer review even though these elements are recognized as valuable pieces of the whole (Hughes, 1993).

The challenge of evaluating students' clinical performance is not new; Slater (1967) provided one of the earliest measures for evaluating individual performance. Wooley (1977) noted a long and anguished history; Bondy (1984) and Krumme (1988) both developed criterion-reference measures for clinical evaluation of student performance. Scheetz (1990) has developed a Clinical Competence Rating Scale for measuring the clinical competence of baccalaureate nursing students.

THE INSTRUMENT

The preceding measures provided direction for utilizing the instrument that facilitated evaluation of this clinical practicum. As Director of Staff Development and Research at The Children's Hospital, Boston, I had assisted in the development of The Professional Advancement Program and in devising a measure to evaluate clinical performance (Hegedus,

Balasco, & Black, 1988). The work of Benner (1984) and Benner and Wrubel (1989) provided the framework for the instrument. Caring is identified by Benner as the major focus of nursing and is presented as an essential experience of human existence. Caring is described by Benner as interactive and ever-changing as in a kaleidoscope with all of its muted hues and contrasting brilliant colors. Benner uses paradigms from nursing practice to portray excellence in the delivery of nursing care.

Members of The Professional Advancement and Evaluation Committee at The Children's Hospital, Boston used Benner's framework, readings from the literature, and their own experience and expertise for devising the measure (Balasco & Black, 1988). The committee had identified four domains of performance expectations: (1) Clinical Practice, (2) Clinical Leadership, (3) Professional Growth/Continuing Education, and (4) Nursing Research/Quality Assurance. Stem statements were generated and critical elements were developed that described specific behaviors for each domain; and content validity was established by using a panel of nursing experts (Waltz, 1984). They judged, independently of one another, the adequacy of each critical element for representing the domain of practice. The measure was revised in 1989 and the evaluative columns were changed to read either Yes or No as is in keeping with the criterion reference format. (Please see Table 20.1, Evaluation Tool.)

Although the original tool had been designed to be used by staff nurses, it was chosen for use with students for several reasons. First, the four domains encompass the expectations that one would have for professional practice and these students were finishing a baccalaureate program. Secondly, it was being used as a frame of reference. Third, it allowed for the qualitative aspect of performance by narrative comments. Fourth, it would serve to validate the verbal comments made by other members of the staff. Lastly, if there were major discrepancies in performance, as determined by student, preceptor, and or faculty, there would be a basis for addressing these diversities (this did not happen).

PROCESS

The tool was introduced to the five students and five preceptors during the initial portion of the clinical experience. Their evaluations and the

Table 20.1   Evaluation Tool

CLINICAL PRACTICE	YES	NO

I. Delivers competent, scientifically based nursing care to patients and families whose needs range from un-complicated to complex.

1. Systematically assesses patient needs from a holistic viewpoint.

2. Engages the patient and family in the formation of an in-dividualized plan of care based upon scientific principles, in which needs are identified and goals are set.

3. Implements nursing care plan in an organized manner; establishes and re-orders priorities as necessary.

4. Consistently evaluates and documents plan of care as needed to achieve identified goals.

5. Conveys, through nursing practice, a clear sense of pro-fessional role and identity.

II. Establishes a helping relationship with the patient and family which uses a holistic approach.

6. Interacts with patients and families in a compassionate and humanistic way.

7. Develops an awareness of the boundaries of the thera-peutic relationship.

8. Identifies and utilizes community resources to promote continuity of care.

9. Identifies learning needs of the patient and family, and develops a teaching plan to meet these needs.

CLINICAL LEADERSHIP

III. Supports the climate for formulating and achieving goals beneficial to patient care and professional practice.

10. Demonstrates evidence of understanding and participa-tion in programmatic goals of the unit.

11. Demonstrates a willingness to be a team member and to work collaboratively and interdependently.

12. Makes clinical and management decisions which reflect awareness of the short term needs of the unit, the ability to prioritize, and the appropriate and timely use of re-sources.

IV. Supports an environment which facilitates growth and development.

13. Shares own knowledge with colleagues; participates in unit-based staff education sessions and staff meetings.

Table 20.1 *(continued)*

	YES	NO
14. Identifies own leadership qualities and learning needs; seeks opportunities to enhance personal growth.		
15. Identifies appropriate leadership role models and seeks their support and counsel.		

PROFESSIONAL GROWTH/CONTINUING EDUCATION

V. Demonstrates commitment to the profession and community at large.

16. Establishes and maintains membership in professional organizations.

17. Daily practice reflects a personal concept of the nursing role.

18. Aware of current health care policies which may influence practice.

VI. Assumes responsibility for own learning.

19. Assumes responsibility for self-evaluation.

20. Formulates yearly goals and objectives and methods for accomplishing these with the Nurse Manager.

21. Participates in the peer review process; identifies areas of merit and need for growth for self and others.

22. Attends conferences, workshops and seminars; shares information gained with colleagues.

23. Reads professional literature which pertains to current practice.

24. Seeks out formal and informal contacts with professional colleagues.

RESEARCH/QUALITY ASSURANCE

VII. Demonstrates competency in critiquing nursing research.

25. Identifies reported clinical research studies that have implications for practice.

26. Identifies clinical nursing problems that may be appropriate for scientific testing.

27. Participates in ongoing research and quality assurance studies.

28. Attends research conferences.

five from the faculty gave a total of 15 measures. For example, each of the five students had one evaluation of self, one from their preceptor and one from the faculty member. The introductory comments provided a brief overview of Benner's work, and some background information regarding how the tool was devised and used in the hospital setting. The students and preceptors agreed to use the tool for evaluating the clinical practicum.

The tool was used by each student, preceptor, and faculty at the end of the semester. Each person worked independently. The preceptors then shared theirs with the student. It was then given to the faculty and the students brought theirs to the final evaluation conference. At this time the student, preceptor, and faculty participated in the evaluation conference. In addition, the student and faculty determined the grade that they mutually agreed upon.

RESULTS

The evaluation tool contains 28 items, nine in the Clinical Practice domain; six in the Leadership domain; nine in the Professional Growth/ Continuing Education domain; and four in the Research/Quality Assurance domain. The following illustrates its use in the evaluation of the student's experience.

One of the students was assigned to work with the staff nurse (preceptor) who worked in the hospice program of the agency. This experience had been arranged based on the student's own educational goal of learning more about the care of dying patients. After an initial orientation period, she accompanied the preceptor on home visits, and selected her own clients for care. Among the families was a frail elderly couple. The wife, 84-years old, was in the late stages of cancer. During the course of the clinical practicum the 86-year-old husband was hospitalized with a heart attack. The student made weekly home visits to the wife at home and to the husband in intensive care. This provided a liaison between the hospital and agency as well as support to both members of the family. The student utilized library resources, research findings, staff counsel and faculty coaching to plan for and provide care as she worked with this family.

The student's performance demonstrated numerous behaviors that were addressed by the tool, for instance: (1) item #1 "Systematically addresses patient needs from a holistic view point" (Practice Domain), (2) item #4 "Identifies own leadership qualities and learning needs;

seeks opportunities to enhance personal growth" (Clinical Leadership), and (3) item #25 "Identifies reported clinical research studies that have implications for practice" (Research/Quality Assurance). This shows the use of the tool from the individual perspective.

The data was also analyzed for aggregate findings. All of the students, preceptors, and faculty each marked 13 (46%) of the items "Yes" demonstrating congruence among the respondents. Those items were the nine items in clinical practice, three items (#11, #14, #15) in Leadership and one item (#17) in Professional Growth/Continuing Education. The consensus in practice items was the same finding as the earlier work with the instrument (Hegedus, Balasco, & Black, 1988). Some interesting patterns emerge when examining the remaining 15 items. For instance, item #10, "Demonstrates evidence of understanding and participating in programmatic goals of the unit," was left blank by one student and preceptor and marked not applicable (NA) by two preceptors. A similar pattern was seen in items #12, 19, 23, and 24. It was noted that the evaluators, who made a determination on these items, tended to "correct" them by writing words in their place.

One of the students put six question marks in the Yes (with a written narrative to illustrate and document the choice). The first two items (#25 and #26) in the Research/Quality Assurance domain were usually marked Yes by most of the evaluators. Items #27 and #28 regarding their participation in research conferences and ongoing research and quality assurance studies were marked NA by the majority of the evaluators.

Some of the preceptors felt that they were not in the position to judge some of the items. For example, item #22 "Attends conferences, workshops and seminars; shares information gained with colleagues," was more evident in the classroom setting than the clinical, and item #19 "Assumes responsibility for self-evaluation" was better determined by faculty and student.

Items were modified, in several instances, to make them more student specific and setting particular. For example, in item #10 the words clinical group were substituted for yearly goals and faculty/preceptor for nurse manager.

DISCUSSION

The instrument spells out behaviors of professional nursing practice that provide a reference for evaluating individual performance. Furthermore, Benner's framework with its focus on caring was operationalized in relation to self and others by the interactive approach between students, preceptors, and faculty. Bevis (1993) advocates "discovery learning" identifying it as a collaborative journey, in a democratic, egalitarian environment where the learner is an equal partner with others. Students seemed to feel that they were team members as is indicated by the following comment, "The atmosphere was relaxed, autonomy was allowed, and we were encouraged to practice in our own personalized and artful way."

Facilitating caring and learning is a privilege for nursing faculty and we must continually examine the activities which accompany the caring/learning process. The learning journey about caring (Nyberg, 1993) is for both teacher and student as was certainly the case here. Nelms, Jones, and Gray (1993), in their study on faculty role modeling as a method of teaching caring, noted that several participants appreciated the freedom to go and do for their patients independently as a way of being cared for by their instructors. The following anecdotal comment by another student concurs with this sentiment, "She treated us like adult learners and provided a positive opportunity for independent nursing practice." Although the students' perceptions of the instructors caring was not formally assessed (Golden, 1993) their unsolicited comments seemed to substantiate this. One student did volunteer the written statement, "This instructor did professional caring."

The amalgamation of students striving, client yearnings, preceptor expertise, and faculty sensitivity were the fragments and compounds of this mosaic reflecting the encirclement of care. Capturing and measuring the colorful flickers of light with the promise of learning and growth for the participants was the driving force behind the undertaking. It is assumed that the process continues but now in new environments for most and with different expectations for all.

REFERENCES

Balasco, E. M., & Black, A. S. (1988). Advancing nursing practice: Description, recognition and reward. *Nursing Administration Quarterly, 12,* 52–57.

Benner, P. (1984). *From novice to expert.* Menlo Park: Addison-Wesley.

Benner, P., & Wrubel, J. (1989). *The Primacy of Caring.* Menlo Park: Addison-Wesley.

Bevis, E. O. (1993). All in all, it was a pretty good funeral. *Journal of Nursing Education. 32*, 101–105.

Bondy, K. (1984). Clinical evaluation of student performance: The effects of criteria on accuracy and reliability.

Golden, D. H. (1993). Development of a tool to measure student perceptions of instructor caring. *Journal of Nursing Education, 32*, 142–143.

Hegedus, K. S., Balasco, E., & Black, A. S. (1988). Measuring clinical performance. In *Measurement of Nursing Outcomes*, 1988, Vol. II (pp. 123–132). Edited by O. Strickland & C. F. Waltz. New York: Springer.

Hegedus, K. S., Micheli, A., & Colangelo, A. (1989). Evaluation of clinical performance monitoring the utilization of standardized tools. In *Proceedings Second Annual Research Day*. Syracuse: Syracuse University.

Hughes, L. (1993). Peer group interactions and the student-perceived climate for caring. *Journal of Nursing Education, 32*, 78–83.

Krumme, U. (1988). Measuring baccalaureate students' nursing process competencies: A nursing diagnosis framework. In *Measurement of Nursing Outcomes*, 1988, Vol. II (pp. 252–284). Edited by O. Strickland, C. F. Waltz. New York: Springer.

Nelms, T. P., Jones, J. M., & Gray, P. D. (1993). Role modeling: A method for teaching caring in nursing education. *Journal of Nursing Education, 32*, 18–23.

Nyberg, J. (1993). Teaching caring to the nurse administrator. *JONA, 11–17.

Scheetz, L. J. (1990). Measuring clinical competence in baccalaureate nursing students. In *Measurement of Nursing Outcomes*, Vol. III (pp. 3–16). Edited by C. F. Waltz & O. Strickland. New York: Springer.

Slater, D. (1967). *The Slater Nursing Competencies Rating Scale*. Detroit: Wayne State University.

Waltz, C. F., Strickland, O. L., & Lenz, E. R. (1984). *Measurement in Nursing Research*. Philadelphia: F. A. Davis.

Woolley, A. (1977). The long and tortured history of clinical evaluation. *Nursing Outlook, 25*, 308–315.